I0727809

Fishes of Edo: A Guide to Classical Japanese Fishes

Planning, Art Director: Kazuhiko Tajima
Supervisor: Masanori Nakae
Designer: Kishiko Omi
Writer: Satoko Monji, Mikako Yamaguchi
Translator: Michael Brucia, Shoko Natori, Brainwoods Corporation, Ltd.
Proofreader: Ouraidou
Editor: Keiko Kinefuchi (PIE International)

Publisher: Hiromoto Miyoshi

PIE International Inc.
2-32-4 Minami-Otsuka, Toshima-ku, Tokyo 170-0005 JAPAN
international@pie.co.jp
www.pie.co.jp/english

ISBN978-4-7562-5652-2 (Outside Japan)
Printed in Japan

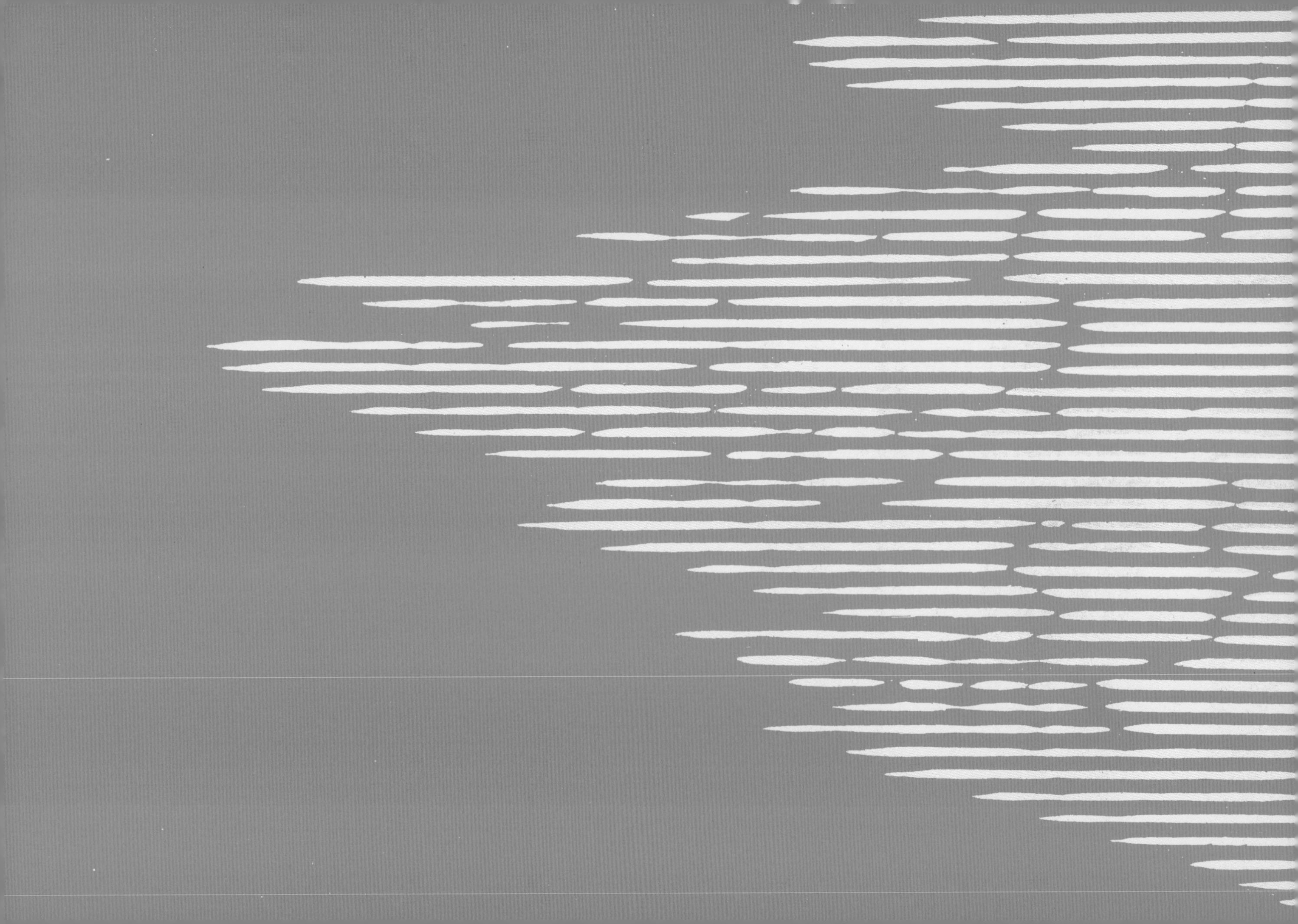

江戸魚図鑑

美し、をかし、の和名由来

Fishes of Edo
A Guide to
Classical Japanese Fishes

江戸の魚類図譜

海洋国で生きる私たちにとって、古くから魚は身近な存在だった。日本人は世界でも類をみない魚食民族だといわれている。例えば、鮨種として人気のマグロ。マグロ漁が始まったのは、縄文、弥生時代だと推測されている。平安時代の歌人で有名な紫式部や和泉式部はイワシが好物だったという。当時イワシは卑しい魚とされ、宮中ではその名前を呼ぶのさえ避けられていたが、人目を忍んで食べていたとか。今日でも生後100日前後の生児のお祝いの儀式「お食い初め」では、尾頭付きの魚を用意する。土用の丑の日には店頭にウナギが並ぶ。魚への愛着は現代でも変わらない。さて、日本人が本草学の視点から魚の探求を始めたのは江戸時代からである。魚類の図譜が初めて登場したのは江戸中期。1731年、神田玄泉によって日本で最初の魚介図説『日東魚譜』が編纂され、約400種の水産動物と製品が記された。さらに本草学をもとに始まった森羅万象を追求する日本の博物学熱は高まり、美術作品のような美しさを併せ持つ図譜も登場する。その代表的なものに、高松藩の5代藩主である松平頼恭（1711〜1771年）が編纂した『衆鱗図』がある。『衆鱗図』は彩色が施され、金銀の箔で光沢を表したり、切り紙細工で立体感を表現したり、その技巧が光る図譜となっている。制作に関わったのは本草家、文芸家、画家、発明家などとして知られる平賀源内（1728〜1779年）だと考えられている。江戸後期になると、江戸時代の代表的な博物画家といわれる毛利梅園（1798〜1851年）によって『梅園魚譜』と『梅園魚品図正』が編纂される。毛利梅園は写生図譜を多く手がけ、植物や鳥類、菌類などの図譜も制作した。これらは総称して「梅園画譜」と呼ばれている。写生にこだわり、繊細な筆致で描かれた毛利梅園の図譜は現代でも定評がある。本書では、毛利梅園が手がけた『梅園魚譜』と『梅園魚品図正』のなかから94種の魚を厳選して紹介する。

季節でみる魚と和名の由来

日本の文献に初めて魚の名前が登場したのはいつ頃か。それは、現存する最古の歴史書『古事記』（712年）まで遡る。『古事記』には「栲縄の千尋縄打ち延へ釣らせる海人が、大口の尾翼鱸（オハタスズキ）さわさわにひきよせあげて、杤竹のとをとをに、天の眞魚咋（アメノマナグヒ）献らむとまをしき」とあり、出雲の国つ神が天つ神に最高のご馳走としてスズキを使った魚料理を献上したと記されている。海に囲まれた日本では、魚は身近な生き物であると同時に主要な食料でもあった。このことは、日本人のなかに海と海の生き物からの恩恵を重んじる心を育んでいったのだろう。江戸時代の頃、熊野灘のある湾にマグロの大群が押し寄せたことで、付近の住人が飢饉から救われた。人々はマグロを「支毘大命神」として崇めて供養塔を建立したという記録がある。古くから私たちは魚に親しみを持ち、観察し、その名前や姿を記してきた。本書では「その魚が日本で旬を迎える季節」という観点から、『梅園魚譜』と『梅園魚品図正』から厳選した94種の図譜を春、夏、秋、冬の章に分けて紹介する。また、魚の標準和名とその由来、地方名や古名、英名を記載している。魚の名前は外見、習性、また伝承などに由来するものが多い。例えば、外見が語源といわれる「サンマ」の名前は、体が細長いところから「狭真魚（サマナ）」が転訛したという説がある。「イシダイ」は、頑丈な顎と歯で貝類などの硬い殻をも噛み砕いて食べる習性から「石をも噛み砕く歯を持つ魚」という意味で名付けられた。「ハタハタ」は、日本海で雷が多い冬に海岸に打ち寄せることから雷神の古名「霹靂神（はたたかみ）」が遣わした魚という伝承から、この名が付けられたという。和名の由来については諸説あり、研究者によって見解が異なる。また本書では割愛した名前や説もあるが、和名の由来とともに日本人の感性と魚にまつわる奥深い物語の一端を堪能していただけたら幸いである。

Illustrated Guide to Fishes
of the Edo Era (1603–1867)

Since olden times, fishes have been a familiar part of life for the people of the maritime country of Japan. It is said that the Japanese are the most fish-eating people in the world. Take tuna, the popular sushi topping, for example. According to one estimate, the beginning of tuna fishing goes back to the Jomon era (12,000 BCE–300 BCE) and the Yayoi era (400 BCE–300 CE). It is said that Murasaki Shikibu and Izumi Shikibu, famous poets of the Heian era (794–1185), were great lovers of Japanese sardine. However, the aristocrats of the era looked down on Japanese sardine as vulgar and even avoided calling them by their names in court. So, they would eat them when no one was looking. Even today, the Japanese prepare a whole fish for "Okuizome," or the first meal, a traditional ritual performed around the hundredth day after the birth of a baby. The Japanese have always felt a strong attachment to fishes. Firstly, it was in the Edo era that the Japanese started studying fishes from the standpoint of botany. The first illustrated fish catalog was published in mid-Edo era. In 1731, a doctor named Kanda Gensen compiled *Nitto-gyofu*, the first illustrated encyclopedia covering approximately 400 species of marine animals and products. Furthermore, guides containing beautiful illustrations, almost equivalent to an artwork, started to appear. One famous example is *Shurin-zu*, compiled by Matsudaira Yoritaka (1711–1771), the fifth lord of Takamatsu. The colored illustrations highlight techniques such as gold and silver leaf decorations that depict the shimmer of the subjects and paper cutouts that express their three-dimensionality. Late in the Edo era, Mori Baien (1798–1851), who is considered to be the most eminent natural history painter of the era, compiled *Baien-gyofu* and *Baien Gyohin Zusei*. With particular attention to realism, his works that showcase his delicate style are highly acclaimed even today. This book features 94 fish species selected from Baien's two works.

Seasonal Fishes and the Origins of their Japanese Names

It was in *Kojiki*, a collection of Japanese mythology compiled in 712, that a fish name appeared for the first time in Japanese literature. Here, the Kunitsukami (gods of land) of Izumo offered dishes featuring Japanese sea bass as the ultimate feast to the Amatsukami (gods of heaven). As Japan is a country surrounded by seas, fishes were not only familiar here, but also important as a food source. This may be the reason why the Japanese nurtured deep respect toward the blessings of the sea and its creatures. During the Edo era, a large school of tuna swam into a bay of the Kumanonada Sea, saving nearby residents from famine. Records state the tuna was worshiped as Shibi Daimyojin, and a memorial tower was erected. Feeling affinity toward fishes since ancient times, the Japanese have observed and recorded their names and forms. This book presents 94 illustrations from *Baien-gyofu* and *Baien Gyohin Zusei*, selected from the perspective of the best time of the year to enjoy that fish. The illustrations are organized into four chapters: spring, summer, autumn, and winter. In addition, it features the standard Japanese name, its origin, local variants, ancient names, and English names. For example, it is said that "sanma (Japanese name for Pacific saury)," whose name originates from its appearance, is a corruption of "samana" (meaning "narrow fish"). Also, "ishidai ("ishi" meaning "rock")," or barred knifejaw, takes its name from its habit of using its powerful jaws and teeth to crack hard shells. And "hatahata," or Japanese sandfish, is related to the legend as the messenger of Hatatakami, the ancient god of lightning, as they come to the coast of the Japan Sea in winter, when lightning is common. But there are various theories. Although it was not possible to include everything in the book, I hope that it allows you to enjoy the fascinating aspects of the Japanese sensibilities and the profound stories related to fish, along with their names.

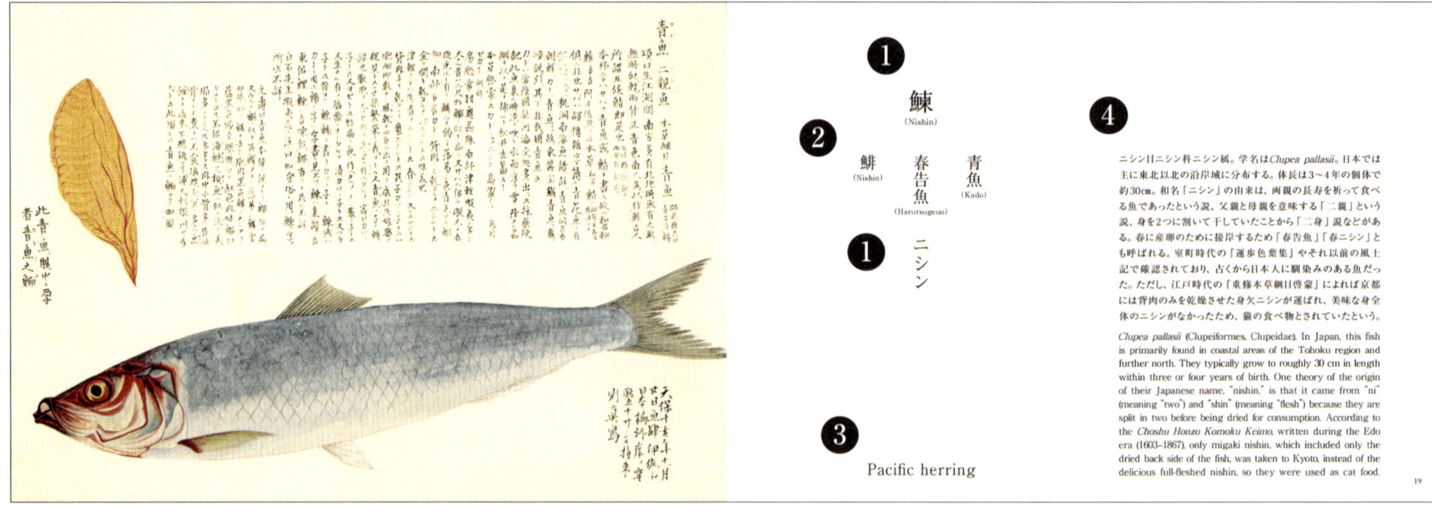

①

鰊
(Nishin)

②

鯡　　春告魚　　青魚
(Nishin)　(Harutsugeuo)　(Kado)

① ニシン

③

Pacific herring

④

ニシン目ニシン科ニシン属。学名は *Clupea pallasii*。日本では主に東北以北の沿岸域に分布する。体長は3〜4年の個体で約30cm。和名「ニシン」の由来は、両親の長寿を祈って食べる魚であったという説、父親と母親を意味する「二親」という説、身を2つに割いて干していたことから「二身」説などがある。春に産卵のために接岸するため「春告魚」「春ニシン」とも呼ばれる。室町時代の『運歩色葉集』やそれ以前の風土記で確認されており、古くから日本人に馴染みのある魚だった。ただし、江戸時代の『重修本草綱目啓蒙』によれば京都には背肉のみを乾燥させた身欠ニシンが運ばれ、美味な身全体のニシンがなかったため、猫の食べ物とされていたという。

Clupea pallasii (Clupeiformes, Clupeidae). In Japan, this fish is primarily found in coastal areas of the Tohoku region and further north. They typically grow to roughly 30 cm in length within three or four years of birth. One theory of the origin of their Japanese name, "nishin," is that it came from "ni" (meaning "two") and "shin" (meaning "flesh") because they are split in two before being dried for consumption. According to the *Choshu Honzo Komoku Keimo*, written during the Edo era (1603–1867), only migaki nishin, which included only the dried back side of the fish, was taken to Kyoto, instead of the delicious full-fleshed nishin, so they were used as cat food.

【凡例】

・収録図版は『梅園魚譜』と『梅園魚品図正』から抜粋した図譜を「その魚が日本で旬を迎える季節」という観点から春、夏、秋、冬の章に分けて掲載している。

・各魚の解説ページは以下の内容を紹介している。

❶ 標準和名、漢字表記、標準和名のローマ字表記

❷ 異名、方言名、古名、漢名などの漢字表記

❸ 英名

❹ 分類、学名、体長、和名の由来などの解説

・魚の科名と学名は主に『日本産魚類全種目録 これまでに記録された日本産魚類全種の現在の標準和名と学名 Online ver. 21』（本村浩之）に、英名は主に『FishBase. World Wide Web electronic publication. Ver.（06 / 2023）』（Froese & Pauly）に基づいて記載している。

【Legend】

・ The illustrations in this book are taken from *Baien-gyofu* and *Baien Gyohin Zusei.* They are selected from the perspective of the best time of the year to enjoy that fish and are organized into four chapters: spring, summer, autumn, and winter.

・ The commentary for each fish features the following:

❶ The standard Japanese name in phonetic Japanese characters, in Romanized Japanese, and in Japanese kanji characters

❷ Different names, local variants, ancient names, Chinese names, etc.

❸ The English name

❹ Commentary including scientific classifications, the binomial name, the body length, and the origin of the Japanese name

・ The family names and scientific names of the fishes are mainly based on *List of Japan's All Fish Species: Current standard Japanese and scientific names of all fish species recorded from Japanese waters. Online ver. 21*" (Hiroyuki Motomura). The English names are mainly from *FishBase. World Wide Web electronic publication. Ver. (06/2023)*" (Froese & Pauly).

【注記】

・収録図版は「国立国会図書館デジタルコレクション」所蔵の『梅園魚譜』と『梅園魚品図正』より転載している。本書掲載にあたって原画の色調補正、絵図をつなぎ合わせる、文字の移動等の画像補正を行なっている。

・収録図版は江戸時代に制作されているため、現代の見解とは異なる点がある。そのため、種の正確な同定が困難なものもある。

【Notes】

・ The illustrations in this book are taken from *Baien-gyofu* and *Baien Gyohin Zusei*" in the National Diet Library Digital Colleciton. The original images have been adjusted for publication in this book. Adjustments include color compensation, image stitching, and relocation of text.

・ The illustrations in this book were created during the Edo era (1603–1867); thus, they contain aspects that differ from modern interpretations, making it difficult to accurately identify some species.

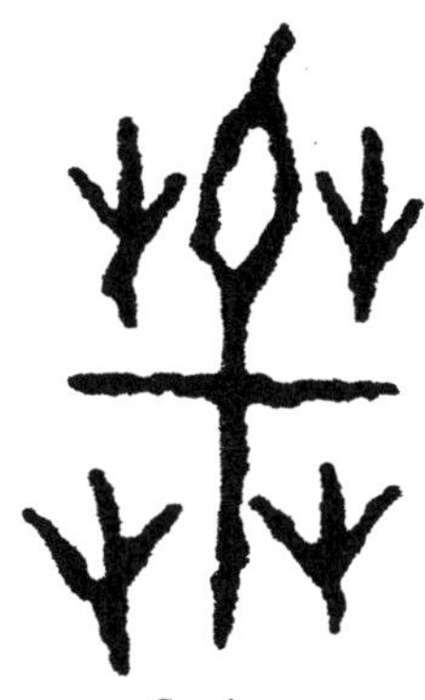

Spring

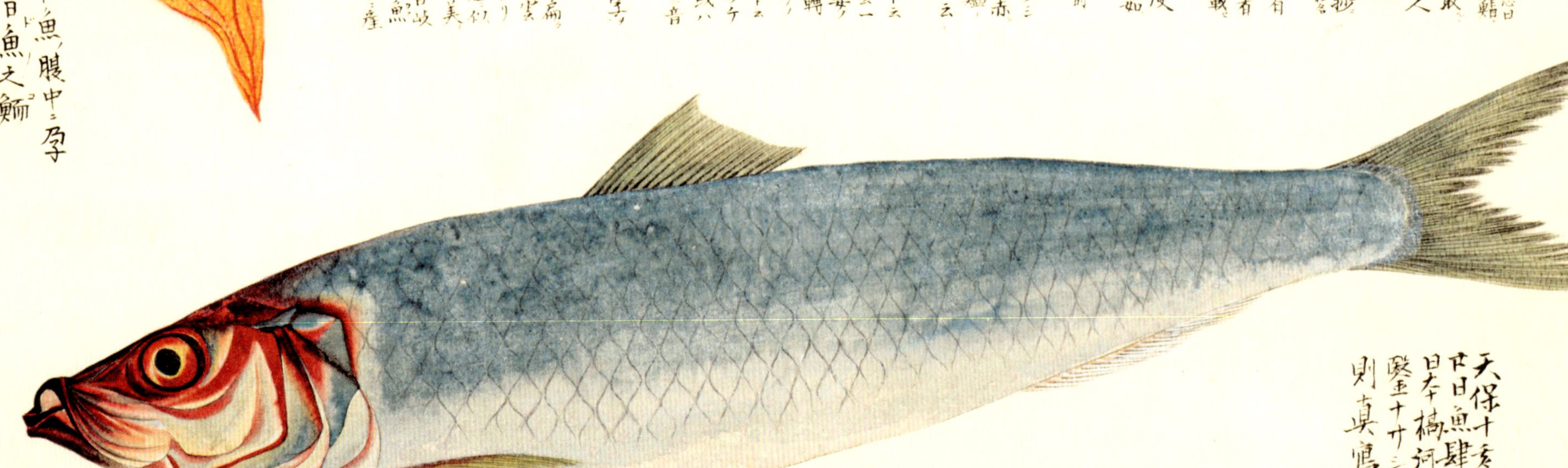

青ノ魚　二親魚　本草綱目　青魚

此青ノ魚ノ腹中ニ子アリ
者青魚之鰊

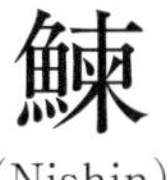

鰊
（Nishin）

鯡　　春告魚　　青魚
（Nishin）　（Harutsugeuo）　（Kado）

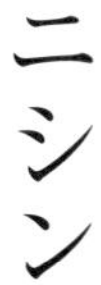

ニシン

Pacific herring

ニシン目ニシン科ニシン属。学名は*Clupea pallasii*。日本では主に東北以北の沿岸域に分布する。体長は3〜4年の個体で約30cm。和名「ニシン」の由来は、両親の長寿を祈って食べる魚であったという説、父親と母親を意味する「二親」という説、身を2つに割いて干していたことから「二身」説などがある。春に産卵のために接岸するため「春告魚」「春ニシン」とも呼ばれる。室町時代の『運歩色葉集』やそれ以前の風土記で確認されており、古くから日本人に馴染みのある魚だった。ただし、江戸時代の『重修本草綱目啓蒙』によれば京都には背肉のみを乾燥させた身欠ニシンが運ばれ、美味な身全体のニシンがなかったため、猫の食べ物とされていたという。

Clupea pallasii (Clupeiformes, Clupeidae). In Japan, this fish is primarily found in coastal areas of the Tohoku region and further north. They typically grow to roughly 30 cm in length within three or four years of birth. One theory of the origin of their Japanese name, "nishin," is that it came from "ni" (meaning "two") and "shin" (meaning "flesh") because they are split in two before being dried for consumption. According to the *Choshu Honzo Komoku Keimo*, written during the Edo era (1603–1867), only migaki nishin, which included only the dried back side of the fish, was taken to Kyoto, instead of the delicious full-fleshed nishin, so they were used as cat food.

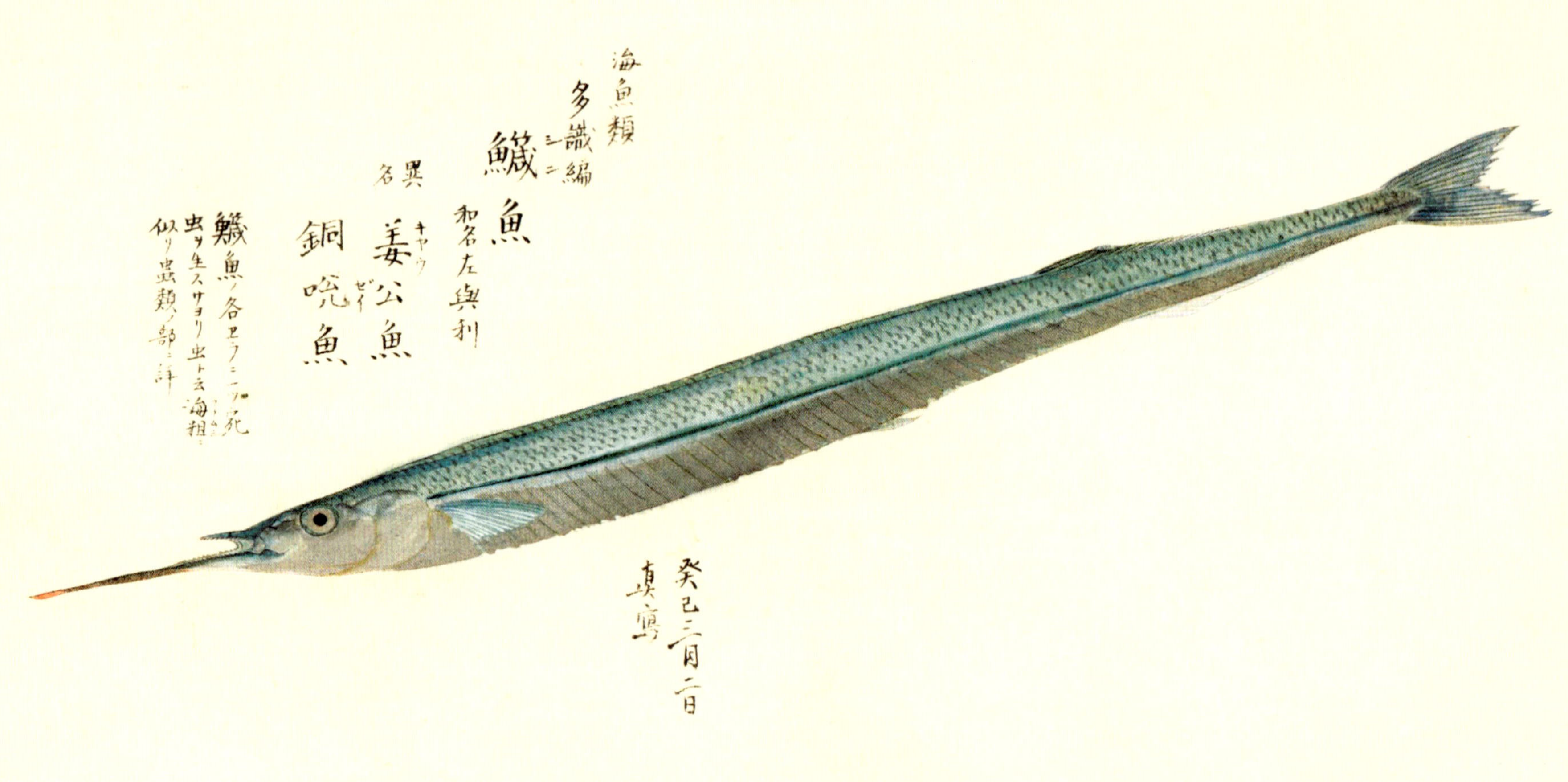

海魚類
多識編 二ノ二二
鱵魚
異名
和名左與利
姜公魚 キャウ
銅呪魚 ゼイ
鱵魚ノ各ヒフ二ツ死
虫ヲ生スサヨリ虫ト云海粗
似リ虫類ノ部ニ詳
癸巳三月二日
眞寫

細魚
(Sayori)

鱵
(Sayori)

鱵魚
(Sayori)

針魚
(Hario)

閂
(Kannuki)

サヨリ

Japanese halfbeak

ダツ目サヨリ科サヨリ属。学名は*Hyporhamphus sajori*。小笠原諸島を除く北海道から九州までの沿岸域、朝鮮半島などに分布する。体長は30〜40cm。白身で上品な味のため刺身や鮨種として人気。「サヨリ」の和名は、群れる習性から魚が群集するさまを表す「さわ寄り」が語源という説や、細長い群れを作ることから「サ（狭い）」と「ヨリ（寄り）」という説、また「サワ（岸辺）」と「ヨリ（寄り）」が由来とする説など多数ある。体が細く、背部が青緑色、腹部が銀白色という外見の美しさから「海の貴婦人」とも称されるが、腹膜が真っ黒なため、悪巧みをする人をたとえて「美人だがサヨリのように腹黒い」ということもあった。

Hyporhamphus sajori (Beloniformes, Hemiramphidae). This fish is found in coastal areas from Hokkaido to Kyushu, except for around the Ogasawara Islands, and around the Korean Peninsula. They typically measure 30 to 40 cm in length. One theory of the origin of their Japanese name, "sayori," is that it comes from "sawayori," meaning "to gather together," because they gather in schools. Due to their beautiful appearance, they have been called "the ladies of the sea," but their abdominal lining is black, so it is sometimes said of devious women that "they're beautiful, but black-hearted, like a halfbeak."

石鰈
(Ishigarei)

鰈
(Karei)

石王余魚
(Ishikarei)

比目魚
(Himokugyo)

イシガレイ

Stone flounder

カレイ目カレイ科ヌマガレイ属。学名は*Platichthys bicoloratus*。日本では九州西岸以北の日本海と東シナ海沿岸、豊後水道以北の太平洋沿岸、瀬戸内海に分布する。体長は約50cm。和名の由来は両眼とも体の右側にあり、成魚になると有眼側に石状の骨質板が発達することから。もともと「カレイ」は「カレエヒ」「カラエイ」と呼ばれており、朝鮮半島南部の「韓に多い鱝のような魚」から派生した名前だと考えられている。カレイの大型のものは「座布団ガレイ」とも呼ばれる。江戸の地誌『江戸名所図会』によると、イシガレイは江戸から明治期にかけての東京で人気の魚で、日本橋魚市などで見られるカレイは全て本種であったという。

Platichthys bicoloratus (Pleuronectiformes, Pleuronectidae). In Japan, this fish is found along the coasts of the Sea of Japan and East China Sea north of the western coast of Kyushu, along the Pacific coast north of the Bungo Channel, and in the Seto Inland Sea. They typically measure 50 cm in length. Both of their eyes are on the right side of their body, and some stone-like plates develop over the side with the eyes as an adult, hence the name "stone flounder." According to the *Edo Meisho Zue*, they were popular in Tokyo throughout the Edo and Meiji periods (1603–1912), and all of the flounders in the Nihombashi fish market were stone flounder.

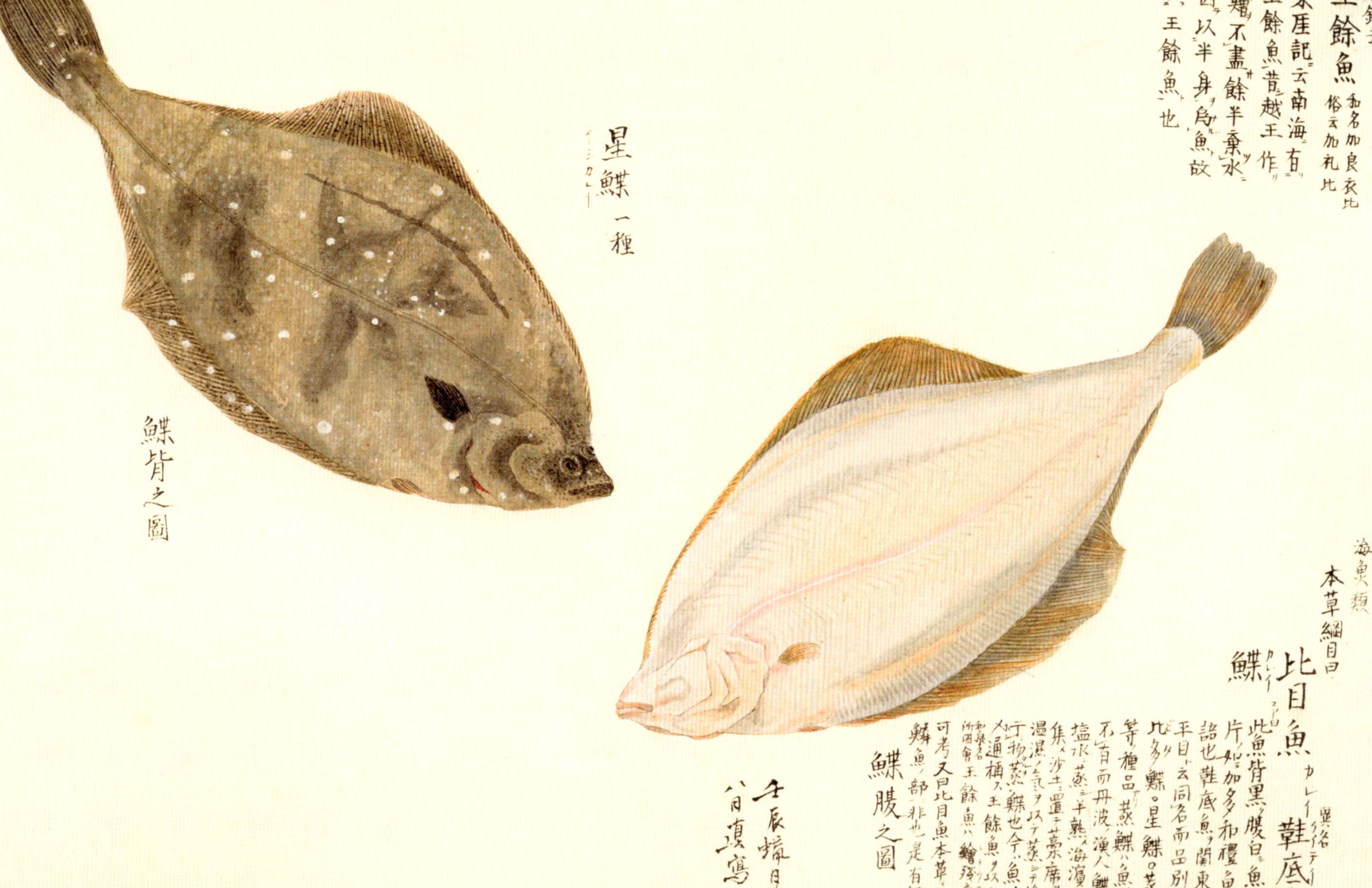

和名鈔ニ云
王餘魚 和名加良衣比 俗云加礼比
朱崖記ニ云南海ニ有リ
王餘魚昔越王ノ作リ
膾不盡餘半棄水ニ
因リ以半身烏魚故
曰王餘魚也
星鰈一種
鰈背之圖
海獣類
本草綱目
比目魚 鞋底魚
鰈
鰈腹之圖
壬辰臘月
八日眞寫

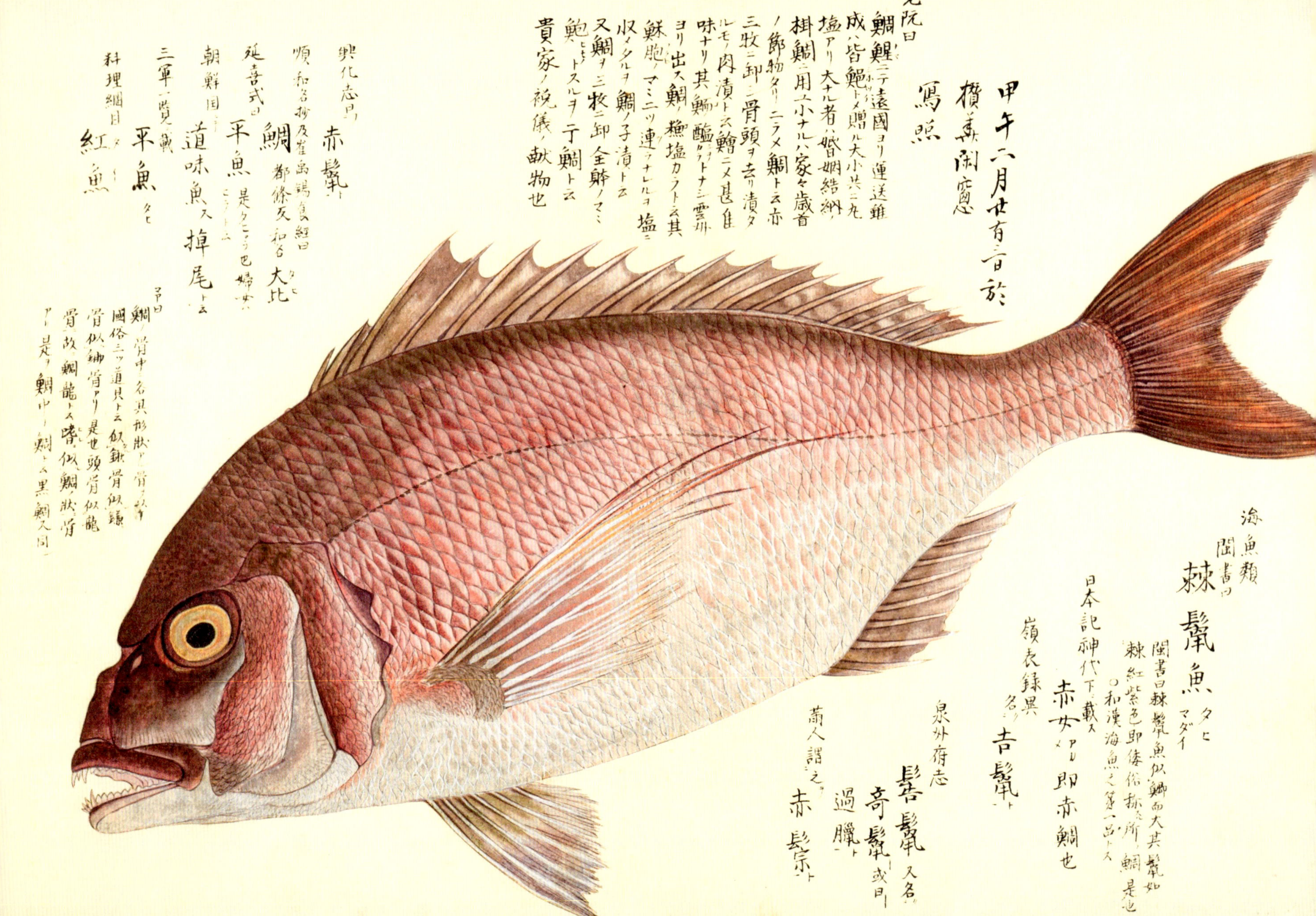

海魚類
閭書曰
棘鬣魚 タヒ マダイ
日本記神代下ニ載ス
嶺表錄異
赤女 アリ 即赤鯛也
赤鬣宗ト
泉外府志
吉鬣 ト
甲午六月廿有二日於
攅簶閑窗
寫照
元阮曰
鯛鯉ニテ遠國ヨリ連送シ雖
成ハ皆鮑トメ贈ル大小共三九
塩アリ大小ハ者婚姻結納
掛鯛用ニ小ナル八家々歲音
興化志曰
赤鬣ト
順和名抄及崔禹錫曰紅日
鯛
延喜式ニ
平魚
朝鮮国ニ
道味魚ニ掉尾
三軍一覧ニ載
平魚 トモ
料理綱目
紅魚

真鯛
（Madai）

赤女
（Akame）　平魚
（Tairauo）　花見鯛
（Hanamidai）　桜鯛
（Sakuradai）　紅魚
（Tai）　太比
（Tai）

マダイ

Red seabream

スズキ目タイ科マダイ属。学名は*Pagrus major*。北海道から九州南岸までの日本周辺海域、渤海、黄海などに分布する。体長は最大で1mを超える。長命で20年以上生きるものもいるといわれている。和名「タイ」の由来は、体形が平らなことから「平魚」が転訛したという説や、恵比寿様が釣る魚であることから「めでたい」の語呂合わせだとする説などがある。体の淡紅色（赤色）が魔除けになると信じられ、さらに立派な姿と上品な味のため、婚礼や祭りなどの祝い事に欠かせない魚として重宝されてきた。奈良時代の皇族や平安時代の貴族、室町時代の足利将軍などの献立の記録に鯛（主にマダイ）の名前がある。織田信長が徳川家康を饗応した際の膳にも鯛が含まれていた。

Pagrus major (Perciformes, Sparidae). This fish is found in the seas around Japan from Hokkaido to the southern coast of Kyushu, the Bohai Sea, and the Yellow Sea. They can grow to sizes over 100 cm in length. They are long-lived, with some said to live for over 20 years. Their Japanese name, "tai," is said to come from their flat shape ("taira" is the Japanese word for "flat"). Due to the reddish rainbow colors of their body, which were believed to ward off evil, their beautiful shape, and their refined taste, they are a mainstay fish in meals eaten at weddings, festivals, and other celebrations.

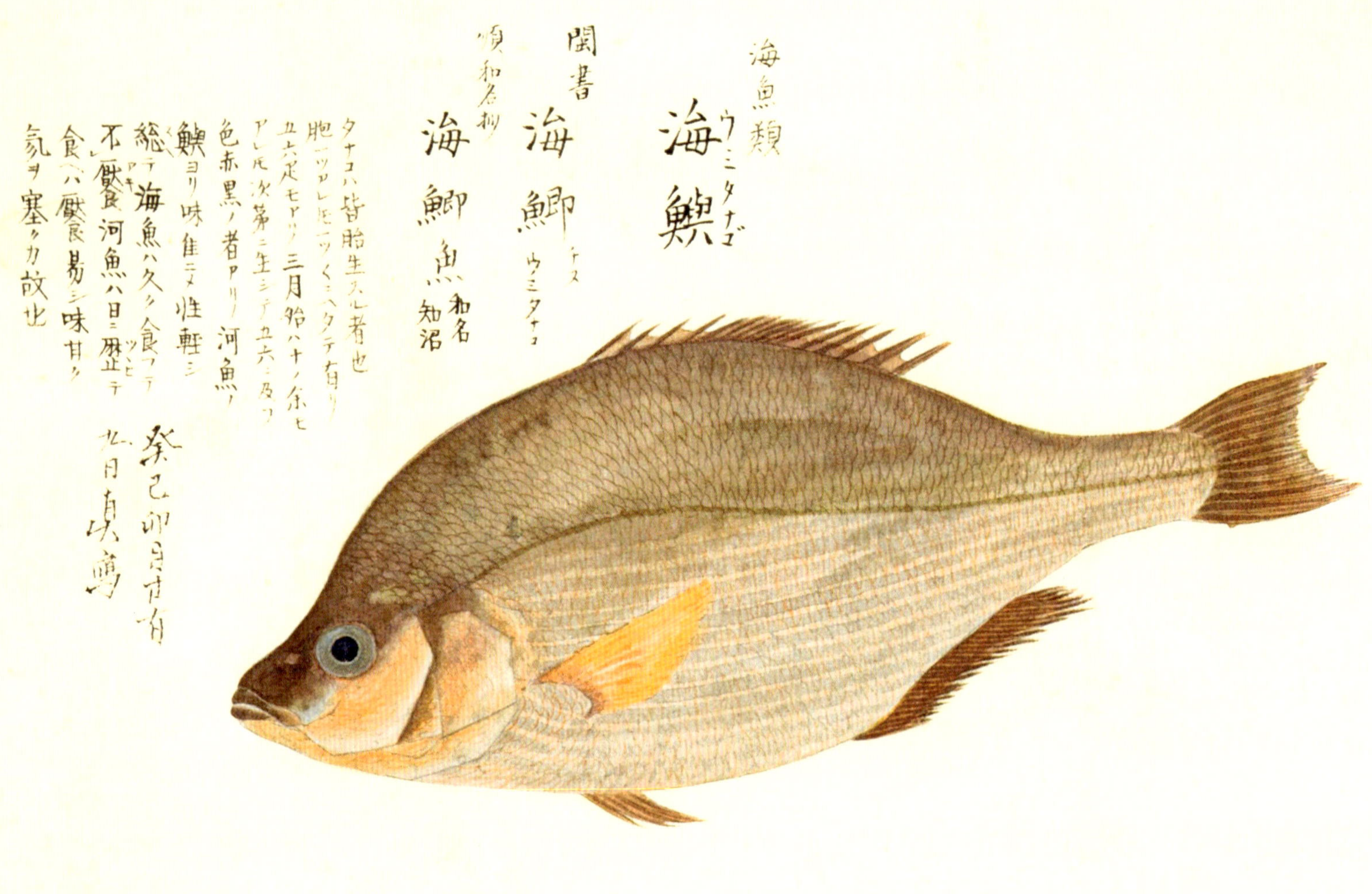
海魚類　ウミタナゴ
海鱮
閩書　海鯽魚　ウミタナコ
順和名栁　海鯽魚　和名　知沼
タナコハ皆胎生ニシテ心者也
胞一ツヅレニ二ツヽミニハクテ有リ
五六足モアリ三月始ハ十ノ余ヒ
アレ死次第二生ニシテ五六ニ及フ
色赤黒ノ者アリノ河魚ノ
鱮ヨリ味隹ニメ性軽シ
総テ海魚ハ久ク食フテ
不厭食河魚ハ八日ニ歴止テ
食ハ厭食易シ味甘ク
気ヲ塞ク力故止
癸巳卯月市有
九月　貞鳶

赤鱏
（Akatanago）

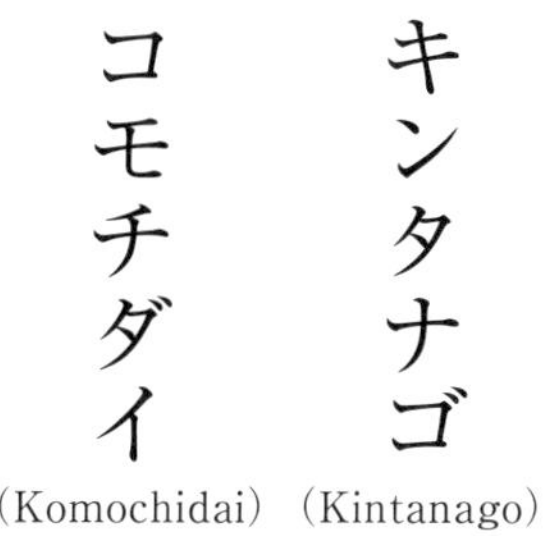

キンタナゴ
（Kintanago）

コモチダイ
（Komochidai）

アカタナゴ

A surfperch (no English name)

図には「海鱏」とあるが、赤い体色などからアカタナゴと考えられる。スズキ目ウミタナゴ科ウミタナゴ属。学名は*Ditrema jordani*。房総半島から紀伊水道までの太平洋沿岸に分布する。体長は20〜25cm。名前の由来は淡水魚の「タナゴ」に似ているので「ウミタナゴ」、体色の赤いものを「アカタナゴ」と呼ぶようになったといわれている。「タナゴ」の名前は平たい魚という意味の古名「タヒラ」「タヒラコ」から、また水田にすむので「田な魚」などが由来といわれている。魚類の中では珍しい胎生。胎内の子は逆子の状態でいるため、山陰地方では妊婦には縁起が悪い魚とする一方、子をたくさん産むことから、東北地方では安産祈願の魚とするなど、地域によって異なる伝承がある。

Ditrema jordani (Perciformes, Embiotocidae). This fish can be found along the Pacific coast, everywhere from the Boso Peninsula to the Kii Channel. They typically measure 20 to 25 cm in length. The Japanese name for surfperch, "umitanago" is said to have come from its resemblance to the freshwater fish "tanago" (bitterlings), of which the red-colored ("aka") ones in particular came to be called "akatanago." "Umi" means "sea," and "tanago" is said to come from the ancient word "tahira" or "tahirako," meaning "flat fish," or from "tanago," meaning "rice field fish." They are unusual fish in that they bear live young.

桜鱒
（Sakuramasu）

紅鱒　本鱒　鱒
（Benimasu）（Honmasu）（Masu）

サクラマス

Masu salmon

サケ目サケ科サケ属。学名は *Oncorhynchus masou masou*。北海道全域、本州の日本海側、神奈川県酒匂川以北の太平洋側、大分を除く九州などに分布する。体長は約60㎝。降海型を「サクラマス」、河川残留型を「ヤマメ」と呼ぶ。和名「サクラマス」の由来には諸説あり、一説では桜が花を付ける頃に川を遡上することから名付けられたといわれている。産卵期になると雄が婚姻色を呈することでも知られ、その婚姻色が桜色をしていることに由来するという説もある。ちなみに「ヤマメ」は漢字で「山女魚」と書き、「山の魚」という意味。どちらも食用とされる。サクラマスを使った料理で特に有名なのは鱒を酢締めにした押し鮨で、富山県の郷土料理「鱒鮨」が知られている。

Oncorhynchus masou masou (Salmoniformes, Salmonidae). This fish can be found throughout Hokkaido, Honshu north of Kanagawa and Yamaguchi Prefectures, and Kyushu, except for Oita Prefecture. They typically measure 60 cm in length. Sea-run masu salmon are called "sakura masu" in Japanese, while river-resident masu salmon are called "yamame." According to one theory, their Japanese name, "sakura masu," is said to come from the fact that they swim upstream when the rivers are dotted with cherry blossoms ("sakura"). One famous sushi dish made with masu salmon is Toyama Prefecture's famous vinegared "masu-zushi."

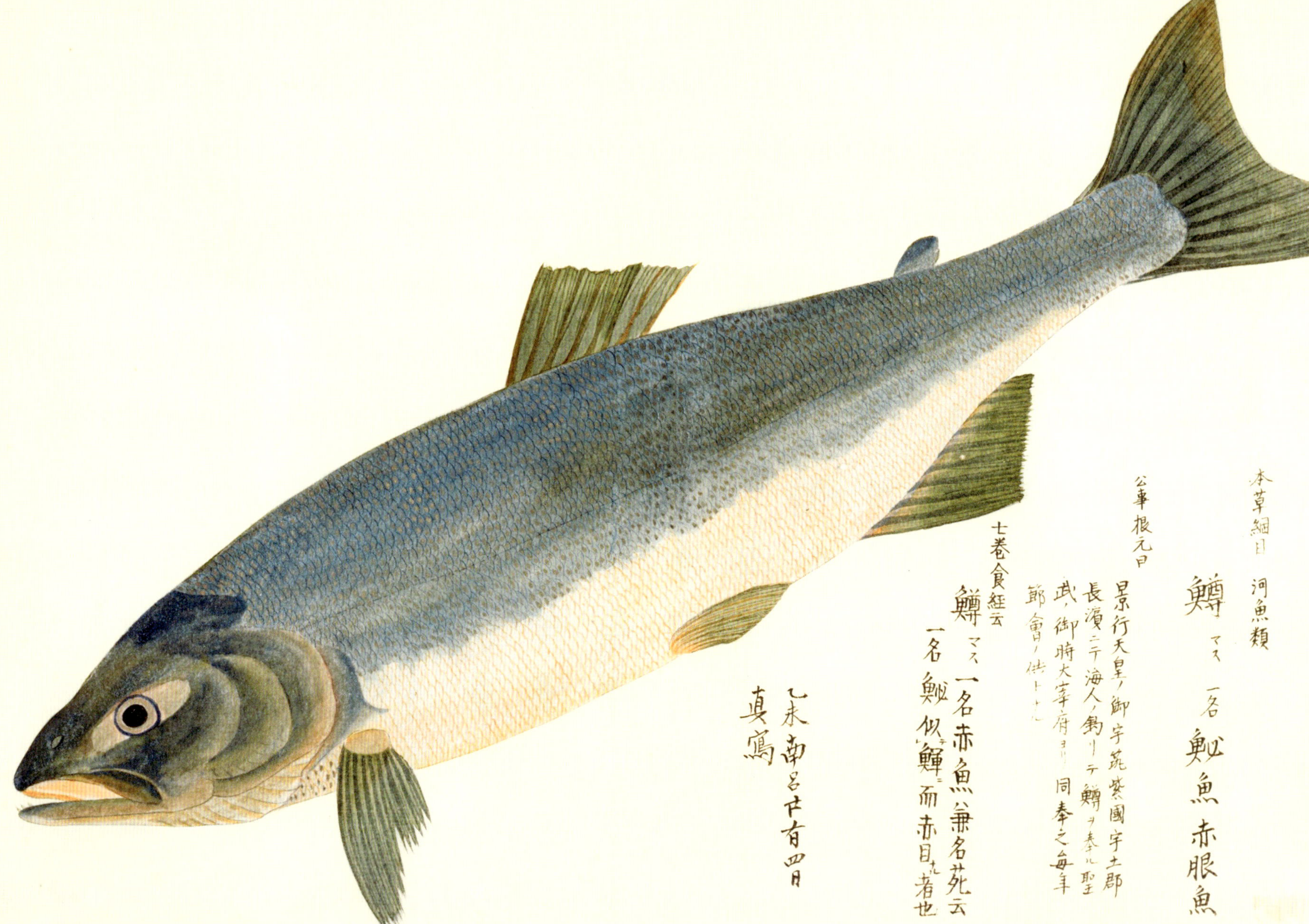

本草綱目　河魚類
鱒　マス　一名　䰲魚　赤眼魚

公車根元曰
景行天皇ノ御宇筑紫國宇土郡
長濱ニテ海人ノ釣リテ鱒ヲ奉ル聖
武ノ御時大宰府ヨリ同奉之毎年
節會ノ供トセリ

七巻食経云
鱒　マス　一名赤魚　兼名苑云
一名䰲　似鱒而赤目九者也

乙未南呂廿有四日
真寫

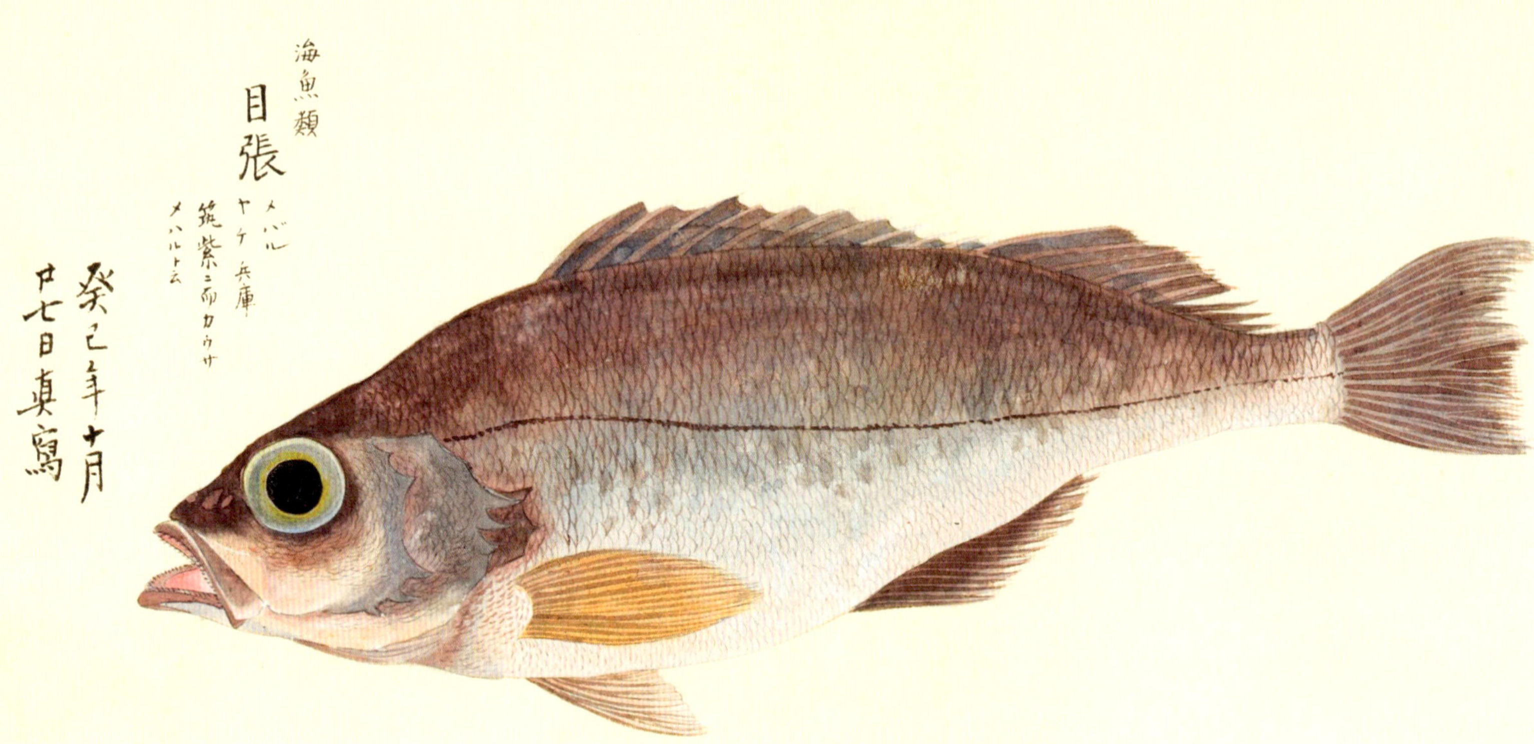

海魚類
目張
メバル
ヤケ　兵庫
筑紫ニ而カゝウ
メバルトモ云
癸巳年十月
廿七日東寫

赤眼張

（Akamebaru）

春告魚
（Harutsugeuo）

赤羽
（Akaba）

アカメバル

Darkbanded rockfish

メバルは体色や体形によって、アカメバル、シロメバル、クロメバルに分けられる。図はアカメバル。スズキ目メバル科メバル属。学名は *Sebastes inermis*。北海道から長崎県までの日本海沿岸、相模湾から紀伊水道までの太平洋沿岸などに分布する。体長は約20cm。和名「メバル」の由来は眼が大きく、出張っていることから。江戸時代の本草書『本朝食鑑』には「黒、赤の二種があり、江戸、相州、豆州、総州、房州の諸州の江浜に多い」とあり、食用とされてきたことがうかがえる。また、江戸時代の百科事典といわれる『和漢三才図会』には「メバルは蟾蜍の化するところなり」とあり、眼の大きさからか、ヒキガエルがメバルになると考えられていたようだ。

Sebastes inermis (Perciformes, Sebastidae). This fish is found along the coast of the Sea of Japan from Hokkaido to Nagasaki Prefecture and along the Pacific coast from Sagami Bay to the Kii Channel. They typically measure 20 cm in length. Their Japanese name, "mebaru," comes from the fact that their eyes ("me") project outward ("haru"). The *Wakan Sansai Zue*, an encyclopedia of the Edo era (1603–1867), states that "Darkbanded rockfish come from toads." Apparently, it was believed, based on the size of their eyes, that toads turned into the fish.

うっかり笠子
（Ukkarikasago）

ウッカリカサゴ

A rockfish (no English name)

スズキ目メバル科カサゴ属。学名は*Sebastiscus tertius*。青森県から鹿児島県までの太平洋沿岸、若狭湾、山口県の日本海沿岸、朝鮮半島南岸などに分布する。体長は20〜40cm。和名の由来は「カサゴ」に似ているため、うっかり「カサゴ」と呼ばれてきたが、別種と判明したため「うっかりカサゴ」となった。「カサゴ」の名前は、体皮が瘡（かさ。皮膚病のこと）になったように見えることから。カサゴは『和漢三才図会』で「肉は淡白で油は少なく、味はよい。どんな病の者が食べてもさしつかえない」と記載されており、当時から食用とされてきたことがうかがえる。また江戸時代には、無骨な見た目から武家の端午の節句の祝い膳に用いられていたという。

Sebastiscus tertius (Perciformes, Sebastidae). This fish is found along the Pacific coast from Aomori Prefecture to Kagoshima Prefecture, in along the coast of the Sea of Japan in Wakasa Bay and Yamaguchi Prefecture, and along the southern coast of the Korean Peninsula. They typically measure 20 to 40 cm in length. They were initially thought to be "kasago" (*Sebastiscus marmoratus*), but it was later discovered that they were actually a different species, so they were renamed "ukkari kasago," which means "inadvertent kasago." Due to its rough appearance, during the Edo era (1603–1867), the fish was used in dishes eaten by samurai families when celebrating Boy's Day.

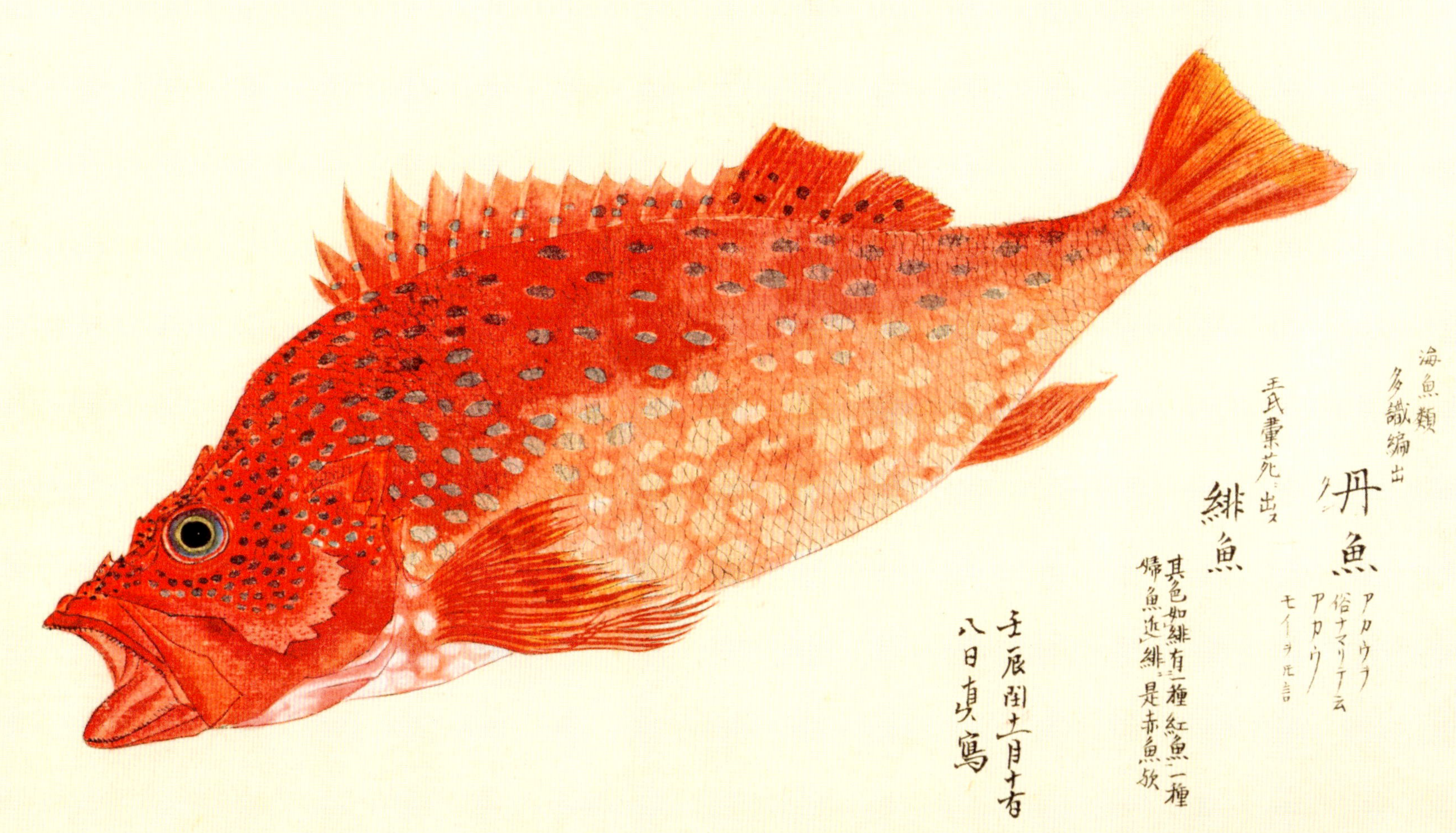

海魚類
多識編出
王氏彙苑ニ出ス
丹魚 アカウラ 俗ナマリテ云 アカウ モイヲ死言
緋魚
其色如緋有一種紅魚一種
帰魚近緋 是赤魚欤
壬辰閏土月十有
八日真寫

鮒
（Funa）

ヒラブナ
（Hirabuna）

金太郎鮒
（Kintarobuna）

真鮒
（Mabuna）

金鮒
（Kinbuna）

フナ

Crucian carps

上の図はキンブナで下の図はギンブナ。キンブナはコイ目コイ科フナ属。学名は*Carassius buergeri*。東北地方の太平洋側と関東地方に分布する。体長は約15 cm。ギンブナに比べて数が少なく、現在は絶滅の危険が増し、環境省のレッドリストにて絶滅危惧II類に指定されている。ギンブナの学名は*Carassius* sp.。日本各地に分布する。体長は12〜30 cm。「フナ」の語源は、水中に伏して隠れるという意味の「伏魚」に由来するという説や、「フ」が古くは産地や田んぼを意味する語であることから田んぼ・養殖池（フ）の魚（ナ）に由来するという説などがある。「キンブナ」の名前は体色が黄色みがかっていること、「ギンブナ」も同様に銀色に近い色であることに由来する。

Carassius buergeri ("kinbuna," above) and *Carassius* sp. ("ginbuna," below) (Cypriniformes, Cyprinidae). Kinbuna is found along the Pacific Ocean side of the Tohoku region and in the Kanto region. They typically measure 15 cm in length. They are rarer than "ginbuna" and are in increased danger of extinction. They have been designated as "Vulnerable" in the Ministry of the Environment's Red List. Ginbuna is found across Japan. They typically measure 12 to 30 cm in length. "Funa" is said to come from "fusu" (to hide) and "na" (fish) because they hide in the water.

本草綱目第四十四卷

鯽魚　鯽資音即　音積

一名鮮千美羨　恩蓬　水族似　フナ　マフナ　釋名　鮒　音附　モブシ　ツカフナ　萬葉集

鱮頮　正字通　逆鱗之魚　事物紺珠　波臣　事物紺珠　皆其上同

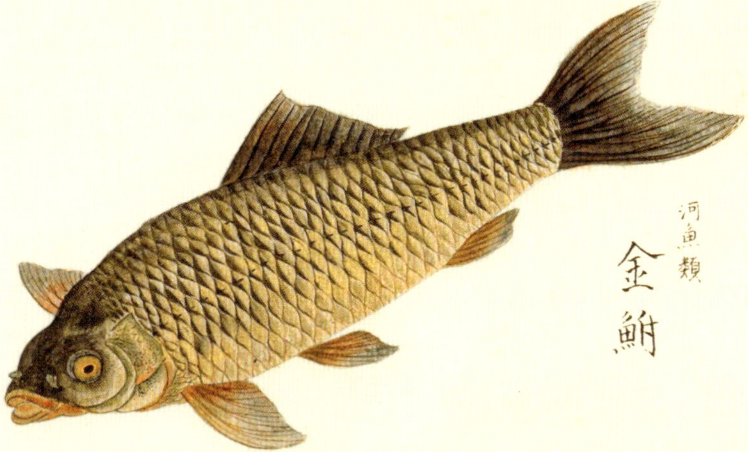

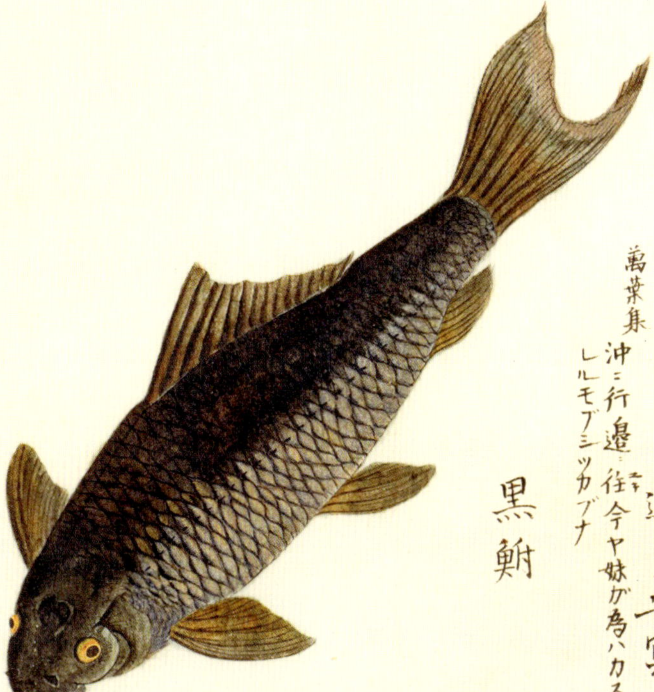

鯽魚　東方朔　神異經

河魚類

金鮒

萬葉集　沖ニ行邊ニ往今ヤ妹が為ハカスト　レルモブ三ツカブナ

黒鮒

甲午二月四日猪江之産曽渕某氏送之真寫

癸巳年十月　廿七日真寫

鮮鯽銀絲繪　香芹碧澗美義　陪鄭廣文作　牡子美

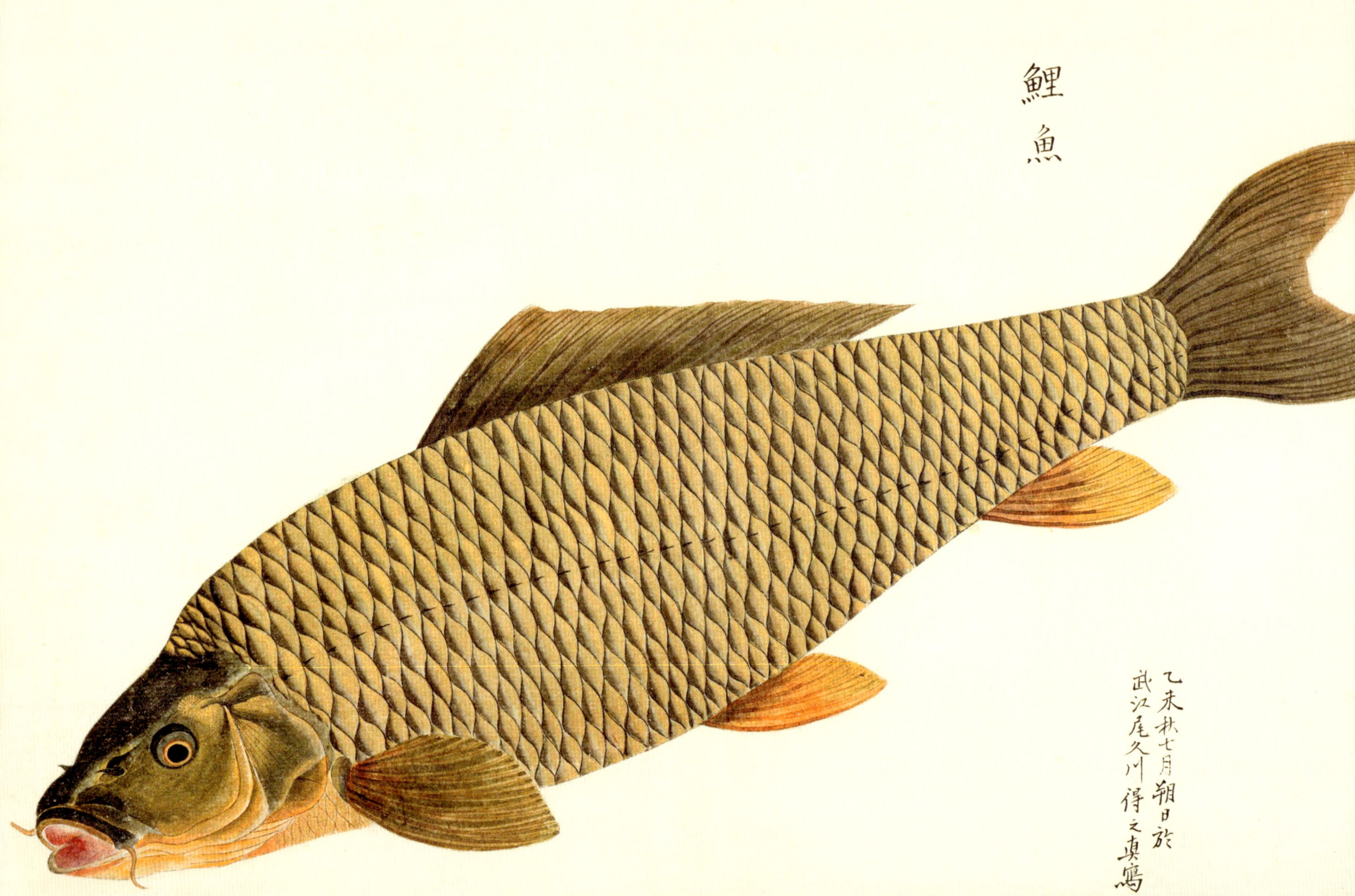

鯉魚
乙未秋七月朝日於
武江尾久川得之真寫

鯉
（Koi）

鮗
（Ko）

六六魚
（Rikurikugyo）

コイ

Common carp

コイ目コイ科コイ属。学名は*Cyprinus carpio*。ユーラシア大陸の温帯域が原産であるが、放流により世界各地で定着している。日本には大陸から人為的に持ち込まれた外来コイと、自然分布していた在来コイが生息している。日本各地で交雑が進んでいるが、琵琶湖の深層に純粋に近い在来コイが残存している。体長は約60cm。「コイ」の語源は、身が肥えていることから「肥」が転じたという説など、多数ある。日本では端午の節句に鯉のぼりをあげて男児の健康や出世を願うように、コイは立身出世の象徴とされてきた。これは中国の「黄河の急流にある竜門をのぼることができた魚は竜に化す」という竜門伝説に由来し、江戸時代の武家では玄関に幟飾りを並べたという。

Cyprinus carpio (Cypriniformes, Cyprinidae). This fish is indigenous to temperate areas of Eurasia, but has been introduced to every part of the world. Both foreign carp brought from the continent and native carp are found in some parts of Japan. They typically measure 60 cm in length. There are many theories regarding the origin of the Japanese name "koi," such as them being fat ("koe"). In Japan, carp are a symbol of advancement in life, and Japanese parents fly carp streamers on Boy's Day in May in the hope that their boys become healthy and prosperous.

丸太
（Maruta）

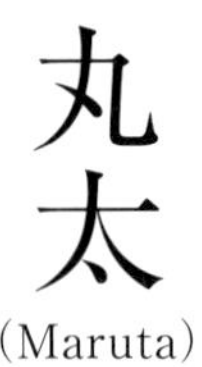

ウシマルタ
（Ushimaruta）

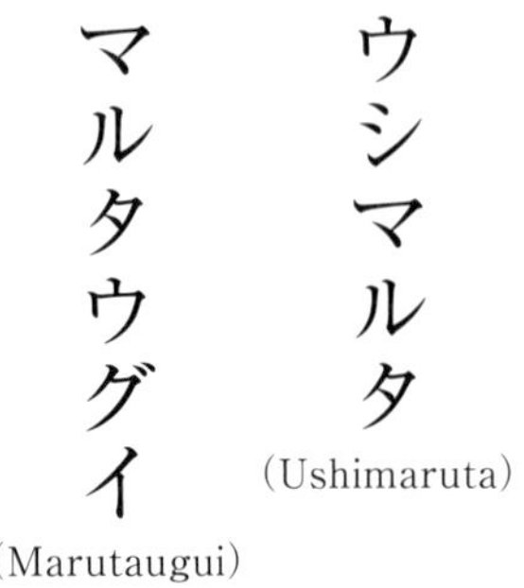

マルタウグイ
（Marutaugui）

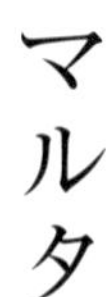

マルタ

Far Eastern dace

コイ目コイ科（またはウグイ科）ウグイ属。学名は *Pseudaspius brandtii maruta*。日本では岩手県から東京湾までの太平洋沿岸およびそこに注ぐ河川に分布する。体長は30〜40cmのものが多いが、50cm以上になるものもいる。体はやや細長い形をしているが、ウグイ類の中では太い方である。産卵期は3月〜6月頃で、産卵のために春に河川を遡上する遡河回遊魚。和名「マルタ」の由来は、体形や大きさが丸太を連想させることから付けられたといわれている。別名に「ウシマルタ」「マルタウグイ」などがある。外見がウグイに似ているが、マルタでは産卵期に出る婚姻色の赤色の帯が腹側に1本現れ、ウグイでは赤色の帯が体側背側にも現れることで区別できる。

Pseudaspius brandtii maruta (Cypriniformes, Cyprinidae (or Leuciscidae)). This fish lives along the Pacific coast from Iwate Prefecture to Tokyo Bay and along the rivers that flow into this area. They typically measure 30 to 40 cm in length, but some exceed 50 cm in length. The body of the fish is somewhat slim, but is comparatively thicker than other daces. Their spawning season is from March to June, and they are anadromous migratory fish, swimming upriver to spawn in spring. Their Japanese name, "maruta," comes from the fact that their shape and thickness are reminiscent of a log ("maruta" in Japanese).

保九戌季九陽武江
綾瀬川釣之十名七日
真寫

泉河魚産
鰷魚　青梅ハヤ
ハイ彦根
ハヱ
赤ハヱ
ハヤ野州
釋名　白條　鮻魚臭
鮈魚
一名　参魚　曲籍便覧
白鰷　同上

湖中産物志曰
ウグヒ雄　漢名不詳
サクラウグヒ

闘魚　一名　文魚也
斑魚　ト云　目高ト名同

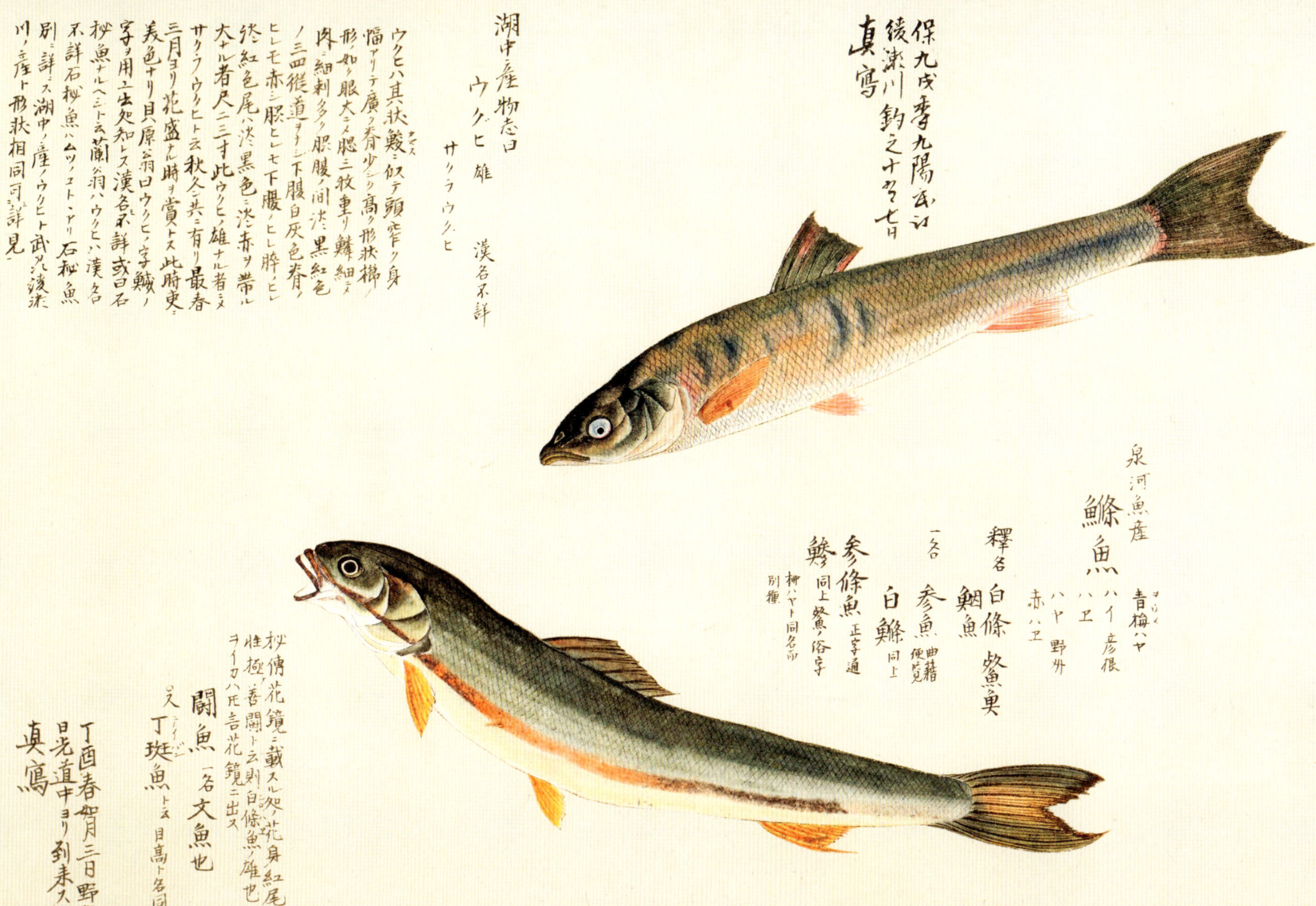

真寫

苦鮊　ベニタナゴ　アカタヒラ京　アカヒレ

鮊魚　釋名　鯿魚　漢名　苗鰱　キタヒラ京　アブラザマ　シブヒラ彦根　一名　金色鰱

河魚類
晴珍曰動ハ充也亦鰱ハ扁也　其形方具身扁也

本草出　與魚　タナゴ　鰱魚
苦鮊　タナヱ　タビラ

料理綱目　鱮　タナゴ

本草綱目云　鰱好群行ノ相與ヲ
タナノ子ハ卵ニ生セス胎生ス他魚ニ異リ海鰷ノ子モ胎生

癸巳十月十四日
掻江領釣诗
真寫

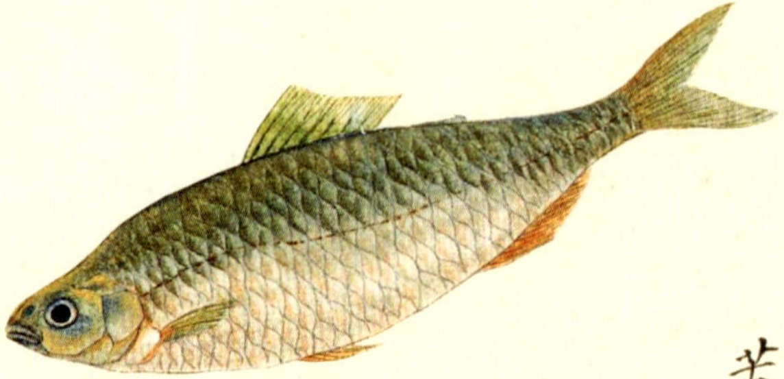

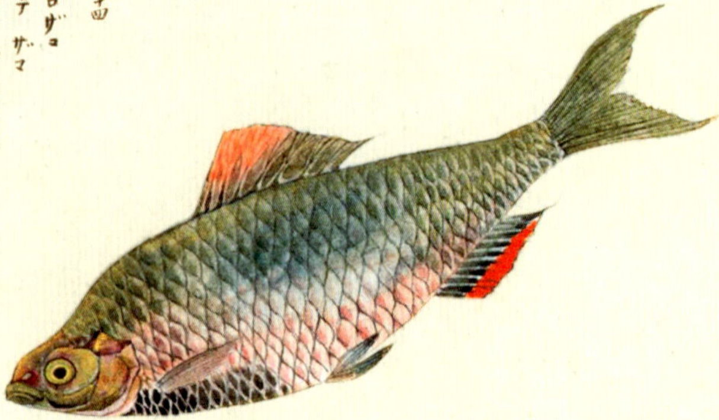

本草綱目卷第四十四

鱮魚　シロザコ　ホテザマ　一サヱ　四名共彦根　クナゴ　伏見　ムシブナ　タビラ　タビラヱ　三名共京

魾魚　網目釋名

乙未五月四日王子川
垂釣得之真寫

賻珍曰酒美者曰鱮　魚美元者曰鱮　佃云好群行ニ相與也故曰鱮　鰱相連也故曰鰱　魾傳曰魚屬蜀連行ス是矣

一名　鰱鰷
青衣魚
鱮鰷
鰕歸　二名亦雅
魚焊　妾魚　亦雅註
鰥魚　亦雅疏
鰟魮鯽　二名共鯽魚註
連魚　八閩通志

槍鱛

（Yaritanago）

ギンタ
（Ginta）

イシボテ
（Ishibote）

ニガフナ
（Nigafuna）

田平子
（Tabirako）

御細
（Ohoso）

ヤリタナゴ

A bitterling (no English name)

コイ目コイ科アブラボテ属。学名は *Tanakia lanceolata*。北海道と南九州を除く日本各地、朝鮮半島から中国の鴨緑江水系に分布する。日本産のタナゴ類において最も分布域が広い種だが、環境省のレッドリストで準絶滅危惧種に指定されている。体長は約10cm。他のタナゴ類より体高が低く、細長い。春から夏の産卵期には雄の鰓蓋の後方は美しい紅色の婚姻色になる。図の左上の個体は「アカタヒラ」と書かれているが、背鰭の前方が赤い、尾柄の縦帯がない、臀鰭外縁が赤いなど、ヤリタナゴの雄の婚姻色の特徴が出ている。右下の個体は口ひげが描かれていないため、タビラ類、タナゴの可能性も残る。和名「ヤリタナゴ」の由来は、細長い体が槍の穂先のように見えることから。

Tanakia lanceolata (Cypriniformes, Cyprinidae (or Acheilognathidae)). This fish is found throughout Japan, except for Hokkaido and Southern Kyushu, and from the Korean Peninsula to China's Yarlung River system. The fish is the most geographically widespread among bitterlings in Japan, but it is designated as a near-threatened species in the Ministry of the Environment's Red List. They typically measure 10 cm in length. The area behind the gill covers of males develops a beautiful red nuptial coloration during the spawning season, from spring to summer. Their Japanese name, "yaritanago," comes from the fact that their slim body resembles a spear ("yari").

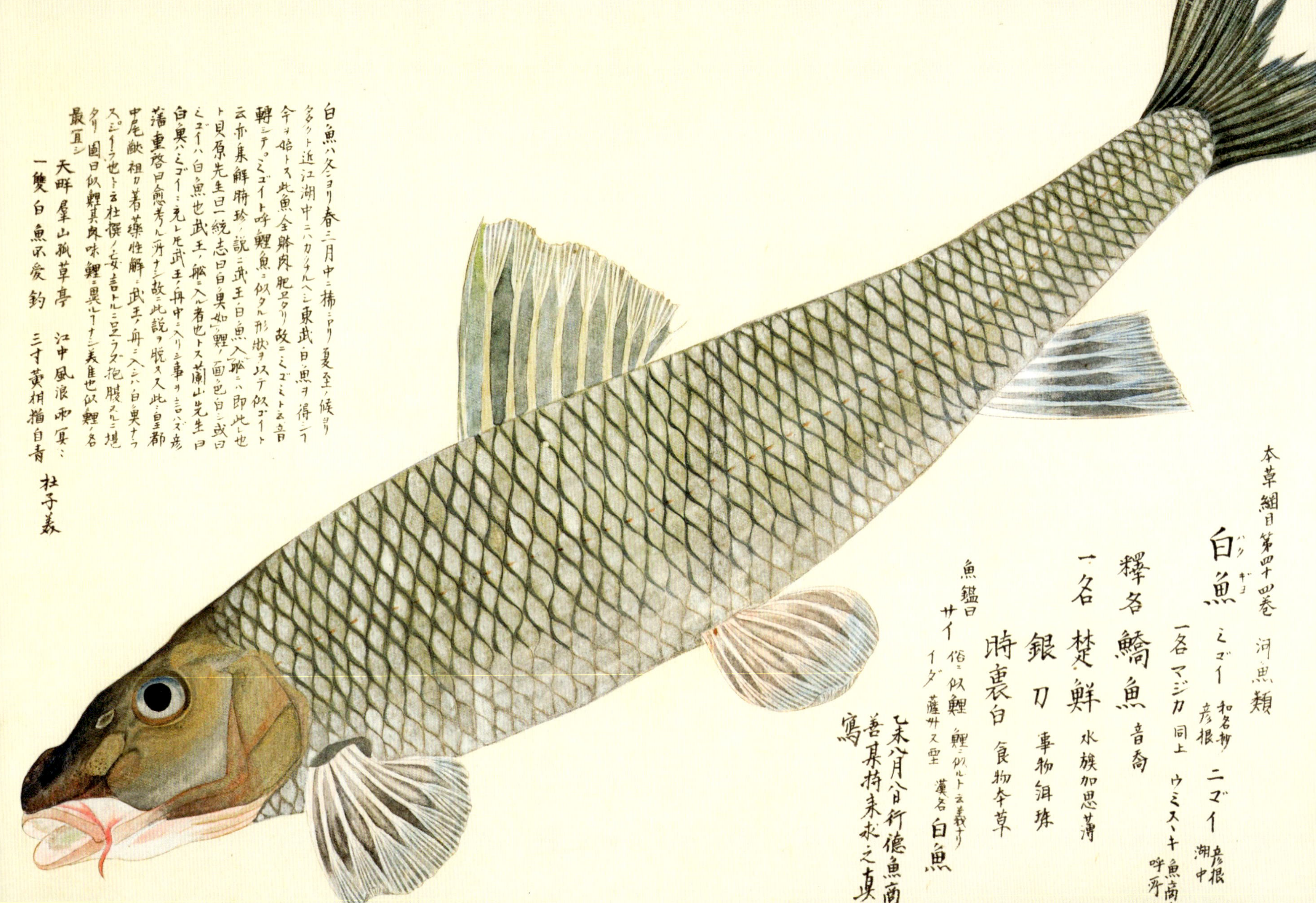
本草綱目第四十四巻　河魚類
白魚
一名マジカ
釋名　鰷魚
一名樊鮮
銀刀
時裏白
魚鑑曰
サイ
白魚
未八月八日行德魚商
善果持末求之眞
寫

似鯉
（Nigoi）

サイ
（Sai）

ミゴイ
（Migoi）

狐鯉
（Kitsunegoi）

丸太魚
（Marutauo）

ニゴイ

Japanese barbel

コイ目コイ科（またはカマツカ科）ニゴイ属。学名は*Hemibarbus barbus*。琵琶湖以東の本州と九州北部などに不連続に分布する。日本固有種。体長は約40cm。最大で60cmになるものもいる。体は細長い。小骨が多いため食用として好まれていないが、天ぷらなどにして食べられる。和名「ニゴイ」の由来は、体形がコイに似ていることから。他に「ミゴヒ（白魚）」が転訛したという説など、諸説ある。古名「丸太魚」の語源は、江戸時代の本草書『本朝食鑑』に「円く肥え長い形で、円材が流れるように泳ぐところから」とある。また江戸時代の生活実用書といわれる『魚鑑』には「形はコイに似て白色で鱗が細く、肉はやわらかいが骨が多く、淡水にすむ」と記されている。

Hemibarbus barbus (Cypriniformes, Cyprinidae (or Gobionidae)). This fish is found in isolated populations in Honshu, from Lake Biwa eastward, and in northern Kyushu. They are endemic to Japan. They typically measure 40 cm in length, but can grow as large as 60 cm in length. Their Japanese name, "nigoi," comes from the resemblance ("ni") of its shape to "koi" (common carp). The *Honchoshokkan*, a book of dietary medicines from the Edo era (1603–1867), says that their ancient name, "maruta-uo," came from the fact that they are round, fat, and long, swimming like a floating log ("maruta").

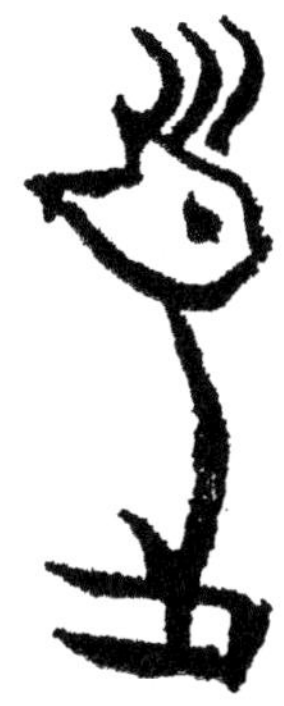

Summer

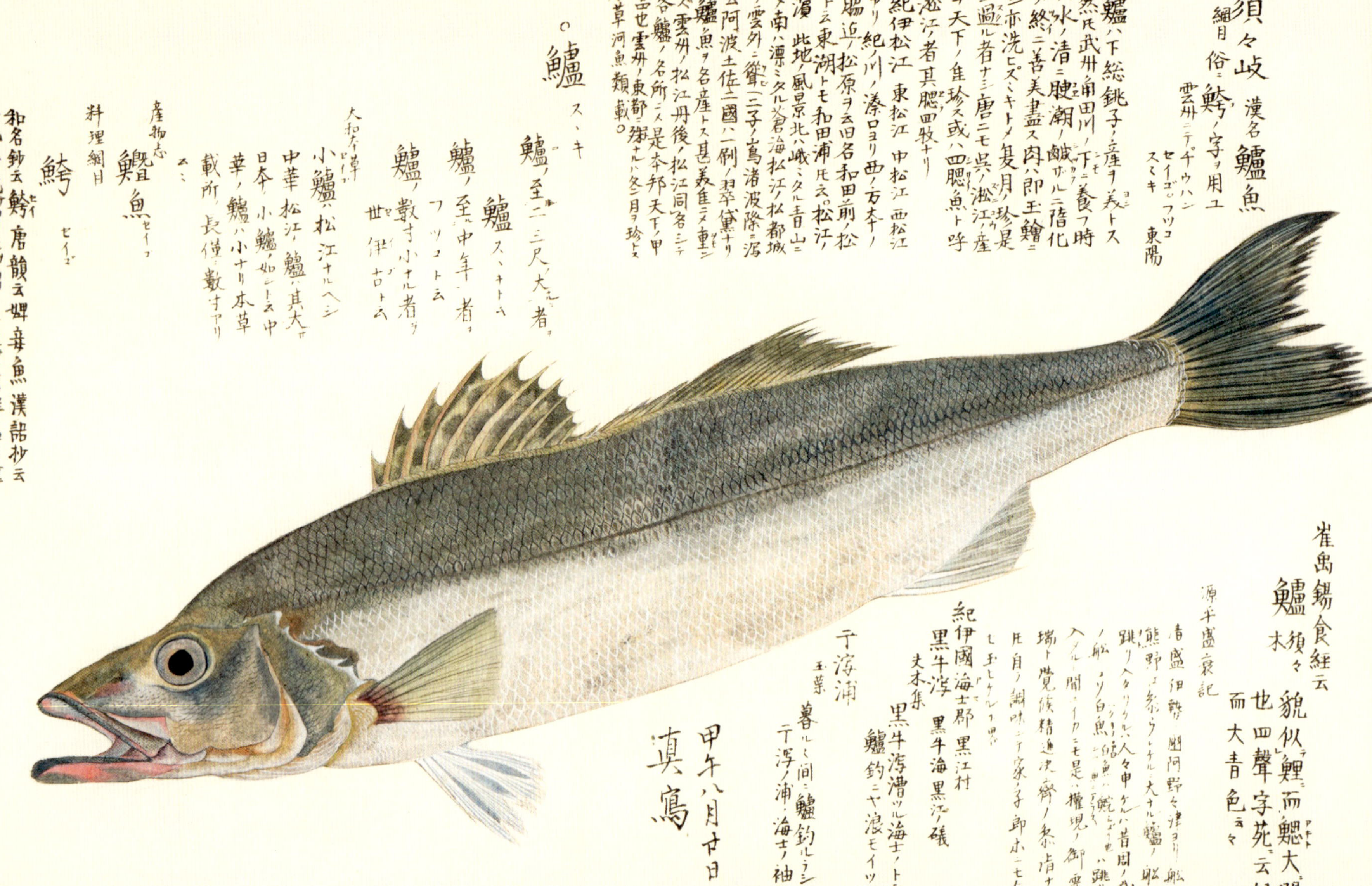

須々岐　漢名　鱸魚
網目　俗に鱸　字を用ユ
雲州ニテスズキ
セイゴ・フツコ　スズキ　東陽

鱸　スヽキ

鱸、至ニ二三尺ノ大ナル者ヲ

鱸、スヽキトヘ

鱸ノ至ニ中年ノ者ヲ
フツコト云

鱸ノ散ス小ナル者ヲ
世ニ伊ト云

小鱸ハ松江ニテルヘニ
中華松江ノ鱸、其大ナルニ
日本ノ鱸ハ小ナリ本草
華ノ鱸ハ小ナリ本草
載所ニ、長倍シ數ナスアリ

鱸八下総銚子ノ産ヲ美ナトス
然氏武州角田川ノ下ニ養フ時
ハ氷ノ清ニ腴ノ潮ノ鹹ナルニ陰化
メ終ニ善美畫ス肉八郎王鱠ニ
シ亦洗ヒスミキトメ復月ノ珍是
ニ區ル者ナシ唐ニモ呉ノ淞江ノ産
ヲ天下ノ隹珍ス或ハ四腮魚ト呼
淞江ノ者其腮四牧ナリ
紀伊松江東松江中松江西松江

崔島錫食經云
鱸　須々　貌似鯉而鰓大唱者
　　也四聲字苑ニ云似鯉
　　而大青色ニ云々

源平盛衰記

紀伊國海士郡黒江村
黒牛潟　黒牛海黒汐ノ礒
干潟浦
玉葉

鱸
（Suzuki）

鱸子
（Seigo）

盧魚
（Suzuki）

須受岐
（Suzuki）

須々支
（Suzuki）

須々木
（Suzuki）

スズキ

Japanese sea bass

スズキ目スズキ科スズキ属。学名は*Lateolabrax japonicus*。北海道から九州南岸までの各沿岸、東シナ海沿岸、朝鮮半島南岸などに分布する。体長は60〜80cmで、1mを超すものもいる。背は褐色で腹部は銀白色をしている。和名の由来は容姿に因んで「すすぎ洗いしたように白く美しい」を由来とする説、「口が大きいわりに尾の小さい魚」として見なされ、小さいことを表す古語「スズ」を語源とする説などがある。鎌倉時代の軍記物語『平家物語』には、平清盛の船にスズキが飛び込んできた後に天下をとったと記されており、スズキは出世を象徴する魚といわれてきた。古くから食用とされ、江戸時代には煎り酒と酢でスズキを煮立たせた「煎り鱸」という料理があった。

Lateolabrax japonicus (Perciformes, Lateolabracidae). This fish is found along the coasts from Hokkaido to southern Kyushu, the East China Sea, and the Korean Peninsula. They typically measure 60 to 80 cm in length. According to one theory, their Japanese name, "suzuki," is said to come from their appearance, a beautiful white like they have been rinsed off ("susugi-arai"). In the *Heike Monogatari*, a military chronicle from the Kamakura era (1185–1333), Taira no Kiyomori conquered the nation after a Japanese sea bass leaped into his boat, so it has been said to be a symbol of success and advancement.

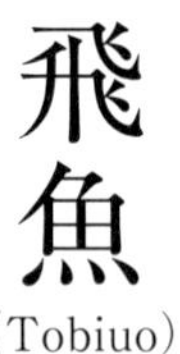

飛魚
（Tobiuo）

燕魚
（Tsubameuo）

止比乎
（Tobiuo）

文鰩魚
（Tobiuo）

飛鳥魚
（Tobiuo）

トビウオ

Japanese flyingfish

図から正確な種の同定は困難だが、ここではトビウオとして扱う。ダツ目トビウオ科。学名は *Cheilopogon agoo agoo*。以前は *Cypselurus* 属に属するとされていたが、近年は *Cheilopogon* 属とする説が有力。日本語での属の名称は未決定。日本では北海道噴火湾から山口県までの日本海沿岸、仙台湾から屋久島までの太平洋沿岸、東シナ海沿岸などに分布する。体長は約35cm。体は細長く、胸びれや腹びれは翼状に、尾びれは長く発達している。和名「トビウオ」の由来は、大きな魚に追われたり、驚いたりすると、尾びれを振って海面から飛び出して胸びれや腹びれを広げて飛行することから。この習性から縁起のいい魚とされ、神饌に使われることもあった。

Cheilopogon agoo agoo (Beloniformes, Exocoetidae). This fish is found along the coast of the Sea of Japan from Hokkaido's Funka Bay to Yamaguchi Prefecture, along the Pacific coast from Sendai Bay to Yakushima Island, and along the coast of the East China Sea. They typically measure 35 cm in length. Their Japanese name, "tobi-uo," comes from the fact that when chased by a larger fish or startled, they will leap out of the water, spreading their fins and flying through the air ("tobi" is the Japanese word for flying). Because of this, they are considered auspicious and sometimes used in shrine offerings.

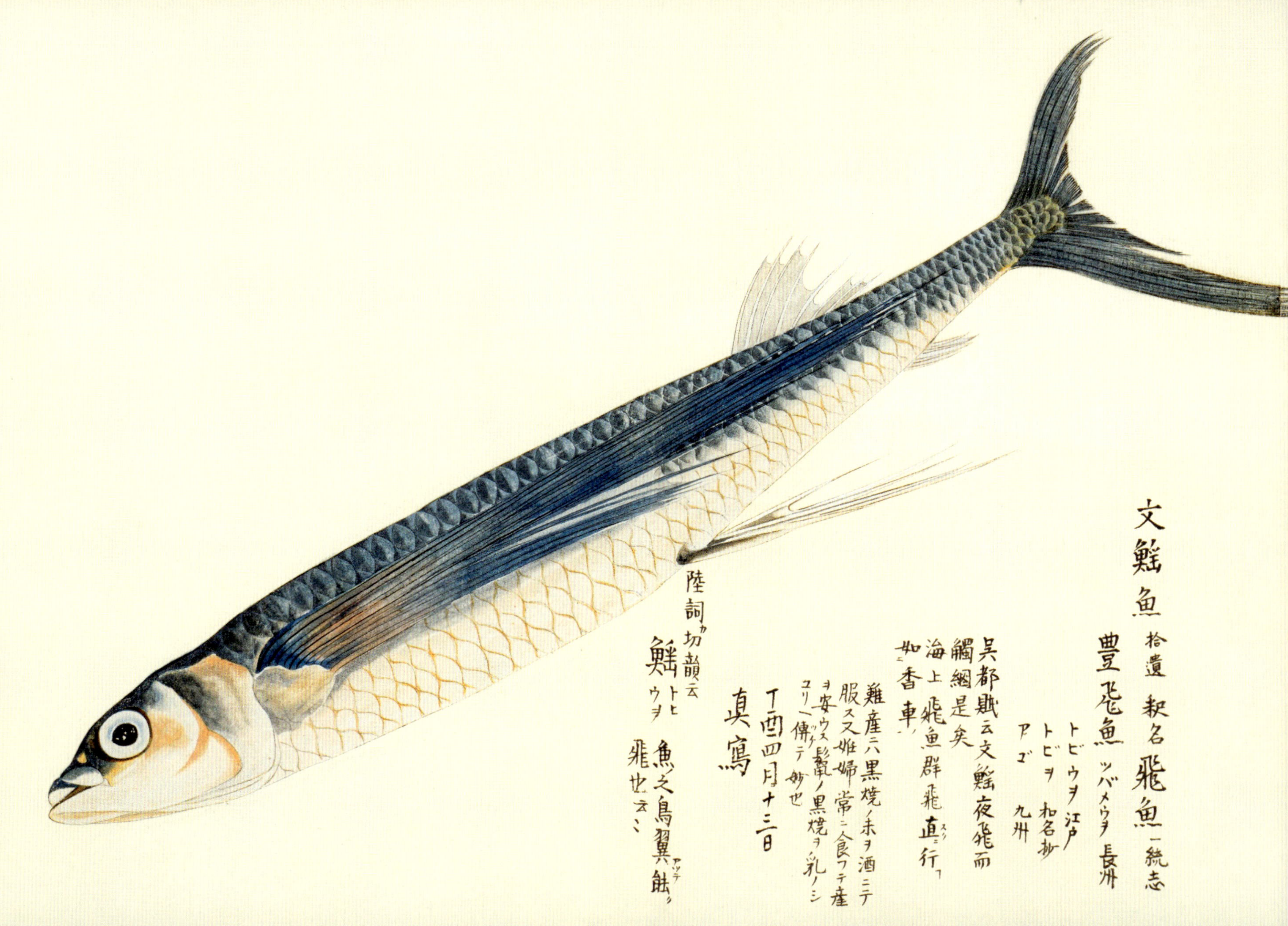

文鰩魚 拾遺 釈名 飛魚 一統志
豊岊魚 ツバメウヲ 長州
トビウヲ 江戸
トビヲ 和名抄
アゴ 九州
陸詞ガ切韻云
鰩 トヒ ウヲ
魚之鳥翼飴ニ
飛也云ニ
呉都賦云文鰩夜飛而
觸網是矢
海上飛魚群飛直行スル
如香車ニ
難産ニ六黒焼ノ未ヲ酒ニテ
服ス又姙婦常ニ食フテ産
ヲ安ウス鬢毛ノ黒焼ヲ
ユリ一佛テ妙也
産ノ黒焼ヲ乳ノシ
丁酉四月十三日
真寫

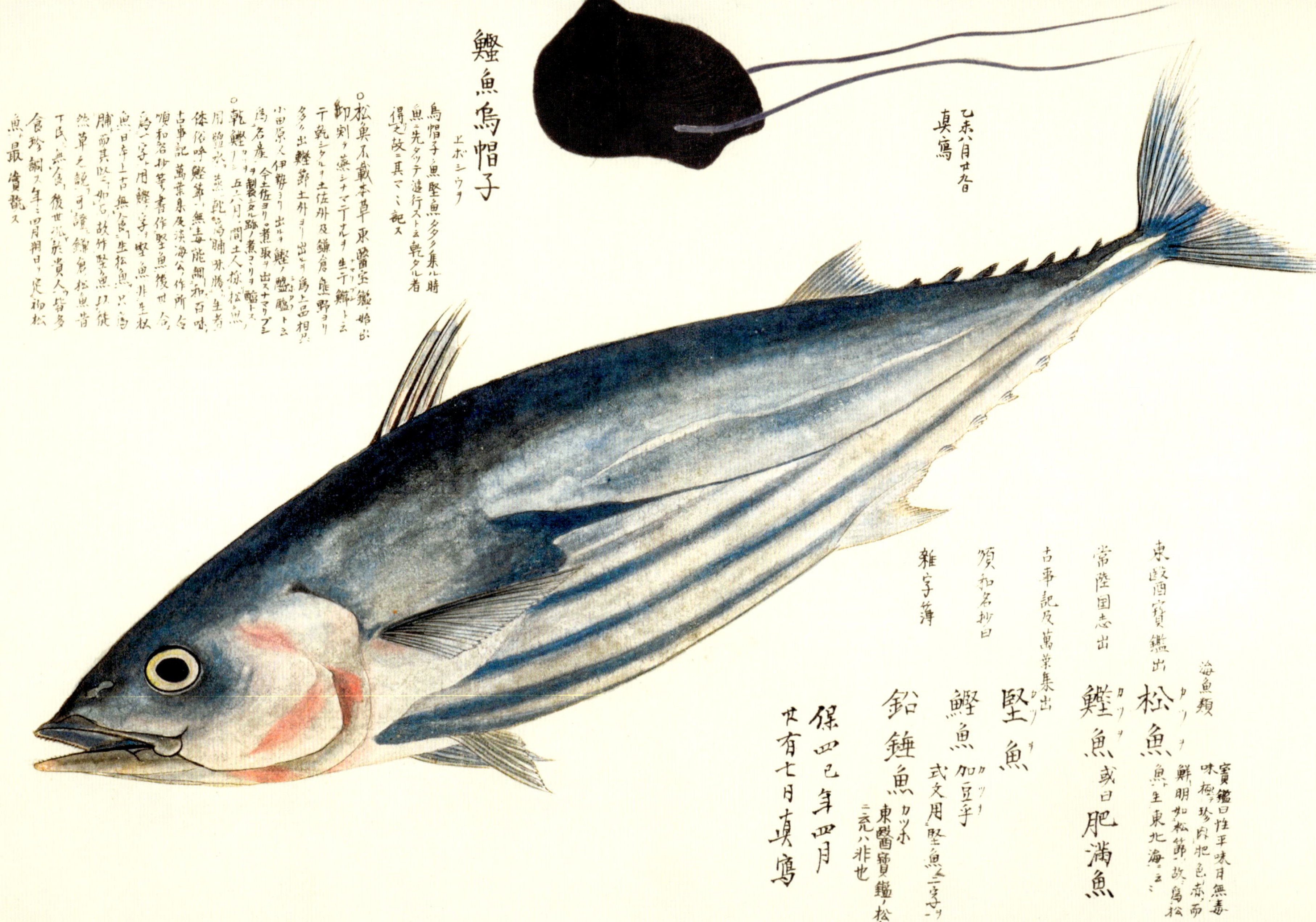

鰹魚烏帽子
ヱホシウヲ
乙未八月廿九日
眞寫
海魚類
東歧酉寶鑑出
松魚
常陸国志出
鰹魚或曰肥満魚
古事記及萬葉集出
堅魚
須和名抄曰
鰹魚加豆子
雜字簿
鉛錘魚
保四巳年四月
廿有七月眞寫

鰹
（Katsuo）

烏帽子魚 （Eboshiuo）
加豆乎 （Katsuo）
古固魚 （Katsuo）
松魚 （Katsuo）
勝魚 （Katsuo）
堅魚 （Katsuo）

カツオ

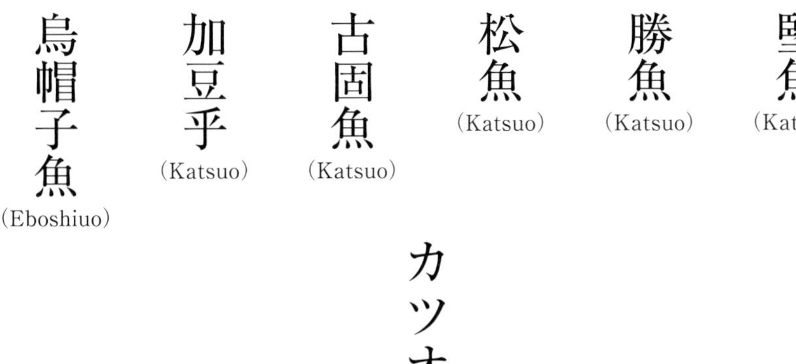

Skipjack tuna

スズキ目サバ科カツオ属。学名は*Katsuwonus pelamis*。世界中の熱帯から温帯域に分布する。日本では太平洋側に多い。体長は約50cmのものが多いが最大で1mを超える。平安時代以前は、鮮度の落ちたカツオで食中毒を起こすことが相次いだことから生食されることは稀で、素干しなどの保存食として重宝された。和名「カツオ」の由来は、乾燥させて鰹節にすると固くなるため「堅魚」が「カツオ」へと転訛したといわれている。『北条五代記』の記録によると、カツオ漁を見物していた北条氏綱の船にカツオが飛び込んできた直後の戦で大勝したことから、武家の間で縁起の良い魚とされ、出陣や元服の祝宴でカツオが供されたという。

Katsuwonus pelamis (Perciformes, Scombridae). This fish is found around the world, from tropical to temperate areas. In Japan, they are found in abundance on the Pacific Ocean side. They typically measure 50 cm in length, but some exceed 100 cm in length. Until the Heian era (794–1185), there were many incidents of food poisoning caused by spoiled skipjack tuna, so eating it raw was rare, but it was often dried in the shade and used as a preserved food. Its Japanese name, "katsuo," is said to come from "kata-uo," meaning "hard fish," because it is dried and used to make bonito flakes.

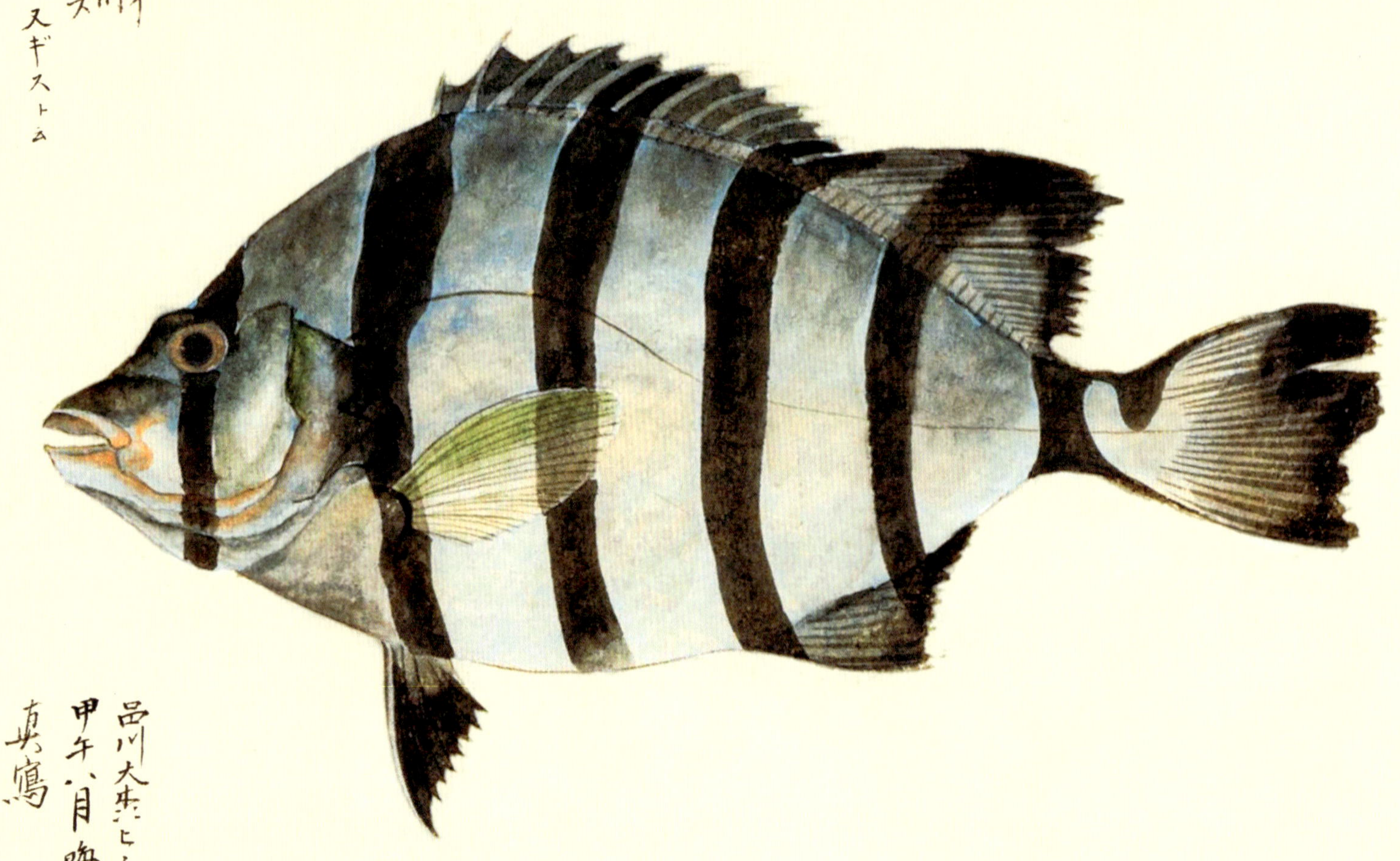

シマダイ
絹鯛
スギストム
品川大森ヒ、之間釣之
甲午八月晦日
真寫

石鯛
（Ishidai）

縞鯛
（Shimadai）

口黒
（Kuchiguro）

三番叟
（Sanbaso）

イシダイ

Barred knifejaw

スズキ目イシダイ科イシダイ属。学名は*Oplegnathus fasciatus*。北海道から九州南岸までの各沿岸域、小笠原諸島、琉球列島、朝鮮半島南岸、台湾などに分布する。満1歳（20cm前後）で成熟する個体が出てくるが、老成した個体では80cmに達するものもいる。体側にある7本の青黒色の横帯が特徴。頑丈な顎と歯で、貝類や甲殻類などの硬い殻をもつ生き物も噛み砕いて食べる。この習性から「石をも噛み砕く歯を持つ魚」という意で、「イシダイ」の名前が付いたといわれる。雄は老成すると尾の部分を残して縞模様が消えて吻から口元が黒くなるため「クチグロ」とも呼ばれる。釣り人の間では引きの強さから「磯の王者」、釣れることが稀のため「幻の魚」とも呼ばれる。

Oplegnathus fasciatus (Perciformes, Oplegnathidae). This fish is found along the coasts from Hokkaido to southern Kyushu, around the Ogasawara Islands, around the Ryukyu Islands, along the southern coast of the Korean Peninsula, and Taiwan. Some reach a mature size of roughly 20 cm in less than a year, but older fish can reach as long as 80 cm. Their Japanese name, "ishidai," is in reference to their having teeth so powerful they could "crush rocks" ("ishi" means "rock"), and comes from their ability to crack shells with their powerful jaws. Anglers call them the "kings of the rocky shores" because of how hard they are to reel in or "the illusive fish" because they are caught so rarely.

鯣烏賊
（Surumeika）

柴烏賊
（Shibaika）

真烏賊
（Maika）

スルメイカ

Japanese common squid

ツツイカ目アカイカ科スルメイカ属。学名は *Todarodes pacificus*。北海道から九州までの日本全域の沿岸、東シナ海、朝鮮半島沿岸などに分布する。体長は約35㎝。日本では漁獲量が最も多いイカだったため、刺身や干物、塩辛などにして食卓で親しまれてきたが、近年では不漁で消費量が減っている。「スルメイカ」の名前は「するめに使うイカ」に由来する。江戸時代の百科事典といわれる『和漢三才図会』には「柔魚は烏賊と同じで、身体は長く大きく、これを乾してするめとする」とある。乾物は日持ちが良いことから縁起物とされ、「寿留女」という当て字で結納時に用いられてきた。「結婚生活が長く幸せに続くように」という願いが込められているといわれている。

Todarodes pacificus (Teuthida, Ommastrephidae). This squid is found along the coasts of Japan from Hokkaido to Kyushu, the East China Sea, and the Korean Peninsula. They typically measure 35 cm in length. Their Japanese name, "surumeika," comes from the fact that they are the squid ("ika") used in making "surume" (dried squid). The *Wakan Sansai Zue*, an encyclopedia from the Edo era (1603-1867), says that their bodies are long and large, and that they can be dried to make surume. They last for a long time when dried, so they are considered auspicious and have been given as betrothal gifts.

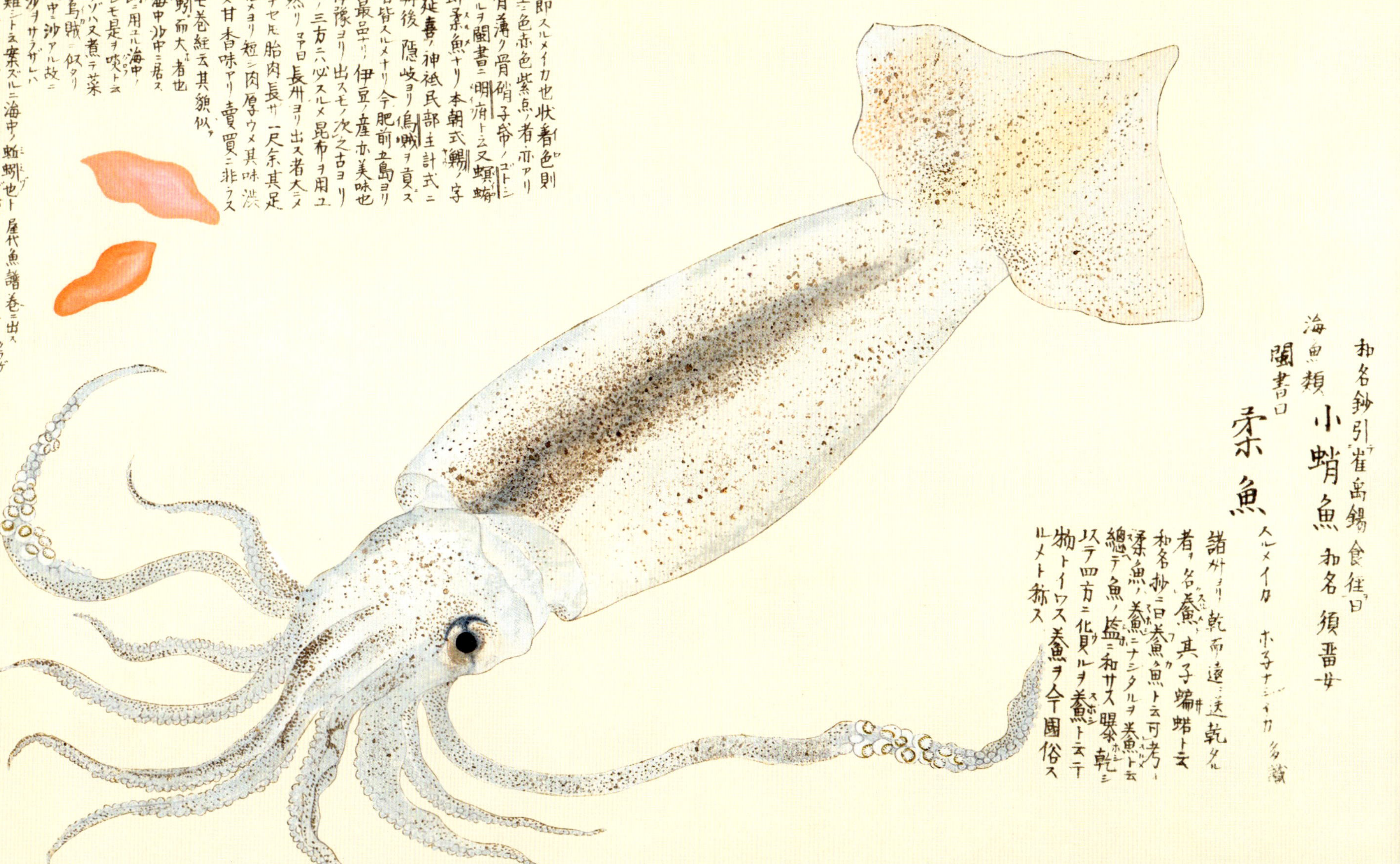
和名鈔云
蝙蛸
柔魚
海魚類 小蛸魚 和名 須晋母
閩書曰
真寫
癸巳十月八日

尻焼烏賊

(Shiriyakeika)

真烏賊
(Maika)

尻腐
(Shirikusari)

墨烏賊
(Sumiika)

シリヤケイカ

Japanese spineless cuttlefish

コウイカ目コウイカ科シリヤケイカ属。学名は*Sepiella japonica*。東北南部から九州南岸までの各沿岸域、東シナ海大陸棚域などに分布する。体長は約25cm。コウイカ類は互いによく似ているが、シリヤケイカは生時では暗褐色の胴の背面に多数の白点があるのが特徴で、他種と区別ができる。外套膜後端にある尾腺の開口部から赤褐色の粘膜が分泌され、外套膜面後半が染まる。この様子から「シリヤケイカ」の名前が付いたといわれている。「尻腐」という別名もある。また、墨汁を多く出すことから「墨烏賊」という俗称も生まれた。コウイカに比べると甘味や旨味はやや少ないとされるが、刺身や天ぷらなどにして食べられている。

Sepiella japonica (Sepiida, Sepiidae). This cuttlefish is found along the coasts from southern Tohoku to the southern coast of Kyushu, along with the East China Sea continental shelf. They typically measure 25 cm in length. Reddish-brown mucus is secreted from the caudal gland at the back tip of the mantle, coloring the back of the mantle. This is why the squid is called "shiriyake-ika" (burnt-bottom squid) in Japanese. The cuttlefish is eaten as sashimi or in tempura more often than other cuttlefish, even though it is slightly less sweet and savory.

海魚類

烏賊魚 イカ　墨魚　烏鰂 素　纜魚 日葦

○海螵蛸（ヘウヒウ）ハ伊加ノ甲ヲ云烏賊　墨有腰中ニ故墨魚ト云

烏賊魚其類多シ
コブイカ。水イカ。
柔魚イカ。
瑣管イカ。スザバイカ此ヲ云
アブリイカ。
小イカナゾノ類多シ
此ニ圖ルル者ハ只イカト
通称ス數類多キ故
此者ヲ国俗ホニイカトス
ホントウトヱナマリ訓也
末烏賊魚俗ニベリト云

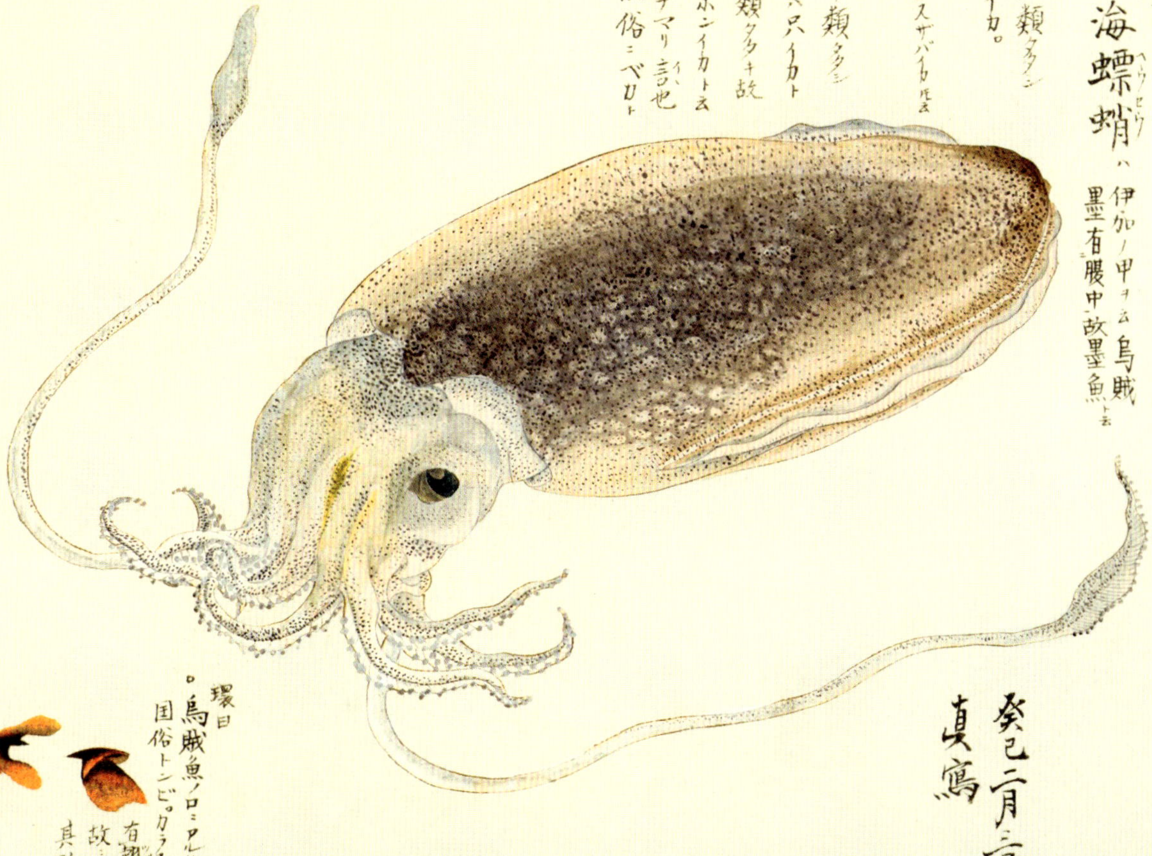

和名鈔
烏賊　加南越志云烏賊　今按烏賊
并従魚作鶏鰂　鰂亦作　常自
鰂見玉篇
浮水上ニ烏見以烏死啄之乃
卷ニ取之故以名之

甲午卯月六日
真寫

環目
○烏賊魚ノ口ニアル者ヲ
国俗トンビ。カラストヱ
有趣如龜　故ニ名ク
其形如此

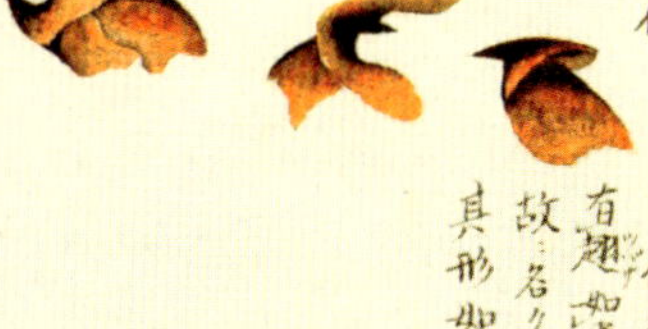

戈鳥鳥（トンビ）ト云者烏賊魚ノ
則歯也如此口中ニテ飲ヒ
シリ飼ノ食フ鯛ニ
三ツ道貝有ガ如ケラス
烏賊魚ニ鳥ノ名アル
丁此歯ヨリ出々子

癸巳二月三日
真寫

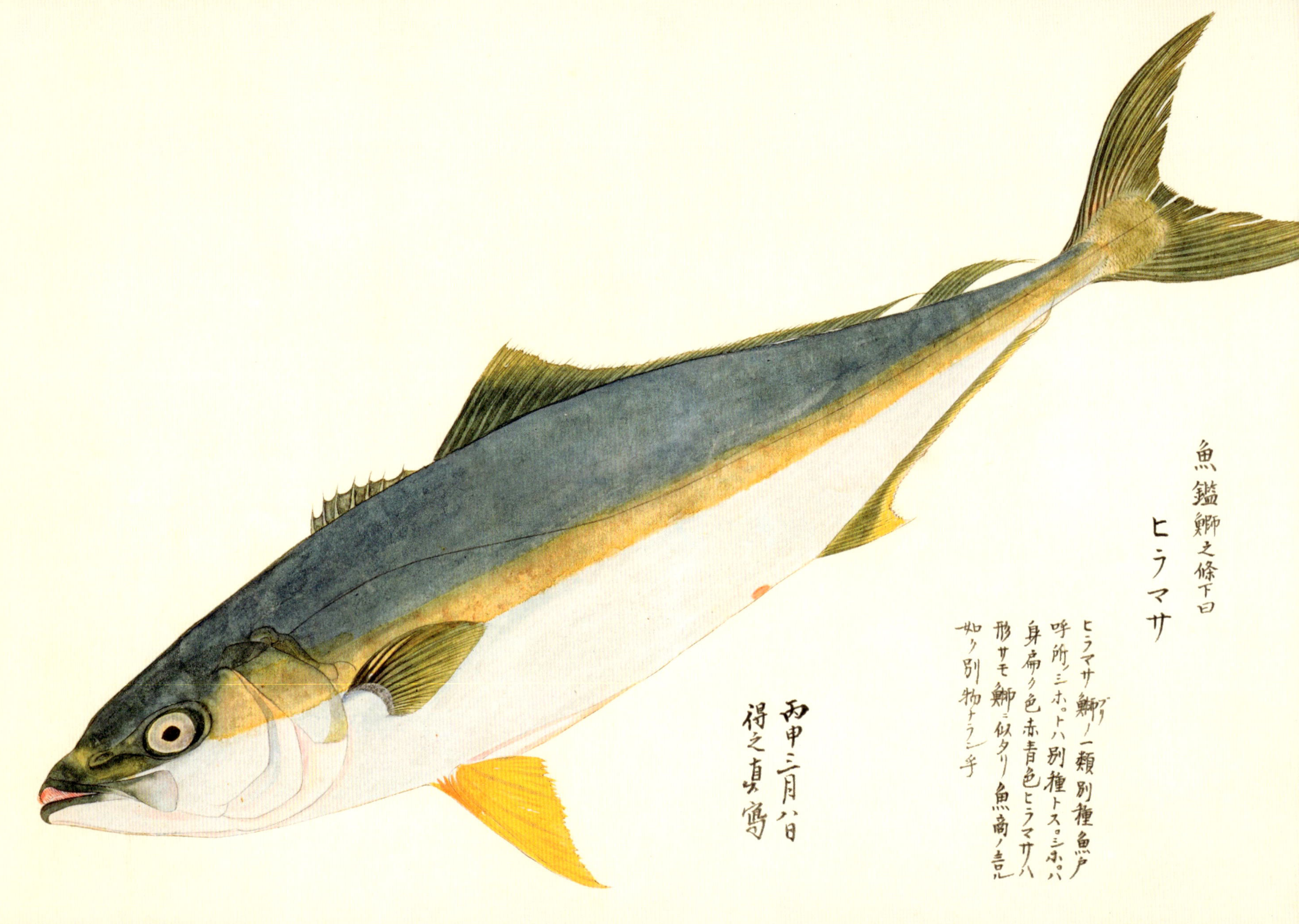

魚鑑鰤之條下曰
ヒラマサ
ヒラマサ鰤ノ一頬別種魚戸
呼所ニホ.ヒ.トハ別種トスヲニホ.ハ
身扁ク色赤青色ヒラマサハ
形サモ鰤ニ似タリ魚商ノ言
如ク別物ナラシ手
丙申三月八日
得之真寫

平政
（Hiramasa）

マサ
（Masa）

ヒラソ
（Hiraso）

ヒラス
（Hirasu）

ヒラ
（Hira）

平鰤
（Hiramasa）

ヒラマサ

Yellowtail amberjack

スズキ目アジ科ブリ属。学名は *Seriola aureovittata*。日本列島の沿岸、朝鮮半島南岸、西部北太平洋外洋域に分布する。体長は約1mだが、大きいものでは1.5mを超す。ブリと似ているが、体の幅が少し狭く、上顎後端の上部が丸みを帯びていること、中央の黄色の縦帯が濃い、胸鰭が腹鰭より短いなどの特徴から区別することができる。「ヒラマサ」の名前の由来は不詳だが、日本では古くから食用として馴染みがあったようで、江戸時代後期の生活実用書『魚鑑』に「ブリに似て、味わい美し」とある。鮨種として使われるようになったのは、昭和の初期頃からといわれている。市場には一年を通して出ているが、旬は夏季で、塩焼きや煮付けなどの調理法で食べられる。

Seriola aureovittata (Perciformes, Carangidae). This fish is found along the coasts of Japan, the southern coast of the Korean Peninsula, and the oceanic regions of the western parts of the northern Pacific. They typically measure 100 cm in length, but some exceed 150 cm in length. They can be distinguished from Japanese amberjack (*Seriola quinqueradiata*) by their slightly thinner body and the rounder rear of their upper jaw. The origin of their Japanese name, "hiramasa," is unknown. The *Uo-kagami*, a how-to book on daily living written in the latter part of the Edo era (1603–1867), says, "Like Japanese amberjack, they are delicious."

二種共乙未閏七月十三日
真寫
海魚類無鱗
嶋鰺
シマアヂ
ヒラアゲ

縞鯵

（Shimaaji）

オオカミ
（Okami）

逆針
（Sakabari）

嶋鯵
（Shimaaji）

島鯵
（Shimaaji）

シマアジ

Striped jack

図から正確な同定は困難だが、ここではシマアジとして扱う。スズキ目アジ科シマアジ属。学名は*Pseudocaranx dentex*。日本では青森県以南の太平洋沿岸、新潟県以南の日本海沿岸、東シナ海などに分布し、世界では東部太平洋を除く暖海全域に分布する。体長は最大で1mを超える。体色は背側が青緑色、腹側は銀白色で、体側の中央に黄色の縦帯があるのが特徴。この黄色の縦帯が、和名「縞鯵」の由来といわれている。東京では「オオカミ」とも呼ばれ、体長1mを超える大型のシマアジのことを指す。アジ類の中で最も美味とされ、高級魚として料亭などで扱われることが多いが、江戸時代の料理書『黒白精味集』では、コイやカツオよりも評価が低い下魚に格付けされている。

Pseudocaranx dentex (Perciformes, Carangidae). This fish is found on the Pacific coast, in Aomori Prefecture and further south; along the coast of the Sea of Japan in Niigata Prefecture and further south, and in East China Sea. Around the world, they live in warm ocean areas except for the eastern Pacific. Their maximum length is over 100 cm. They are called striped jacks due to the yellow stripe along the middle of their side. The fish is considered the most delicious fish among the jacks (carangids), but *Kokubyaku Seimishu*, a cookbook from the Edo era (1603–1867), ranked them as a lower class, below common carp and skipjack tuna.

太刀魚

（Tachiuo）

刀刃
（Katanaba）　　刀（Katana）　　立魚（Tachiuo）

タチウオ

Largehead hairtail

スズキ目タチウオ科タチウオ属。学名は *Trichiurus japonicus*。北海道から九州南岸までの各沿岸域、東シナ海大陸棚域などに分布する。体長は約1.5m。体は細長く、薄い。無鱗の銀白色で、口は大きく、鋭い歯を持つ。和名の由来は、この銀白色に輝く美しい姿が太刀に似ていることから「太刀魚」になったという説と、静止時には頭を上にして立ち泳ぎをすることから「立魚」になったという説がある。外見の特徴から、鎌倉時代の武将が太刀を海に投げたところ、太刀が魚に化けたという伝説が残っている。また『大日本魚類画集』の解説文には、暗い海底から浮上してくるタチウオの姿が白刀を持った平家の幽霊だと信じられていたとの記述がある。

Trichiurus japonicus (Perciformes, Trichiuridae). This fish is found along the coasts from Hokkaido to southern Kyushu, along with the East China Sea continental shelf. They typically measure 150 cm in length. The largehead hairtail's Japanese name, "tachi-uo," is said to either come from the resemblance of their beautiful silvery-white body to a sword ("tachi") or because they rest standing up (in Japanese, standing is "tachi"). Due to their appearance, there is a legend that a general in the Kamakura era (1185–1333) threw his sword into the sea and it became the largehead hairtail.

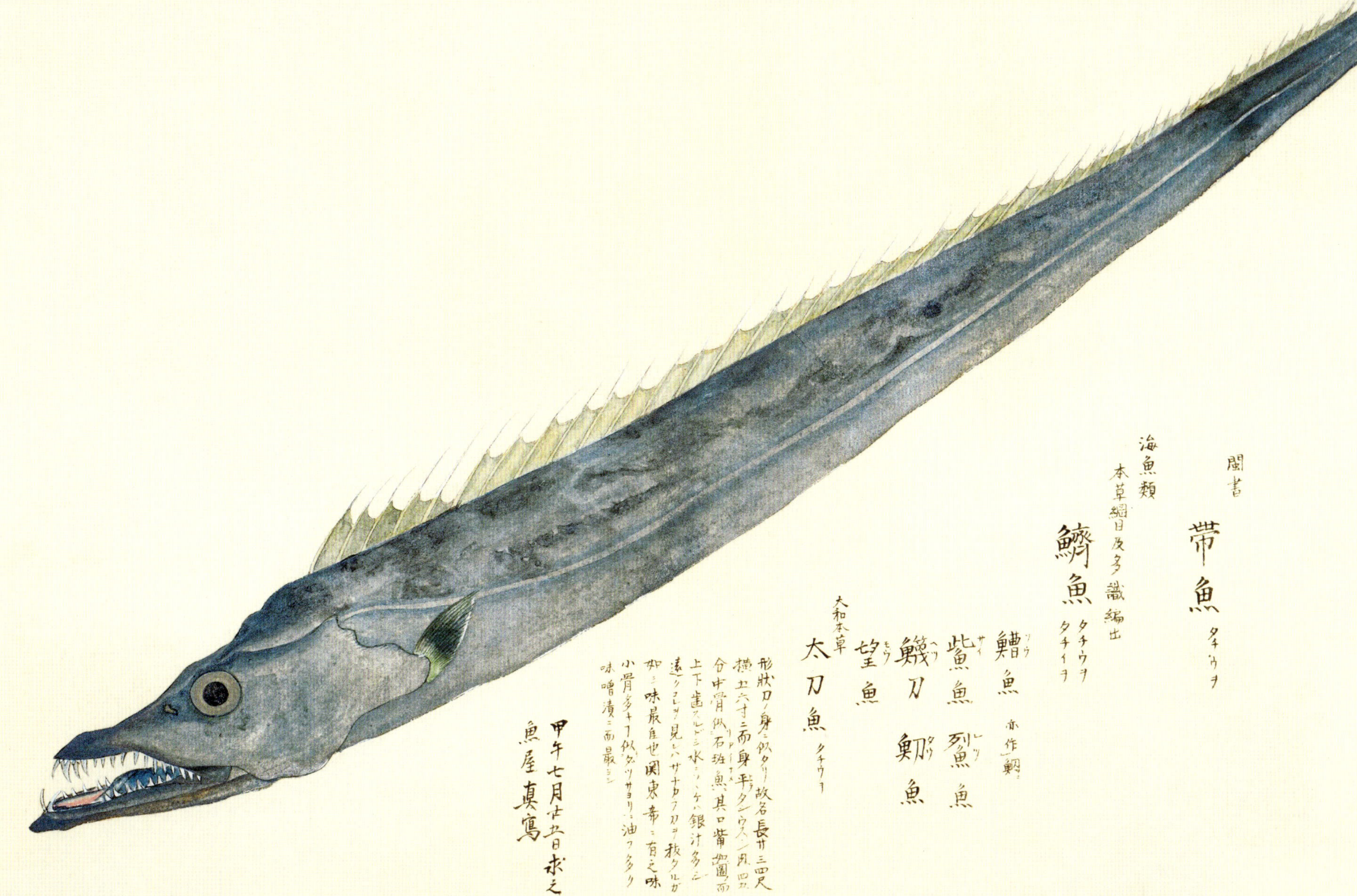
閣書
帯魚 タチウヲ
海魚頬
本草綱目及多識編出
鱗魚 タチウヲ
タチイヲ
鱛魚 亦作𩾃
鮆魚 サイ
烈魚 ヒツ
望魚 モウ
鱴刀 ヘツ
魛魚 タウ
大和本草
太刀魚 タチウヲ
形狀刀ノ身ニ似タリ故名長サ三四尺
横ニ六寸三而身平タシ又ノ丹四ツ
分中骨似石斑魚其口嘴盤ノ圖而
上下歯スルドシ水ニ入ケハ銀汁多ニ
遠クヨレリ見ハサナカフカヲ抜クルガ
如ニ味最産也関東帝ニ百之味
小骨多キ丁似ダツサヨリニ油フ多り
味噌漬ニ而最シニ
甲午七月廿五日求之
魚屋真寫

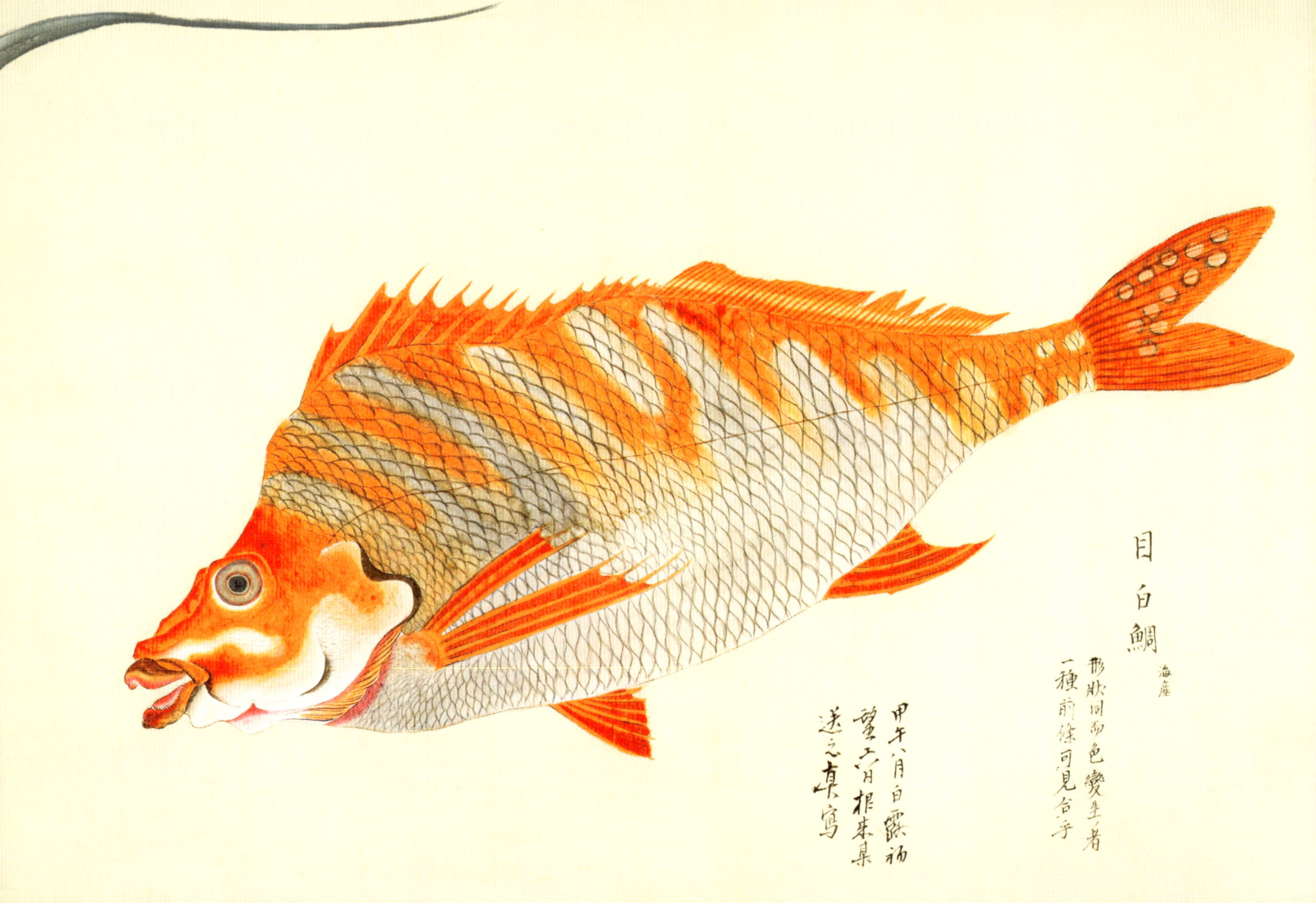

目白鯛　海産
形狀同却色變生ノ者
一種前條ニ見合ヂ
甲午八月白露禱
翌二月根末景
送之　真寫

鷹羽鯛

（Takanohadai）

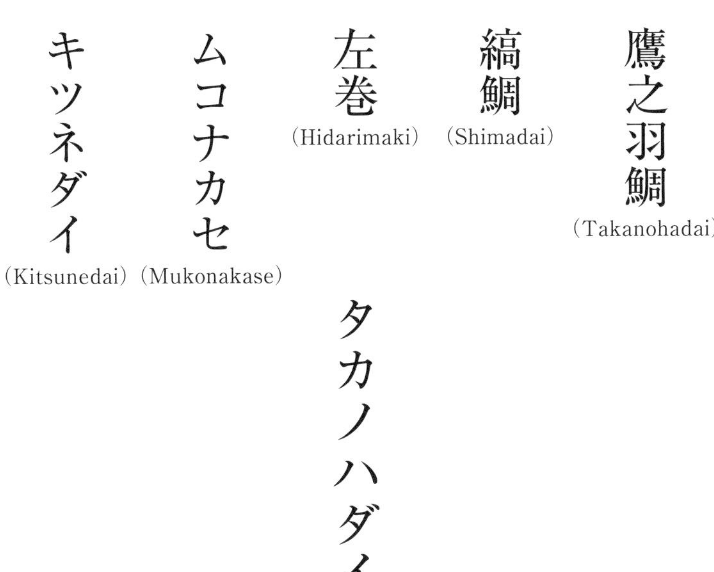

Spottedtail morwong

スズキ目タカノハダイ科タカノハダイ属。学名は*Goniistius zonatus*。青森県から九州南岸までの各沿岸域、沖縄島、伊豆諸島などに分布する。体長は約40㎝。江戸時代の『本朝食鑑』には、和名「タカノハダイ」の由来として「鷹の斑のような鱗紋があるため」と記されている。磯臭さが弱くなる晩秋から初春は美味とされる場合もあるが、基本的に臭みが強いため、食用としてはあまり好まれない。釣り人の中には、タカノハダイが釣れるのは水温が低いということであり、目当てのメジナが釣れないという人もいる。伊豆地方や神奈川県の三浦では「ムコナカセ」と呼ばれる。鱗が取れにくいので料理をする婿が苦労するから、または不味な魚を婿に食わせるからと解釈されている。

Goniistius zonatus (Perciformes, Latridae). This fish is found in coastal areas from Aomori Prefecture to the southern coast of Kyushu, near Okinawa-jima Island, and by the Izu Islands. They typically measure 40 cm in length. The *Honchoshokkan*, a book of dietary medicines from the Edo era (1603–1867), says that their Japanese name, "takanohadai," comes from their scales having a pattern like the mottled appearance of a hawk ("taka"). In the Izu region and in Kanagawa Prefecture's Miura Peninsula, they are called "mukonakase." This is because their scales are hard to remove, driving a son-in-law ("muko") to tears ("nakase") when cooking them.

赤太刀
（Akatachi）

巫女の帯
（Mikonoobi）

菜刀
（Nagatana）

元結
（Motte）

アカタチ

Red-spotted bandfish

スズキ目アカタチ科アカタチ属。学名は *Acanthocepola krusensternii*。新潟県から九州南岸までの日本海・東シナ海沿岸、相模湾から九州南岸までの太平洋沿岸、東シナ海大陸棚、中国南シナ海沿岸、フロレス島などに分布する。体長は約50㎝。細長い体がタチウオに似ていること、および体色が赤いことから「アカタチ」の名前が付いた。赤色の体に黄色の丸い点が一列に並んでいるのが特徴。水深100ｍ前後の砂泥底に生息し、小型の甲殻類や魚類を補食する。市場に出回ることは少なく、練り製品の材料にされる。幕末に来日してオランダ医学を伝えたポンペ・ファン・メーデルフォールトが、日本で収集して母国に送った魚類の中にアカタチも含まれていたといわれる。

Acanthocepola krusensternii (Perciformes, Cepolidae). This fish is found along the coasts of the Sea of Japan and East China Sea from Niigata Prefecture to southern Kyushu, on the Pacific coast from Sagami Bay to southern Kyushu, on the East China Sea continental shelf, along the coast of the South China Sea, and around the island of Flores. They typically measure 50 cm in length. They resemble largehead hairtail, called "tachi-uo," but their bodies are red, hence their Japanese name, "akatachi" ("aka" means "red"). Pompe van Meerdervoort, a Dutch physician of the mid-1800s, sent red-spotted bandfish back to the Netherlands.

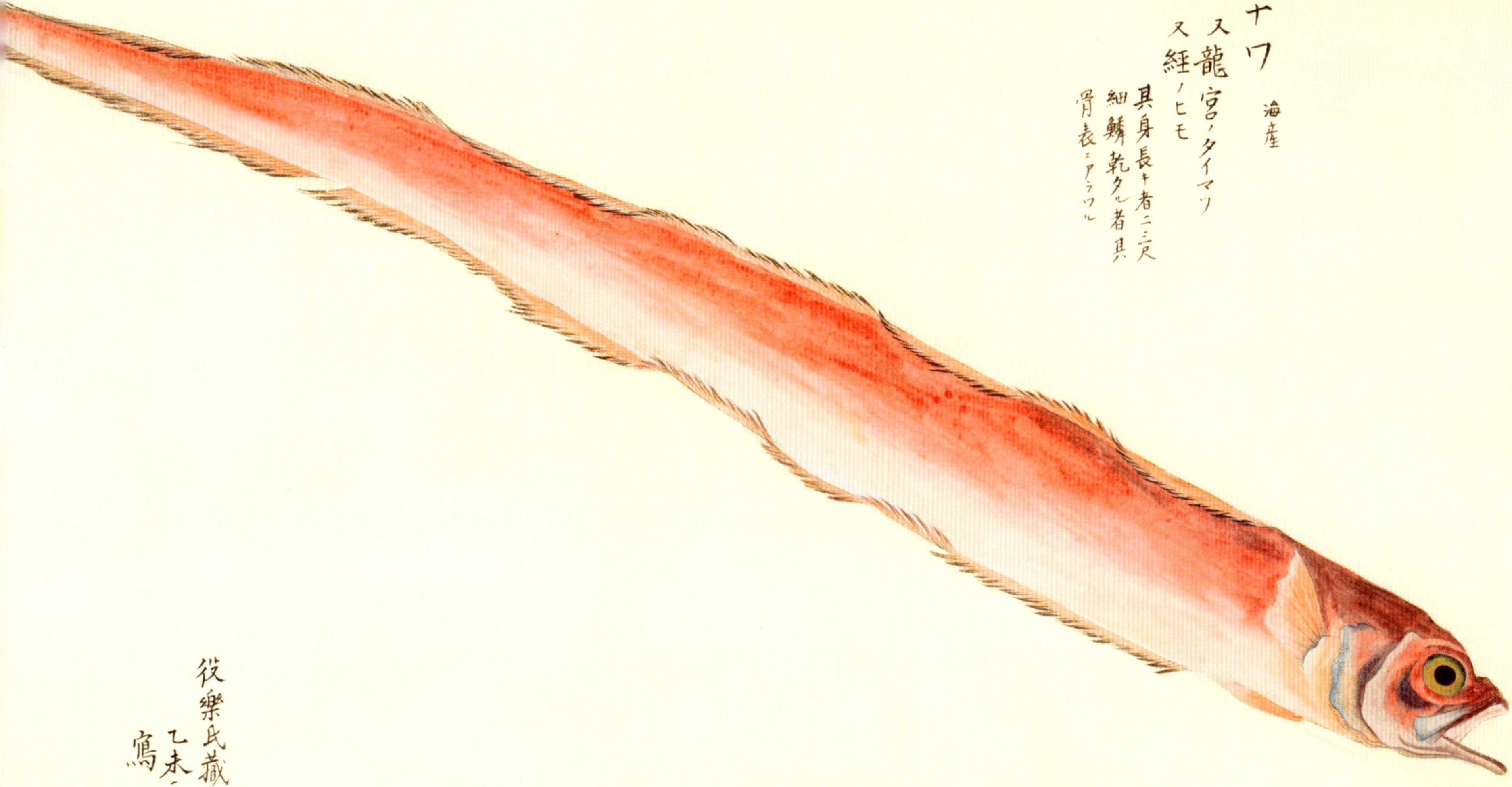

アナワ　海産

又龍宮ノタイマツ
又經ノヒモ
其身長十者二三尺
細鱗乾クル者其
骨長ニアラワル

従樂氏藏
乙未三月上巳之日
寫

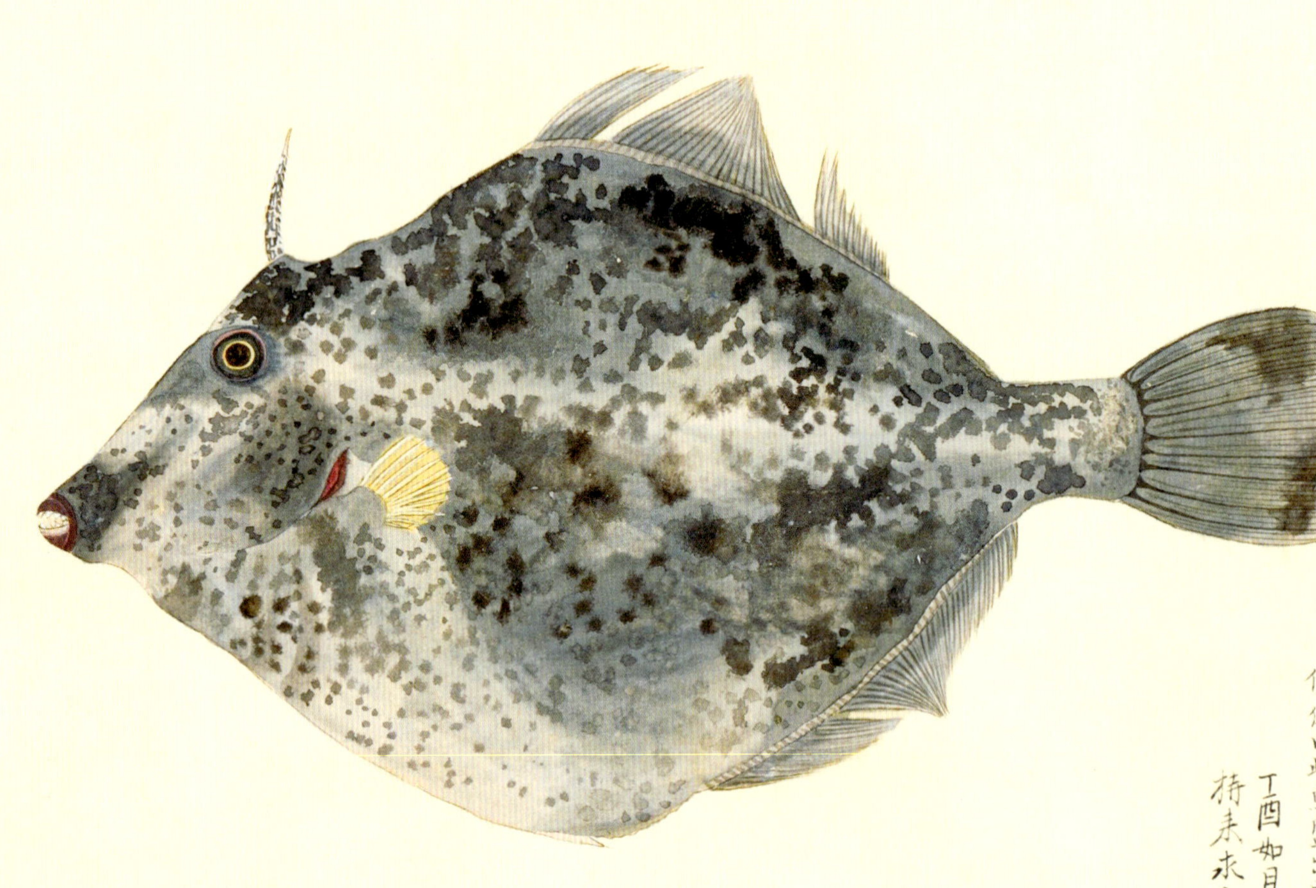</br>

海産
日東魚譜
鮫魚 和名 釈各加波破岐
皮剝
カワハギ ハクチョキ加丹
モチカワハギ 兵庫

此者皮ニ砂アリテ鮫ノ如ニ皮剝ゲハ
圓ニテムケル其身至テ白ニ惣身
無鱗ノ魚ノ如之味羨ニメ海豚ニ似
タリ人首ニ角ノナキ者アリ下品
魚也野人食之耳
俚俗曰此魚盛出則禾穀踊貴

丁酉如月廿一日魚商
持未求之真寫

皮剥
(Kawahagi)

ゲンパ
(Genpa)

ゲバチ
(Gebachi)

ゲバ
(Geba)

ハゲ
(Hage)

千歯
(Senba)

カワハギ

フグ目カワハギ科カワハギ属。学名は*Stephanolepis cirrhifer*。青森県から九州南岸までの各沿岸域、朝鮮半島南岸・東岸、台湾などに分布する。体長は約30cm。体表はざらざらとした硬い皮に覆われ、不規則な黒褐色の斑紋がある。口は小さいが頑丈な歯を持ち、貝なども砕くことができる。和名「カワハギ」の由来は、調理の際にまず硬い皮を剥がないといけないことから。ざらざらの皮から「おろし金」という意味の「千歯」、皮を剥いだ姿から「ハゲ」などの地方名もある。江戸時代の『和漢三才図会』には「形状は大へん醜く、頭は方頭魚に似、状はほぼ鮫に似ている」と記述されている（ただし、同じカワハギ科のウマヅラハギと混同している可能性もある）。

Stephanolepis cirrhifer (Tetraodontiformes, Monacanthidae). This fish is found along the coasts from Aomori Prefecture to southern Kyushu, along the southern and eastern coasts of the Korean Peninsula, and Taiwan. They typically measure 30 cm in length. They are covered in tough skin which has irregular brownish-black spots. Their Japanese name, "kawahagi," is said to come from the need to peel ("hagu") their tough skin ("kawa") before cooking. They also go by regional names, such as "senba," which means "grater," due to their rough skin, or "hage" ("bald") because of how they look when peeled.

Thread-sail filefish

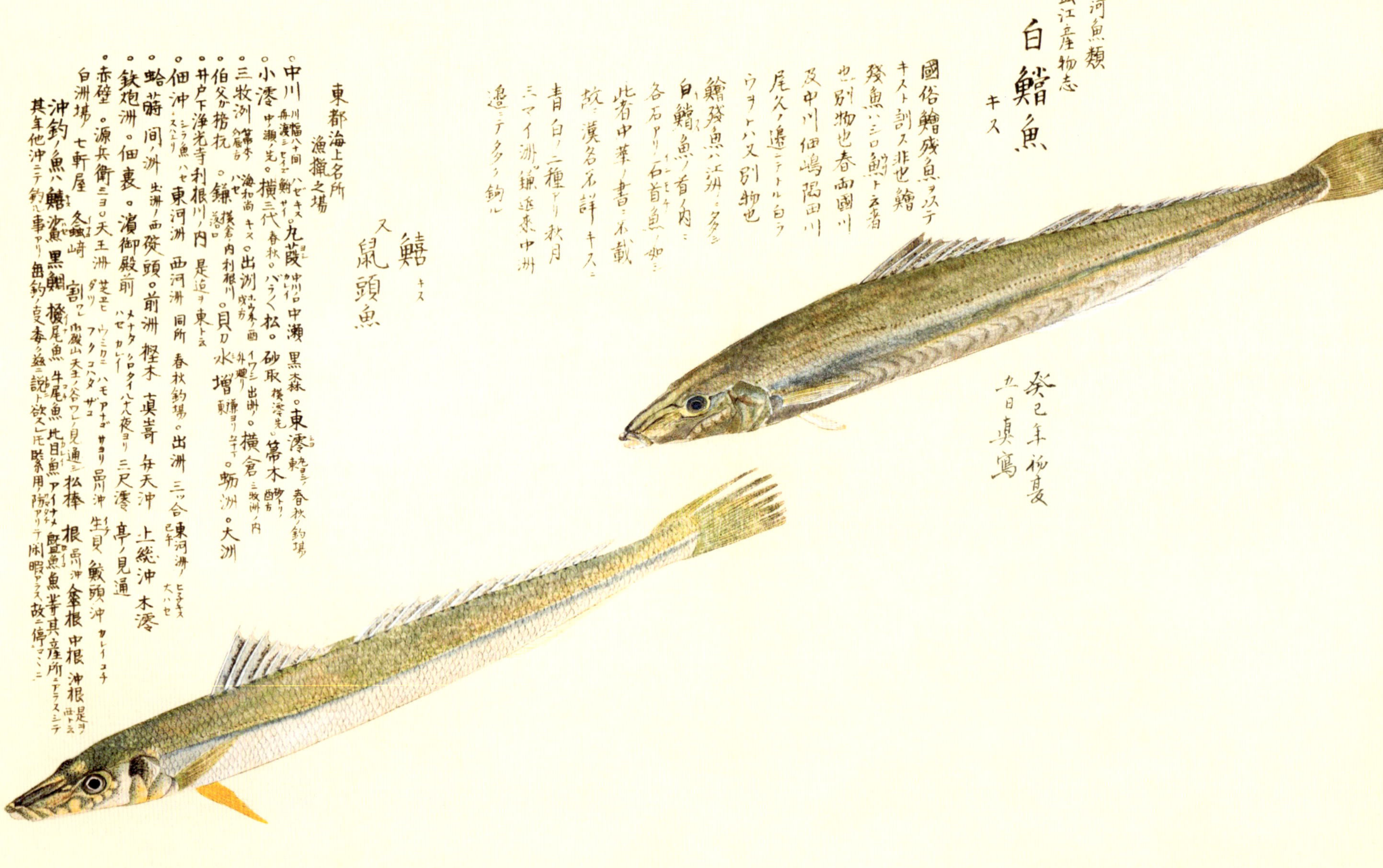

海河魚類
武江産物志
白鱚魚
キス

鱚
キス
又
鼠頭魚

東都海上名所
漁撿之場

白鱚
（Shirogisu）

鱚
（Kisu）

鼠頭魚
（Kisu）

幾須吾
（Kisugo）

シロギス

Japanese whiting

スズキ目キス科キス属。学名は*Sillago japonica*。北海道から九州南岸までの各沿岸域、台湾などに分布する。体長は約20cm。一般的に「キス」というと「シロギス」のことを指す。体は細長く、体色は背が灰黄色で、腹部は白銀色。砂底や砂泥底に生息していて、危険を察すると砂の中に潜る習性がある。和名「キス」の由来は、淡白な味を意味する「潔し」が転訛したという説など、諸説ある。漢字では「鱚」と書き、縁起の良い魚とされてきた。海釣りの人気魚種で、刺身や塩焼き、天ぷらなどにして賞味される。江戸の地誌『江戸名所図会』でも、武士や町人が中川で競ってキス釣りをする様子が記されており、古くから釣り人の間で人気の魚だったことがうかがえる。

Sillago japonica (Perciformes, Sillaginidae). This fish is found along the coasts from Hokkaido to southern Kyushu and in Taiwan. They typically measure 20 cm in length. Their Japanese name, "kisu," is said to come from their clean, light flavor ("kiyoshi" means "pureness" or "cleanliness"). They are popular with anglers and are eaten as sashimi, salted and broiled, or in tempura. The Edo topographical book *Edo Meisho Zue* records that samurai and merchants competed to catch Japanese whiting in the Nakagawa River, showing how long this fish has been popular for fishing.

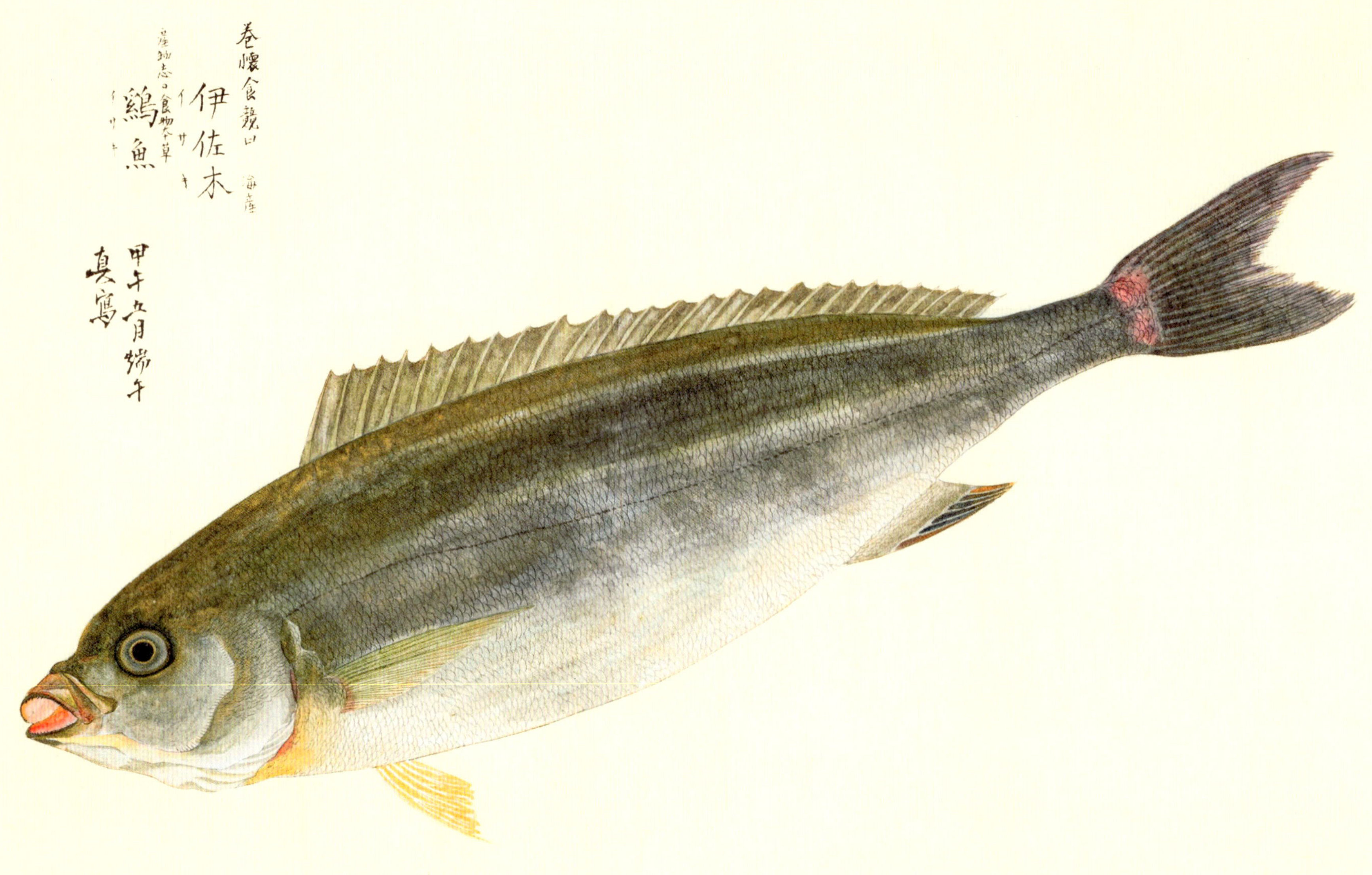
巻懐食競曰　海産
伊佐木
イサキ
鶏魚
甲午九月端午　真寫

伊佐木
（Isaki）

磯魚
（Isoki）

斑魚
（Isagi）

瓜坊
（Uribo）

伊佐幾
（Isaki）

カジヤコロシ
（Kajiyakoroshi）

イサキ

Chicken grunt

スズキ目イサキ科イサキ属。学名は*Parapristipoma trilineatum*。日本では新潟県から九州南岸までの日本海・東シナ海沿岸、宮城県から九州南岸までの太平洋沿岸などに分布する。体長は約45cm。幼魚は体に3本の縦縞があり、この模様がイノシシの子どもに似ていることから「ウリボウ」などと呼ばれる。和名の「イサキ」は縞模様を表す「斑（イサ）」と魚を示す「魚（キ）」に由来するという説や、磯に生息することから「磯魚（イソキ）」が語源という説など多数ある。和歌山の地方名「カジヤコロシ」は鍛冶屋がイサキを食べたところ、鋭い骨が喉に刺さって死んだという俗説による。『本朝食鑑』には「味が良くなく下の魚であるが、庶民に食べられている」という記述が残っている。

Parapristipoma trilineatum (Perciformes, Haemulidae). This fish is found along the coasts of the Sea of Japan and East China Sea from Niigata Prefecture to southern Kyushu and on the Pacific coast from Miyagi Prefecture to southern Kyushu. They typically measure 45 cm in length. There are many theories for their Japanese name, "isaki," such as it coming from "isa" ("mottled"), representing their stripes, and "ki" ("fish"). In the Wakayama area they are called "kajiya-koroshi" (literally "blacksmith killers") because a blacksmith ate one and its sharp bones pierced his throat, killing him.

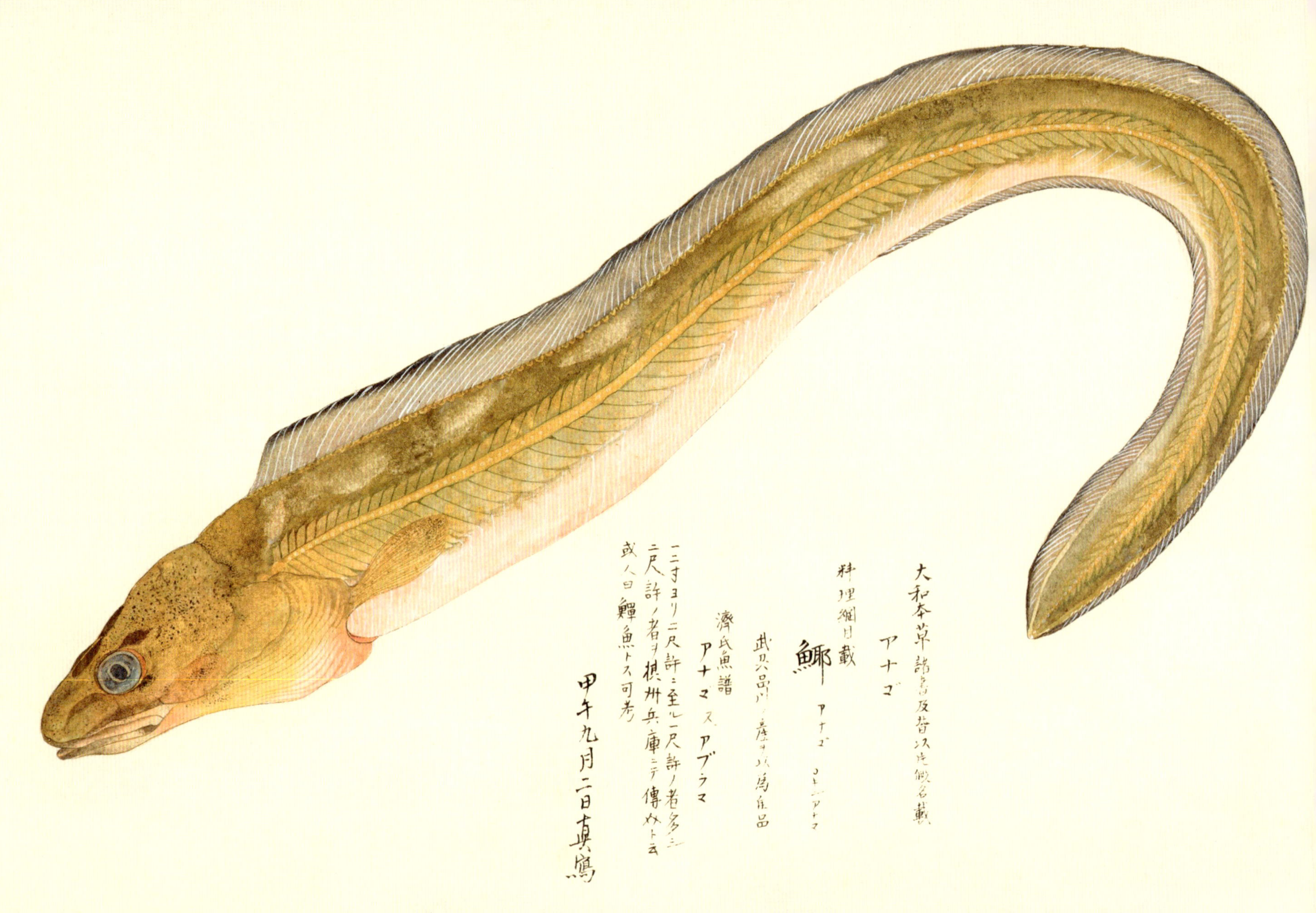

大和本草諸書及皆以此ノ個名載
アナゴ
料理綱目載
鯏 アナゴ コレアナゴ
武以品川ノ産ナ以為佳品
濟氏魚譜
アナマス アブラマ
二寸ヨリ二尺許ニ至ル一尺許ノ者多シ
二尺許ノ者ヲ摂州兵庫ニテ傳メ卜云
或人曰鱧魚卜ス可考
甲午九月二日眞寫

御殿穴子

(Goten-anago)

ギン
(Gin)

ハカリメ
(Hakarime)

ゴテンアナゴ

Silvery conger

ウナギ目アナゴ科ゴテンアナゴ属。学名は *Ariosoma meeki*。仙台湾から九州南岸までの太平洋沿岸、新潟県から九州北西岸までの日本海・東シナ海沿岸、東シナ海大陸棚域などに分布する。体長は約60cm。背側は暗褐色、腹側は白色で、浅海の砂泥底に生息する。砂泥底に潜入する習性があり、昼は頭だけを水中に出し、夜に活動する。眼の後方に黒い2つの斑点があるのが特徴。和名「ゴテンアナゴ」はこの斑点に由来するもので、御殿に仕えていた女性が眉を剃り落として眉墨で描いた下り眉に似ていることから、この名前が付けられたという。マアナゴに比べると味は落ちるといわれているが、蒲焼きや塩焼き、天ぷらにするとおいしく、蒲鉾などの練り製品の材料としても使われている。

Ariosoma meeki (Anguilliformes, Congridae). This fish is found along the Pacific coast from Sendai Bay to southern Kyushu, along the coasts of the Sea of Japan and the East China Sea from Niigata Prefecture to northwest Kyushu, and on the East China Sea continental shelf. They typically measure 60 cm in length. They have two black spots behind their eyes, and these spots are behind their Japanese name, "goten-anago," because of their resemblance to the eyebrows of women serving in palaces ("goten"), who would shave off their eyebrows and redraw them with pencil.

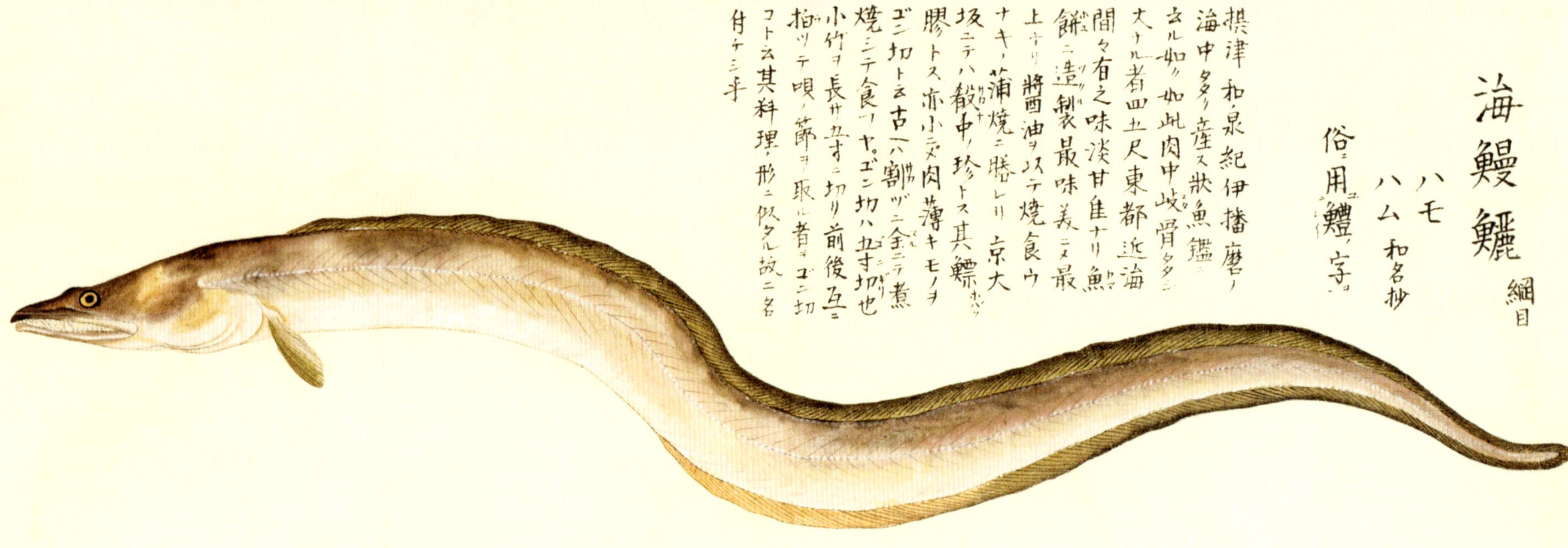

海鰻鱺 細目

ハモ
ハム 和名抄
俗用鱧ノ字

摂津 和泉 紀伊 播磨ノ
海中タリ産ス状魚鑑ニ
云ル如ク此肉中岐骨多シ
大ナル者四五尺東都近海
間々有之味淡甘佳ナリ鮓
餅ニ造製最最味美之最
上ナリ
醤油ヲ以テ焼食ウ
蒲焼ニ膾トレリ 京大
坂ニテハ殻中ノ珍トス其鰾
膠トス亦小之メ肉薄キモノヲ
ナキノ
ゴニ切トス古ハ六割ツ全ニテ煮
焼ニテ食フヤゴニ切ハ丑寸切也
小竹ヲ長廿五寸ニ切リ前後互
拍ツテ唄ノ節ヲ取ル者ヲゴニ切
コトヲ其料理ノ形ニ似タル故ニ名
付ケ三チ

多識編ニ云
海鰻鱺 宇美宇 狗魚華
慈鰻鱺 那岐

邦各鈔引ニ本草ニ云鱧。鱧魚ヲ載ス國
俗皆鱧ノ之字ヲ用ユル也鱧ト鱧トハ
異名ニメ皆ハモトメ鱧チモ海ウナキト謂ル
書アリ海鰻鱺 鱧各々多識ニ分チ載
ス皆一物予

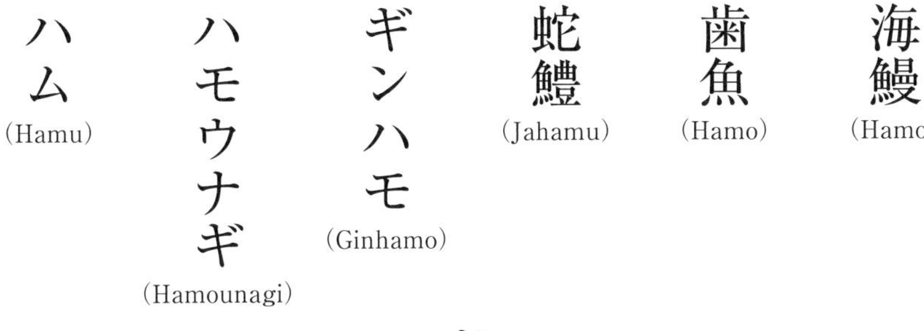

鱧
(Hamo)

ハム
(Hamu)

ハモウナギ
(Hamounagi)

ギンハモ
(Ginhamo)

ハモ

蛇鱧
(Jahamu)

歯魚
(Hamo)

海鰻
(Hamo)

Daggertooth pike conger

図から正確な同定は困難であり、スズハモの可能性もあるが、ここではハモとして扱う。ウナギ目ハモ科ハモ属。学名は*Muraenesox cinereus*。新潟県から九州南岸までの日本海・東シナ海沿岸、福島県から九州南岸までの太平洋沿岸、朝鮮半島南岸・西岸などに分布する。体長は60㎝〜1mのものが多いが、2mを超える記録もある。細長い体で、大きな口と鋭い歯を持つのが特徴。和名の由来は鋭い歯でエサを食べることから「咬む」、「食べる」を意味する「食む」が転じて「ハモ」になったという説や、「歯魚」という説など諸説ある。ハモは生命力が強く、保冷手段が乏しい時代でも生きたまま大阪や京都に届いたため、今でも大阪の天神祭や京都の祇園祭で欠かせない食材となっている。

Muraenesox cinereus (Anguilliformes, Muraenesocidae). This fish is found along the coasts of the Sea of Japan and East China Sea from Niigata Prefecture to southern Kyushu, on the Pacific coast from Fukushima Prefecture to southern Kyushu, and on the southern and western coasts of the Korean Peninsula. They typically measure 60 to 100 cm in length. According to one theory, their Japanese name, "hamo," comes from a Japanese word for "to bite," because of their sharp teeth. They are very resilient and could be transported live to Osaka and Kyoto in times before refrigeration, so even now they are essential ingredients in these areas.

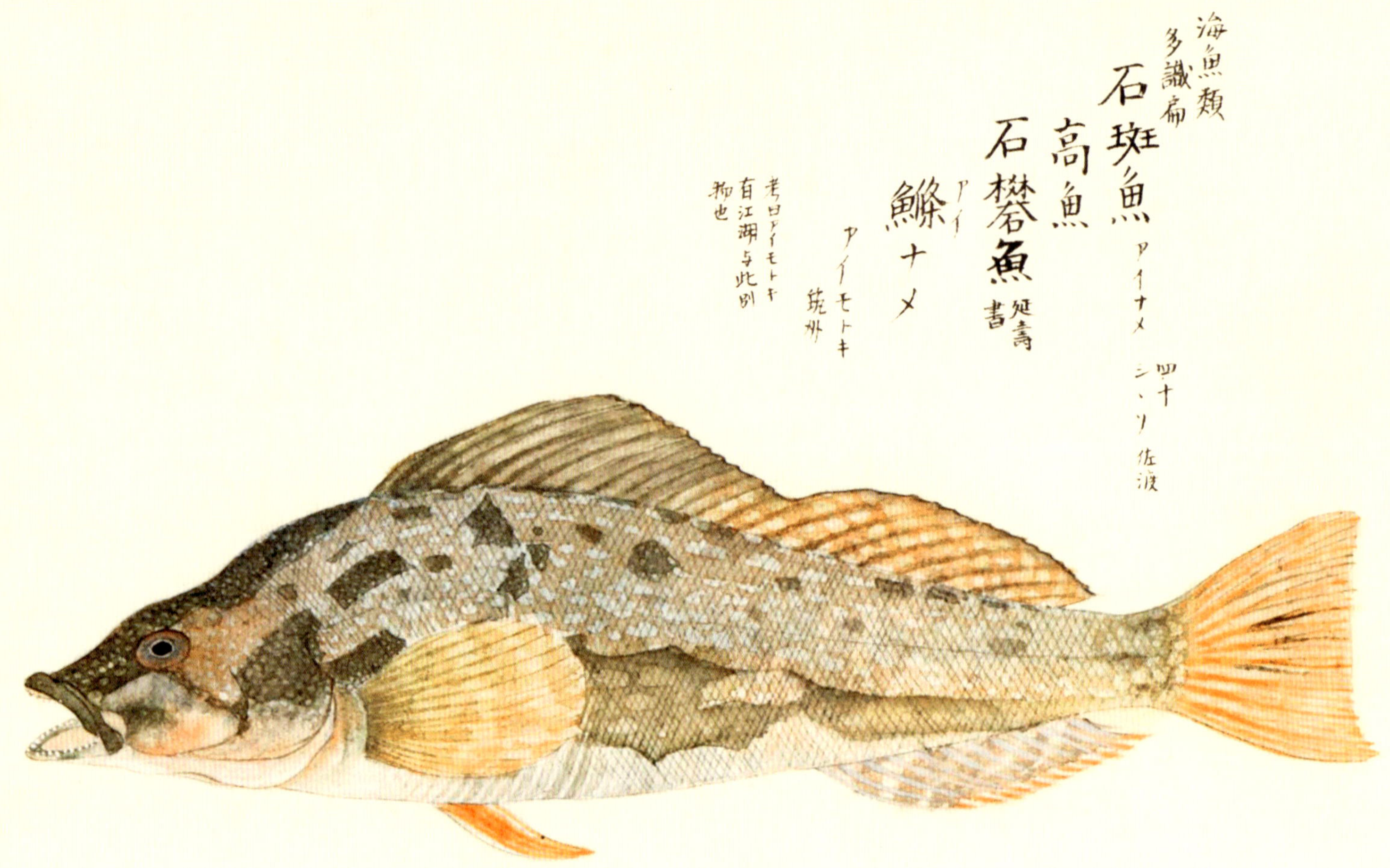

海魚類
多識篇
石斑魚 アイナメ ニシノ 佐渡
高魚 ツナ
石䱜魚 延壽書
鰷 ナメ
アイモトキ 筑州
考曰アイモトキ
有江湖与此別
柳也
癸巳丑月八日
眞寫

鮎並
（Ainame）

籾種失い
（Momidaneushinai）

寝所
（Shinjo）

寝魚
（Neuo）

愛魚女
（Ainame）

鮎魚女
（Ainame）

アイナメ

Fat greenling

スズキ目アイナメ科アイナメ属。学名は*Hexagrammos otakii*。北海道から九州南岸までの各沿岸域、朝鮮半島全沿岸、渤海・黄海などに分布する。体長は約40cmで、60cmを超えるものもいる。和名「アイナメ」の由来は、アユと同様に縄張りを持つ性質から「鮎並」が転じたという説や、アユに形が似ていることから「鮎魚女」、古くからおいしい魚と称賛されていたことを意味する「愛魚女」、柔らかい体形から「愛な女」という説など多数ある。地方名の「籾種失い」は、アイナメがおいしいあまりに貴重な籾種を買うお金までつぎこんでしまった、という故事に由来する。白身で脂肪分が多く、刺身や煮付けなどにして食べられる。

Hexagrammos otakii (Perciformes, Hexagrammidae). This fish is found along the coasts from Hokkaido to southern Kyushu, along all of the coast of the Korean Peninsula, and in the Bohai Sea and Yellow Sea. They typically measure 40 cm in length, but some exceed 60 cm in length. Their Japanese name, "ainame," is said to come from "ayu nami," meaning "on the level of an ayu" because they are fiercely territorial, like ayu sweetfish. In some regions, they are called "momidane-ushinai" meaning "losing seed rice" because they are so delicious that farmers would spend their precious seed rice money to buy them.

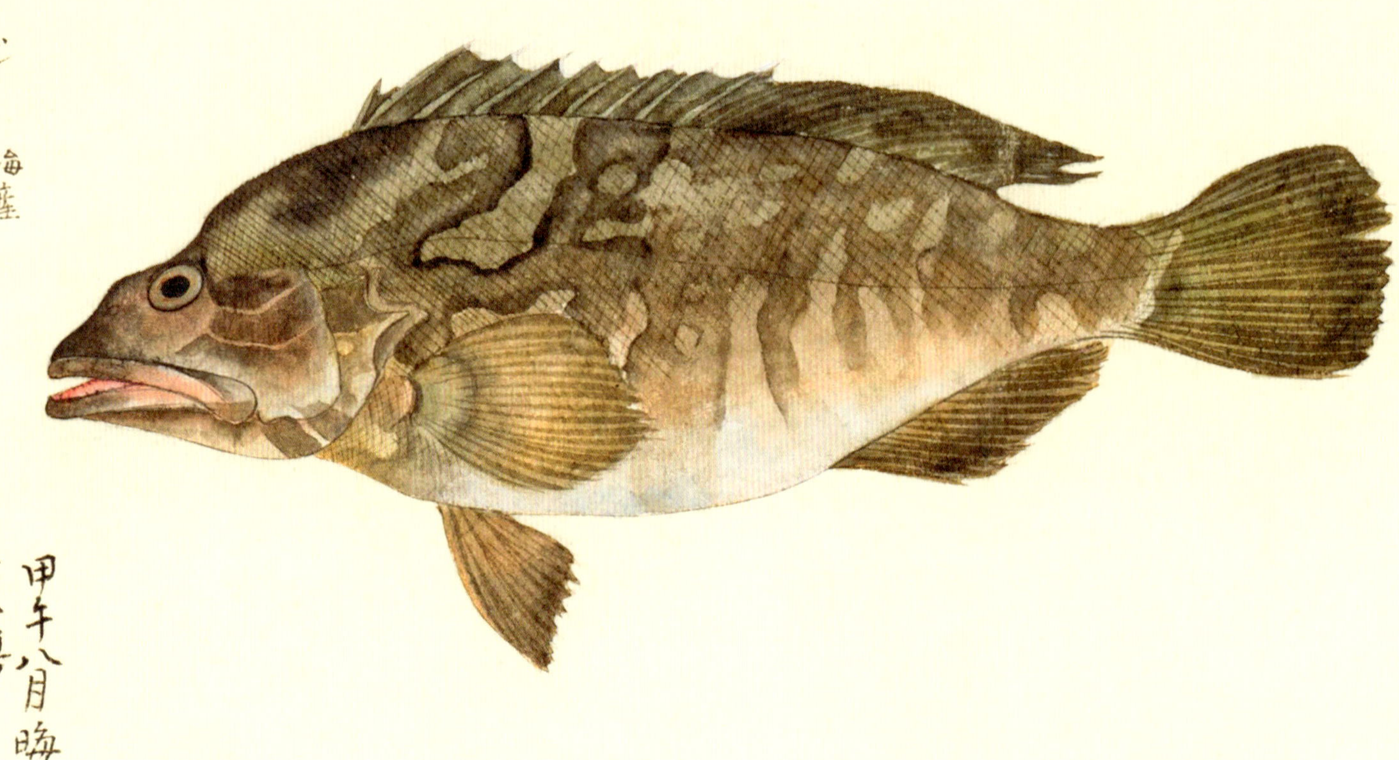

クジメ　海産
似タアイナメニ頭大ニ異リ味隹品也
甲午八月晦日
真寫

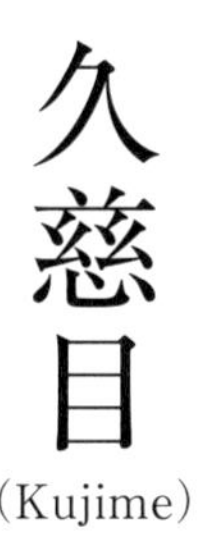

久慈目
（Kujime）

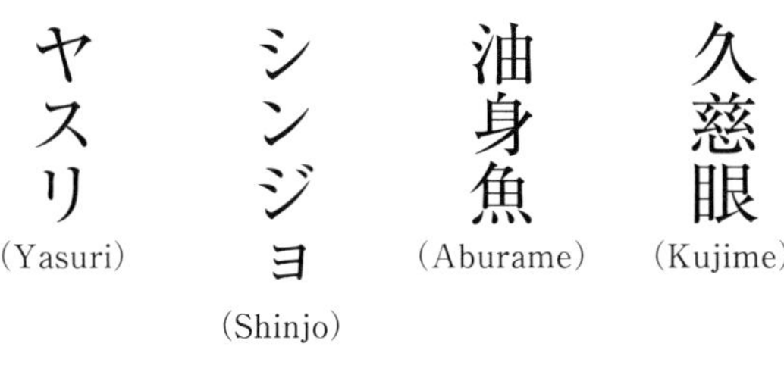

ヤスリ
（Yasuri）

シンジョ
（Shinjo）

油身魚
（Aburame）

久慈眼
（Kujime）

クジメ

Spotty-bellied greenling

スズキ目アイナメ科アイナメ属。学名は*Hexagrammos agrammus*。北海道から九州北岸までの日本海沿岸、北海道から土佐湾までの太平洋沿岸、朝鮮半島全沿岸などに分布する。体長は約30㎝。アイナメと容姿が似ているため混同されるが、アイナメは側線が5本あるのに対してクジメは1本しかないこと、尾びれの後縁が丸みを帯びていること、体がアイナメほど大きくないことなどで区別される。また、痘痕のような斑紋があるのが特徴で、九州の方言で痘痕のことを「クジ」と呼び、魚介の総称を「メ」ということから、「痘痕のような斑紋のある魚」を意味する「クジメ」という名前が付けられたといわれている。漢字では「久慈目」「久慈眼」と書く。

Hexagrammos agrammus (Perciformes, Hexagrammidae). This fish is found along the coast of the Sea of Japan from Hokkaido to northern Kyushu, along the Pacific coast from Hokkaido to Tosa Bay, and along the entire coast of the Korean Peninsula. They typically measure 30 cm in length. Although they resemble fat greenlings, they can be distinguished because they have only one line on their sides and the back edges of their tail fins are rounded. They are notable for their pockmark-like spots. In a Kyushu dialect, "pockmarks" are called "kuji," and "me" is the collective term for sea life, so they are named "kujime," meaning "fish with pockmark-like spots."

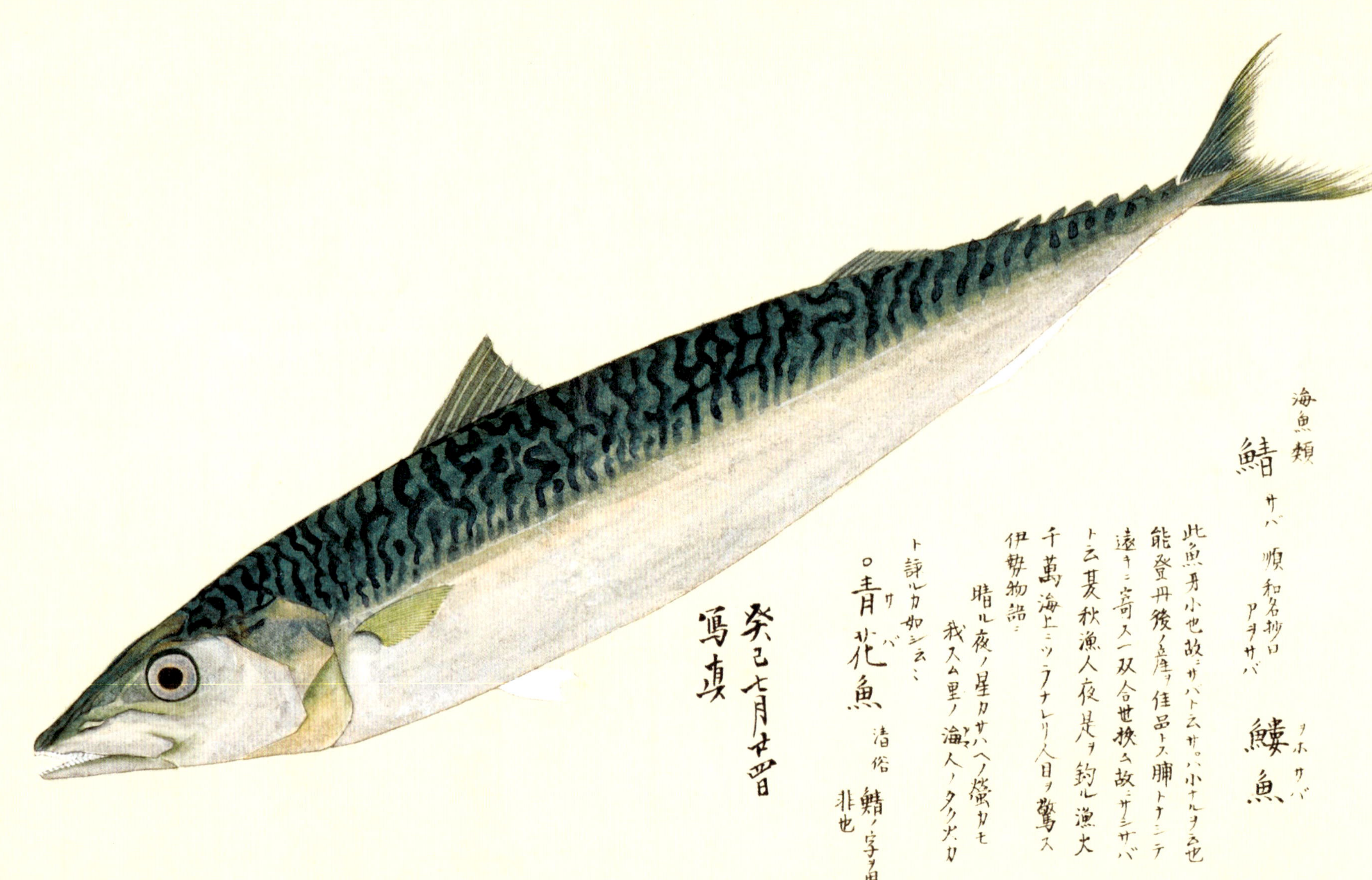

海魚類

鯖　サバ　順和名抄曰　アヲサバ

鰺魚　ヲホサバ

此魚身小也故ニサバト云。小サキヲ云也
能登丹後ノ産ヲ佳品トス脯トナシテ
遠キニ寄入ニ一双合世換ユ故ニサシサバ
ト云其秋漁人夜是ヲ釣ル漁大
千萬海上ニツラナレリ人日ヲ驚ス
伊勢物語ニ
晴ル夜ノ星カサバヘノ燈カモ
我スム里ノ漁人ノタク火カ
ト詠ルカ如シ云ニ、

〇青花魚　俗　鯖ノ字ヲ用ルハ　非也

癸巳七月廿四　寫真

真鯖
（Masaba）

平鯖　本鯖　鯖
（Hirasaba）（Honsaba）（Saba）

マサバ

Club mackerel

スズキ目サバ科サバ属。学名は*Scomber japonicus*。北海道から九州南岸までの各沿岸域、朝鮮半島全沿岸、フィリピン諸島、ハワイ諸島などに分布する。体長は30cmほどのものが多いが60cmを超える記録もある。背部は青緑色で、黒い縞状紋が特徴。和名「マサバ」の由来は、「マ」は同類の中において代表的なものを表し、「サバ」は歯が小さいことから「小歯」という説や、群れをなすことから「多」が転じたなど、諸説ある。日本では古くから大衆魚として親しまれ、贈り物にも用いられてきた。江戸時代には七夕の前夜に大名から将軍家にサバを献上する慣習があったという。後にサバの代わりに金銀が使われ、さらに時を経て今日の「お中元」の風習になったといわれている。

Scomber japonicus (Perciformes, Scombridae). This fish is found along the coasts from Hokkaido to southern Kyushu, along the coast of the Korean Peninsula, around the Philippine Islands, and around the Hawaiian Islands. They typically measure 30 cm in length. One theory holds that their Japanese name, "masaba," comes from "ma," indicating a representative of a group of similar things, and "saba," from a Japanese term for small teeth. In the Edo era (1603–1867), it was customary for daimyo lords to present club mackerel to the family in line to accede to the shogunate on the night before Tanabata (July 7). This is said to be the origin of Japan's ochugen summer gift-giving custom.

真鯵
（Maaji）

アヂジャコ
（Ajijako）

アヅ
（Azu）

ガソン
（Gason）

マルワリ
（Maruwari）

メダマ
（Medama）

マアジ

Japanese jack mackerel

スズキ目アジ科マアジ属。学名は *Trachurus japonicus*。北海道から九州南岸までの各沿岸域、沖縄島、黄海、朝鮮半島全沿岸、台湾西岸などに分布する。体長は30cmほどのものが多いが、大型になると50cmほどにもなる。刺身や塩焼きなどで食べることが多く、日本の食卓では馴染みのある魚の一つ。かつてアジは高級魚として神饌や行事食として用いられたという。「アジ」の名前は味の良さに由来するもので、「真」はアジの代表種であったことを示している。他にも「ア」は愛称語、「ジ」は魚を表す語尾で、昔から大量に獲れる魚であったことに因むという説もある。江戸っ子たちは夏季の食中毒予防のため、毒消しになると信じられていたなすと一緒に食べたといわれている。

Trachurus japonicus (Perciformes, Carangidae). The fish is found along the coasts from Hokkaido to southern Kyushu, around Okinawa-jima Island, the Yellow Sea, along all of the coast of the Korean Peninsula, and western Taiwan. They typically measure 30 cm in length, but large individuals may be as large as 50 cm in length. Their Japanese name, "maaji," comes from their delicious taste ("aji" means "flavor") and "ma," indicating that they are a representative of the jack mackerels. The people of Edo ate them along with eggplant, which was believed to act as an antidote, to prevent food poisoning during the summer.

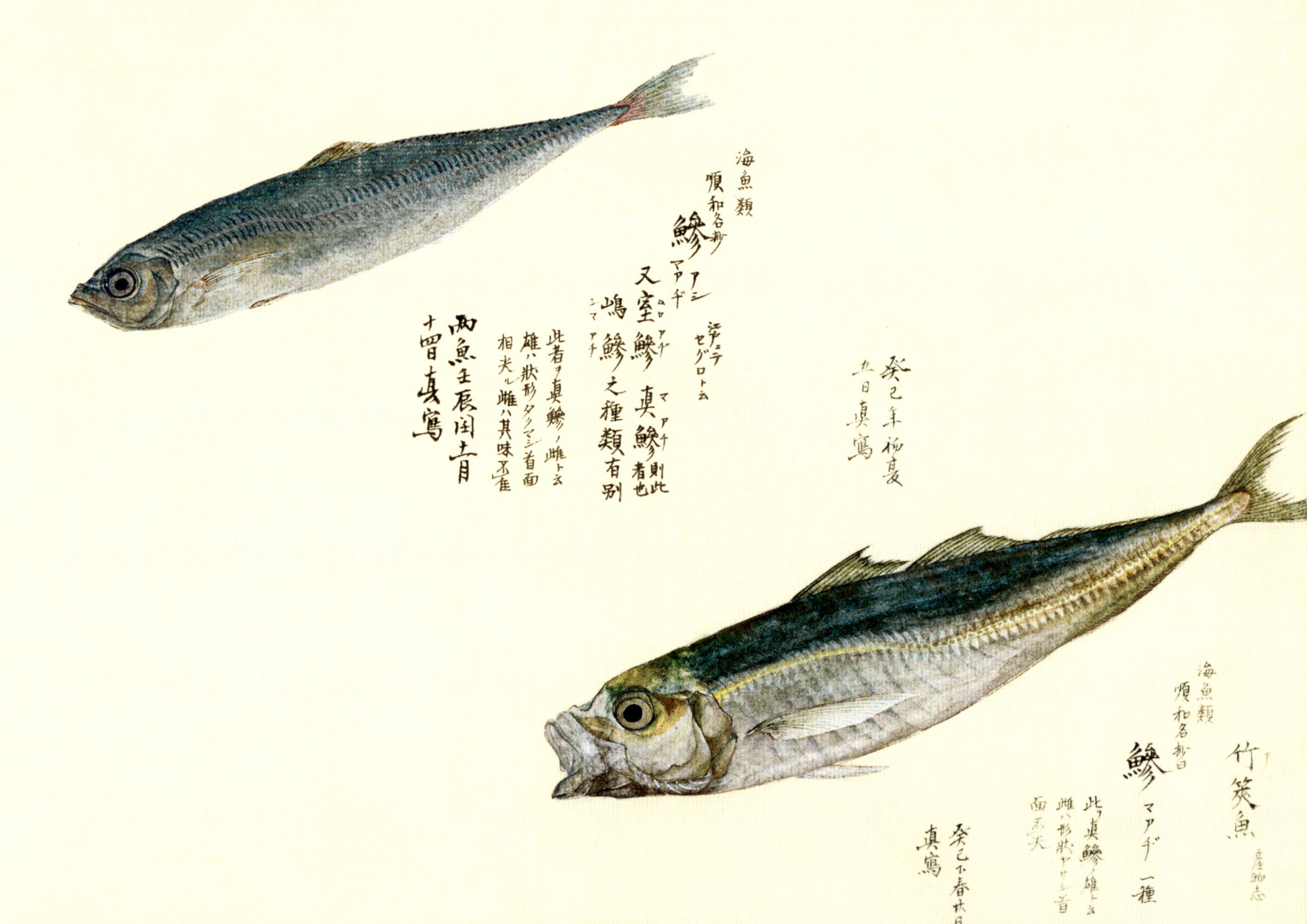

海魚類
順和名抄
鯵 アヂ
又室鯵 真鯵ノ則チ此者也
嶋鯵 真鯵之種類有別
此者ヲ真鯵ノ雌ト云
雄ハ狀形タクマシ首面
相夫ル雌ハ其味不雀
兩魚壬辰閏十二月
十日真寫
癸巳年初夏
五日真寫
海魚類
順和名抄曰
鯵 マアヂ一種
竹筴魚
此ノ真鯵ノ雄ト云
雌ハ形狀ヤヤ音
面示大
癸巳下春廿六日
真寫

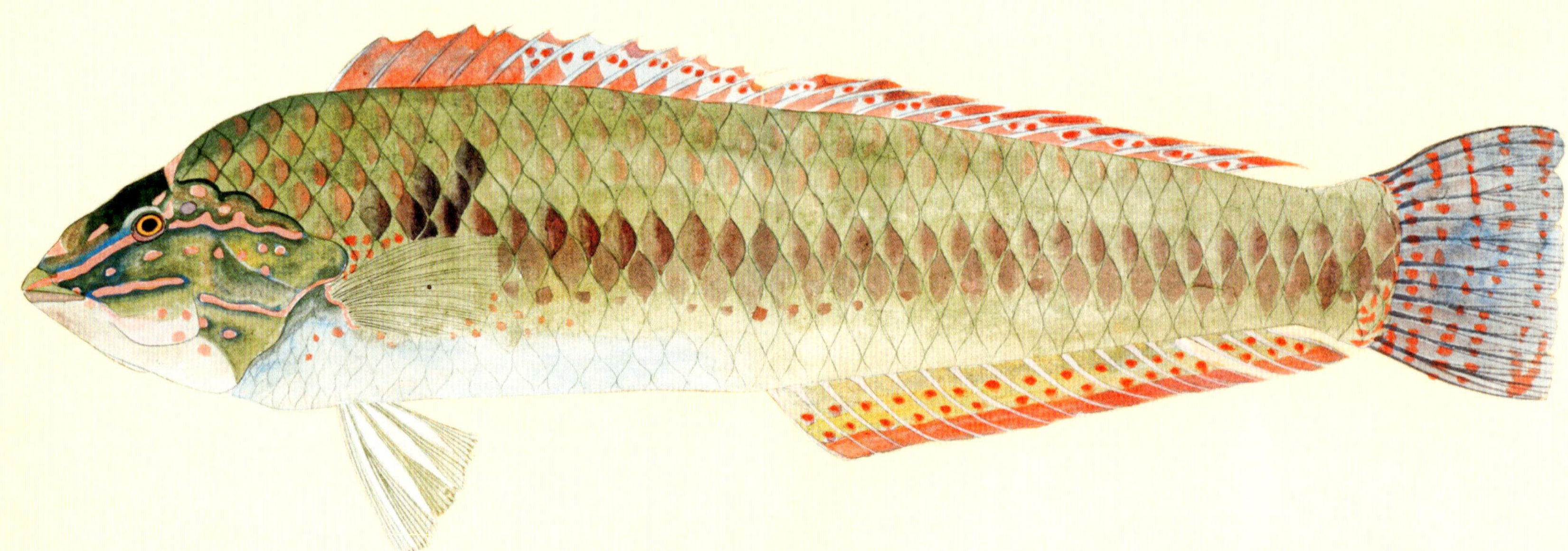

大和本草出
クサビ 海魚
ベラ 魚扁呼
所
前條ニ載スクサビノ大十八者ニ
彩色異也其大一尺二至ニ
身ニヌメリ多シ鱗スルトセ
肉白メ味目類ニ鮒魚
乙未八月二日送之
鷹若子真寫

九線
（Kyusen）

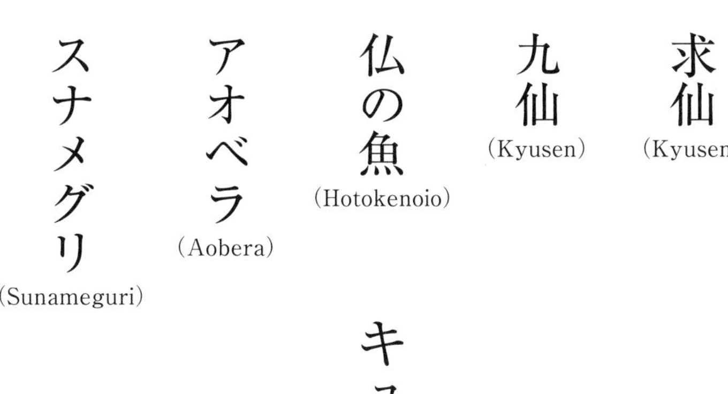

スナメグリ（Sunameguri）　アオベラ（Aobera）　仏の魚（Hotokenoio）　九仙（Kyusen）　求仙（Kyusen）

キュウセン

Multicolor fin rainbowfish

図はキュウセンの雄である。スズキ目ベラ科キュウセン属。学名は*Parajulis poecilepterus*。日本では北海道から九州南岸までの各沿岸域、伊豆大島の日本海側などに分布する。体長は20㎝ほどのものが多いが、30㎝を超えるものもいる。雄は青緑色であることから「アオベラ」、雌は赤みがかっていることから「アカベラ」とも呼ばれ、明治時代の末期頃までは雄雌で別の種とされていた。雌から雄に性転換する個体がいるのが特徴で、性転換した雌は体色が変化する。和名「キュウセン」の由来は、雌の体表の縦帯と赤点の縦列が合わせて9本あることから。砂に潜る性質から「スナメグリ」、仏様でなければ食べてくれないような不味い味から「仏の魚」とも呼ばれる。

Parajulis poecilepterus (Perciformes, Labridae). The fish shown in the figure is a male. This fish is found along the coasts from Hokkaido to southern Kyushu, along the coast of the Sea of Japan, and around Izu Oshima Island. They typically measure 20 cm in length. They are notable for the ability of females to become males. When they change sex, the color of their body also changes. Their Japanese name, "kyusen," is said to come from the nine ("kyu") bands and lines of red dots ("sen") on the female's body. They taste so bad that only the Buddha could eat one, so they are also called "hotoke-no-io" (literally "Buddha fish").

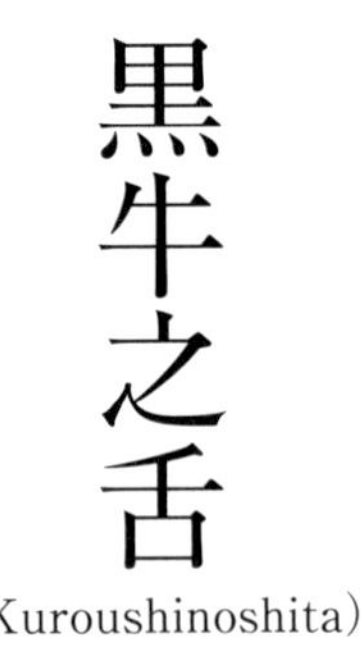

黒牛之舌

（Kuroushinoshita）

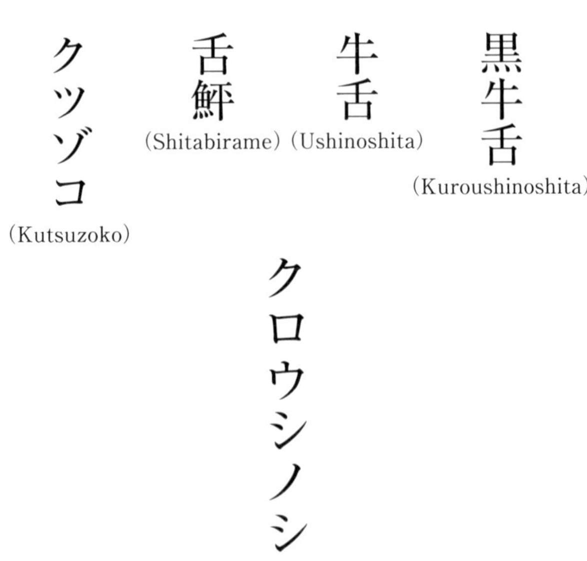

Black cow-tongue

カレイ目ウシノシタ科タイワンシタビラメ属。学名は*Paraplagusia japonica*。北海道から九州南岸までの各沿岸域、朝鮮半島、中国東シナ海・南シナ海北部沿岸などに分布する。体長は20〜35cm前後。体は扁平な長楕円形で両眼が体の左側にある。口唇にひげがあること、体の有眼側に3本の側線があること、黒っぽい体色などで他のシタビラメ類と区別される。和名「クロウシノシタ」は「体の色が黒いウシノシタ（ウシノシタ科とササウシノシタ科の魚類の総称）」という意。体形が舌や靴底を連想させることから「シタビラメ」「クツゾコ」などの地方名もある。味は近縁種のアカシタビラメやイヌノシタなどより劣るともいわれるが、ムニエルやフライにして食べられる。

Paraplagusia japonica (Pleuronectiformes, Cynoglossidae). This fish is found along the coasts from Hokkaido to southern Kyushu, the Korean Peninsula, and along the coasts of the East China Sea and northern South China Sea in China. They typically measure 20 to 35 cm in length. Their Japanese name, "kuro-ushinoshita," comes from them being "ushinoshita"(soles and tongue soles) with a black ("kuro") body. They are eaten deep-fried or as a meuniere, although they do not taste as good as the related species of red tonguesole (*Cynoglossus joyneri*) or robust tonguefish (*Cynoglossus robustus*).

鞋底魚　舌ビラメ
　　　　赤シタ

乙未十月廿六日
至康貞寫

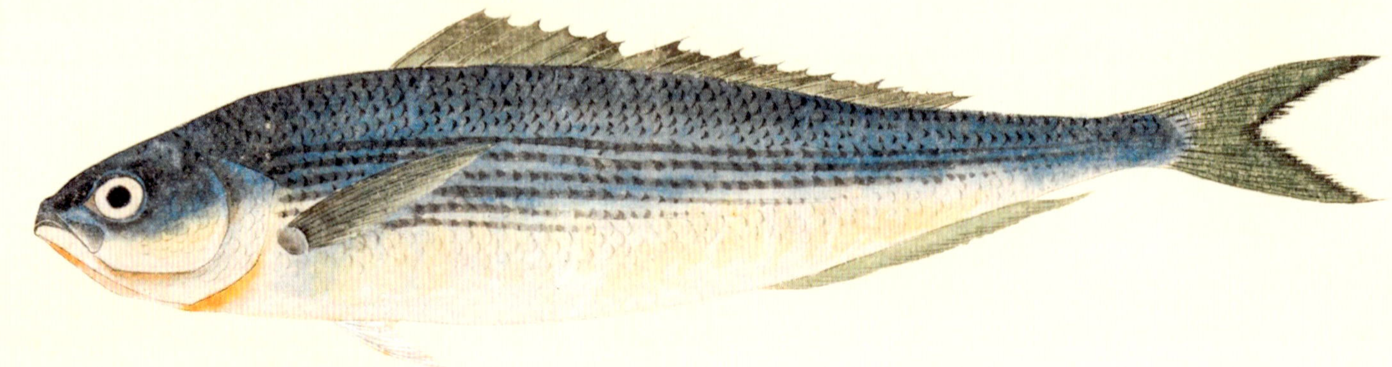

海産
タカベ
此者ヲ真トス
鱠魚　釈各多加部　各義不詳
日東魚譜
丙申十二月十六日到来
真寫

鰖
（Takabe）

ホタ（Hota）　ベント（Bento）　シャカ（Shaka）　シマウオ（Shimauo）　タカベ

Yellowstriped butterfish

スズキ目タカベ科タカベ属。学名は*Labracoglossa argentiventris*。茨城県から九州南岸までの太平洋沿岸、若狭湾以西の日本海沿岸、小笠原諸島、朝鮮半島南岸、済州島などに分布する。体長は約20㎝。和名「タカベ」は、「タカ」は漁村用語で海中の岩礁、「ベ」は魚名語尾で、「岩礁の魚」を意味する。能登では海藻が少ない磯を「トコ」といい、本種がトコに多いことから「トコヤ」と呼ぶ。他にも「シマウオ」「シャカ」「ベント」などの地方名がある。関東では伊豆諸島での漁獲量が多い。食用とされ、肉は柔らかく、脂肪分が多く美味とされる。江戸時代の本草書『大和本草』には「形アヂニ似又コノシロ似タリ関東ニアリ味淡シ」と記述されている。

Labracoglossa argentiventris (Perciformes, Scorpididae). This fish is found along the Pacific coast from Ibaraki Prefecture to southern Kyushu, on the coast of the Sea of Japan from Wakasa Bay westward, around the Ogasawara Islands, on the southern coast of the Korean Peninsula, and around Jeju Island. They typically measure 20 cm in length. Their Japanese name, "takabe," combines "taka," a fishing village term for reef, and "be," a suffix used in fish names, to mean "reef fish." In the Kanto region they are caught in especially high numbers near the Izu Islands. They are a delicious fish, with soft flesh and high in fat.

赤鱏
（Akaei）

潟掘
（Gatahori）

赤魚
（Akayo）

赤海鷂魚
（Akaei）

赤鱝
（Akaei）

アカエイ

Red stingray

トビエイ目アカエイ科アカエイ属。学名は*Hemitrygon akajei*。日本では北海道から九州南岸までの各沿岸域、小笠原諸島、東シナ海などに分布する。体長（体盤長）は約90cm。和名「アカエイ」の由来は、「赤みを帯びたエイ」という体色によるもの。尾に鋭い毒棘があるのが特徴で、アイヌ語で棘や尖ったものを表す「アイ」から、「アイコットチェップ（棘を持った魚）」と呼ばれ、「エイ」の語源となったという説もある。英名「Red stingray」も「赤い刺すエイ」という意味。江戸時代の地理書『三国通覧図説』には約200mのアカエイがいると記され、江戸時代後期の『絵本百物語』にも体長が12km以上ある妖怪として紹介されるなど、その巨大さが誇張されていた。

Hemitrygon akajei (Myliobatiformes, Dasyatidae). This fish is found along the coasts from Hokkaido to southern Kyushu, around the Ogasawara Islands, and the East China Sea. They typically measure 90 cm (not including their tails). Their Japanese name, "akaei," comes from the fact that they are red ("aka") rays ("ei"). Their size has been greatly exaggerated. The *Sangoku Tsuran Zusetsu*, a geography book written in the Edo era (1603–1867), says that there are red stingrays that measure 200 meters, and the *Ehon Hyakumonogatari*, from the late Edo period, introduces a monster red stingray over 12 kilometers long.

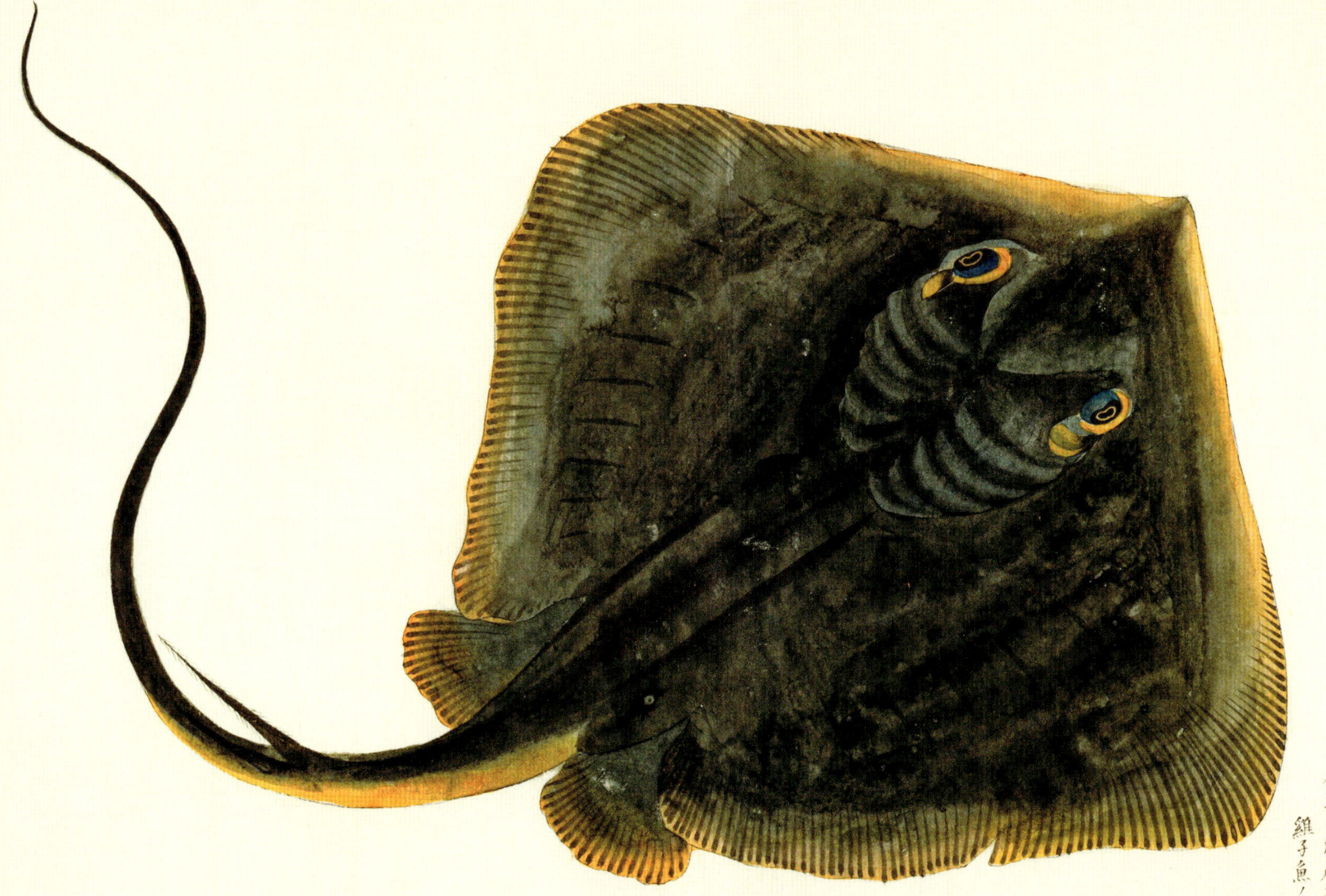

エイ　海鷂魚脊之圖

海鷂魚ハ以ガヲ此アトンビト云不然
トンビト称スル者ハ別種ニ而、鳥アイト
云海鷂魚ニ一種也最エイノ少尤ハ
味不美鳥アイハ胼形鳥ニ似タリ味
不好　アイモ中品ナルヲ以爲隹品鳥
アイ本草ニ曰鼠尾魚、地青魚
鱝子魚ノ屬ナルヘシ

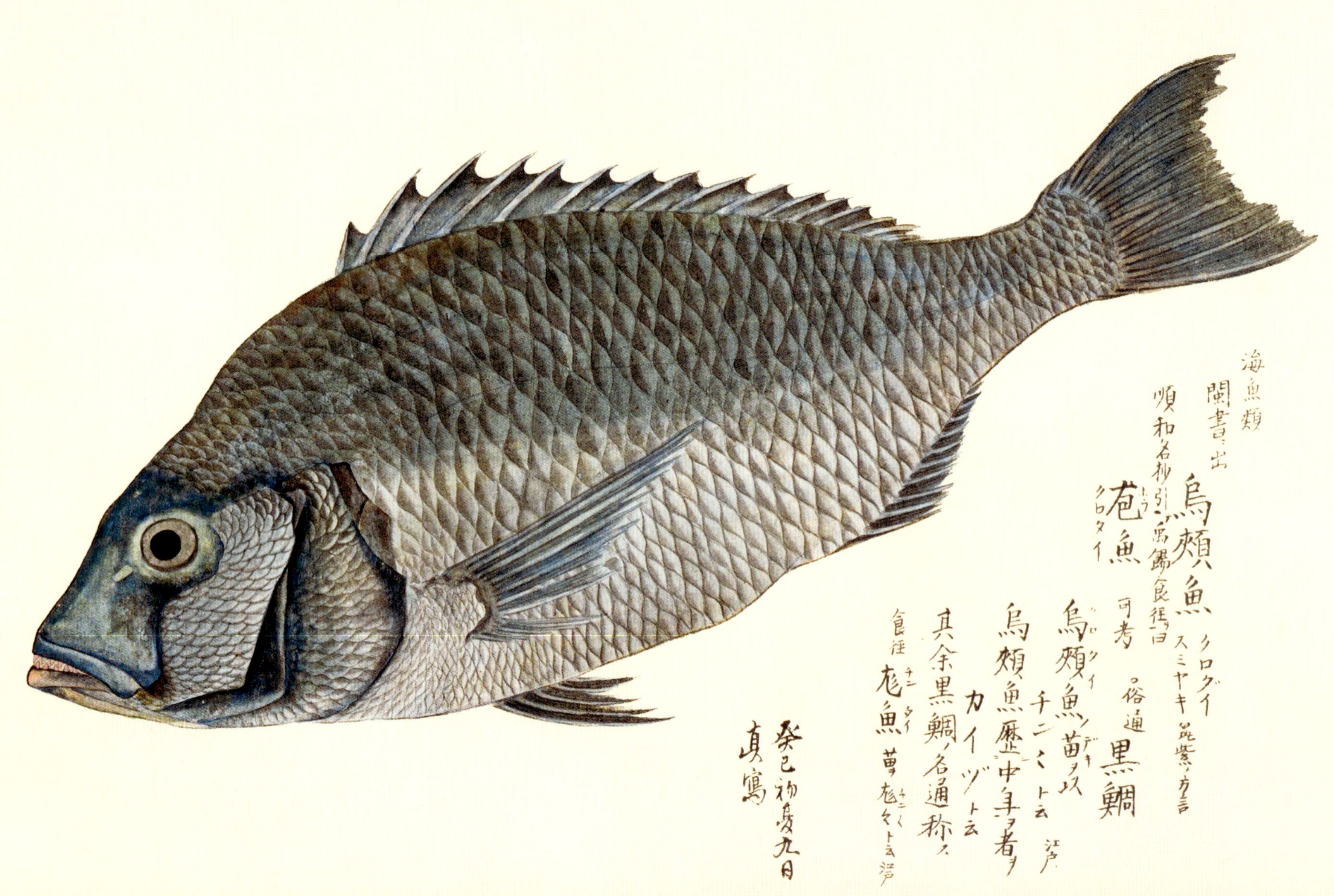

海魚類
閩書ニ出
順和名抄引ニ萬鬣食猶當白
烏頬魚 クロダイ スミヤキ 荒紫ノ方言
苞魚 クロタイ
可考
俗通 黒鯛
烏頬魚ンデキ チニくトニ云 江戸
烏頬魚苗ヲ以
烏頬魚歴中手ヲ者ヲ カイヅトニ云
其余黒鯛ノ名ヲ通称ス
食任 苞魚 ナニタイ 苔苞々くトニ云江戸
癸巳初夏九日
貞寫

黒鯛
(Kurodai)

貝津
(Kaizu)

海鯽
(Chinu)

茅渟
(Chinu)

茅渟鯛
(Chinudai)

烏頬魚
(Kurodai)

クロダイ

Black porgy

スズキ目タイ科クロダイ属。学名は*Acanthopagrus schlegelii*。北海道から九州南岸までの各沿岸域、屋久島、朝鮮半島全沿岸、渤海、黄海、済州島、台湾などに分布する。体長は約50cm。性転換する魚として知られている。釣り人の間では人気のターゲットであり、生育環境によって磯臭い場合もあるが、食用にもされる。和名「クロダイ」は、体の色が暗灰色なことから「黒っぽいタイ」という意味で名付けられた。奈良時代の歴史書である『日本書紀』には、神功皇后が船上で食事をしているときにクロダイが船に集まってきたので酒をかけたところ、酔って浮かんだため、クロダイは6月になると酔ったように傾いて浮かぶという話が残されている。

Acanthopagrus schlegelii (Perciformes, Sparidae). This fish is found along the coasts from Hokkaido to southern Kyushu, around Yakushima Island, along the coast of the Korean Peninsula, the Bohai Sea, the Yellow Sea, around Jeju Island, and Taiwan. They typically measure 50 cm in length. They are known to be a hermaphroditic species. They are a popular target for anglers, and although they can have a strong sea smell depending on their living environment, they are also used for food. Their Japanese name, "kurodai," comes from the fact that its body is a dark gray ("kuro" is Japanese for "black") and that they are a porgy ("tai").

真蛸
（Madako）

蛸
（Tako）

明石蛸
（Akashidako）

マダコ

East Asian common octopus

八腕形目マダコ科マダコ属。学名は*Octopus sinensis*。青森県から九州南岸までの各沿岸域、東シナ海、台湾などに分布する。従来は*Octopus vulgaris*として世界の温暖海域に広く分布すると考えられていたが、日本でマダコと呼ばれている種は東アジア周辺だけに分布する別種だと近年明らかになった。全長40〜60cm。日本で食用とされるタコ類で最も多いのが本種。和名「マダコ」の由来は、「タ」は「手」の転、「コ」は「たくさん」という意味で、「手が多い」を意味するという説など、多数ある。「マ」は同類の中において代表的なものを表す。日本では有史以前から食用とされてきたといわれ、弥生・古墳時代の遺跡から蛸壺らしきものが出土している。

Octopus sinensis (Octopoda, Octopodidae). This octopus is found along the coasts from Aomori Prefecture to southern Kyushu, the East China Sea, and Taiwan. They typically measure 40 to 60 cm. This octopus is the most commonly eaten type of octopus in Japan. There are many theories regarding their Japanese name, such as "madako," coming from "ta," which derives from "te" ("hand"), and "ko" ("many"). The "ma" indicates that they are a representative variety of octopus. They are said to have been eaten in Japan since prehistoric times, and what appear to be octopus traps have been found in archaeological sites from the Yayoi and Kofun eras (from roughly 300 BCE to 700 CE).

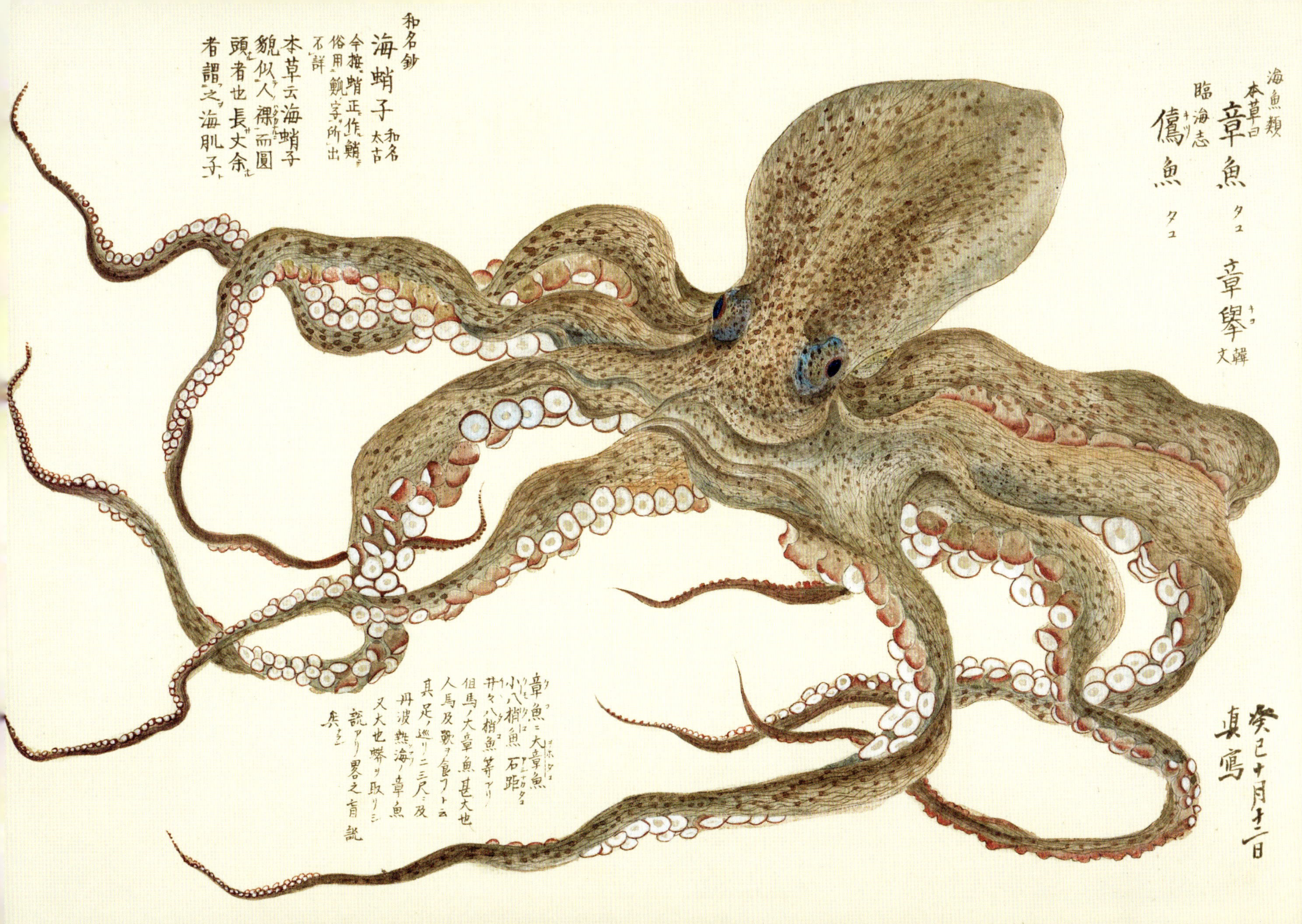

海魚類
本草曰　章魚　タコ
臨海志　章擧　文輯
鮹魚　タコ

和名鈔
海蛸子　和名　太古
今按鮹正作鮹
俗用蛸字所出
不詳
本草云海蛸子
貌似人裸而圓
頭者也長丈餘
者謂之海肌子

章魚ニ大章魚
小八梢魚　石距
廾々八梢魚等アリ
但馬ノ大章魚甚大也
人馬及歌ヲ食フト云
其足ノ巡リ二三尺及
丹波難海ノ章魚
又大也帶リ取リシ
説アリ畧之肯説
俟之

癸巳十月十二日
眞寫

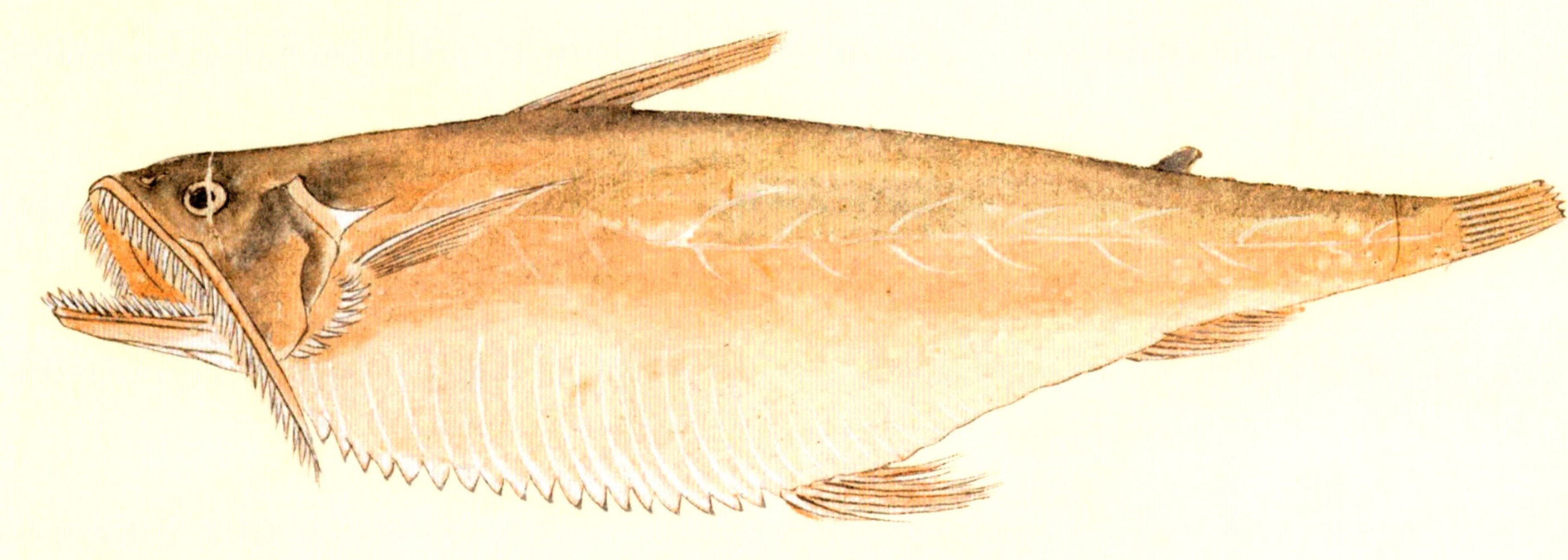

己亥八月八日求之
真寫

海産
網目出
勤魚　ミイラ　クマ足
　　　俗トフヤク　クマ足
　ヒラ
　鰯ノ字ヲ用
　アソニ似テ腹ニ
　硬キ針アリ
　テクル者好子
　家某送之

勤魚是々足ト云
數万群游ス故ニ九
万足ト云此魚紀伊
土佐肥前肥後又
薩州ニ産ス又相
外其州ニモ産ス
鱗細ク皮厚ク
肉白ク味隹カラ
ストヱ氏未生魚
ヲ不見

斉魚

（Etsu）

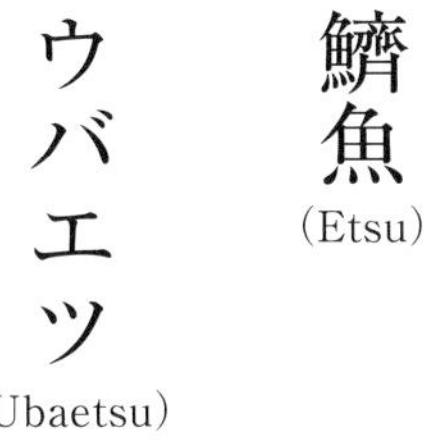

鱭魚
（Etsu）

ウバエツ
（Ubaetsu）

エツ

Japanese grenadier anchovy

図から正確な同定はできないが、上顎後端が鰓蓋を越えることや体高などから、エツの尾部再生個体を描いた可能性が高い。エツはニシン目カタクチイワシ科エツ属。学名は*Coilia nasus*。体長は約30cm。有明海と有明海に注ぐ河川に分布する。体は側扁し、尾部にかけて体高が低くなる。体色は青みのある銀白色。和名「エツ」の由来は「エツボ」の略とする説、「鱭」の中国語音「ヘツ」が転訛したとする説がある。食用とされ、流網や刺網で漁獲される。筑後川には「行脚中の僧が川を渡れずにいたとき、親切な漁師が船で向こう岸に渡した。僧がお礼にと岸辺のヨシ（アシ）の葉を取って川へ流したところ、葉がエツに変わった。実はその僧は弘法大師だった」という伝説が残っている。

Coilia nasus (Clupeiformes, Engraulididae). This fish is found in the Ariake Sea and the rivers that flow into it. They typically measure 30 cm in length. Their Japanese name, "etsu," is said to be short for "etsubo," or to come from the Chinese reading ("hetsu") of the Chinese character used in their name. In the Chikugo River area, there is a legend that "a monk on a pilgrimage found himself at a river he could not cross when a kind fisherman took him across in his boat. In thanks, the monk took a reed and floated it down the river, where it turned into a Japanese grenadier anchovy. That monk was the great Kobo Daishi."

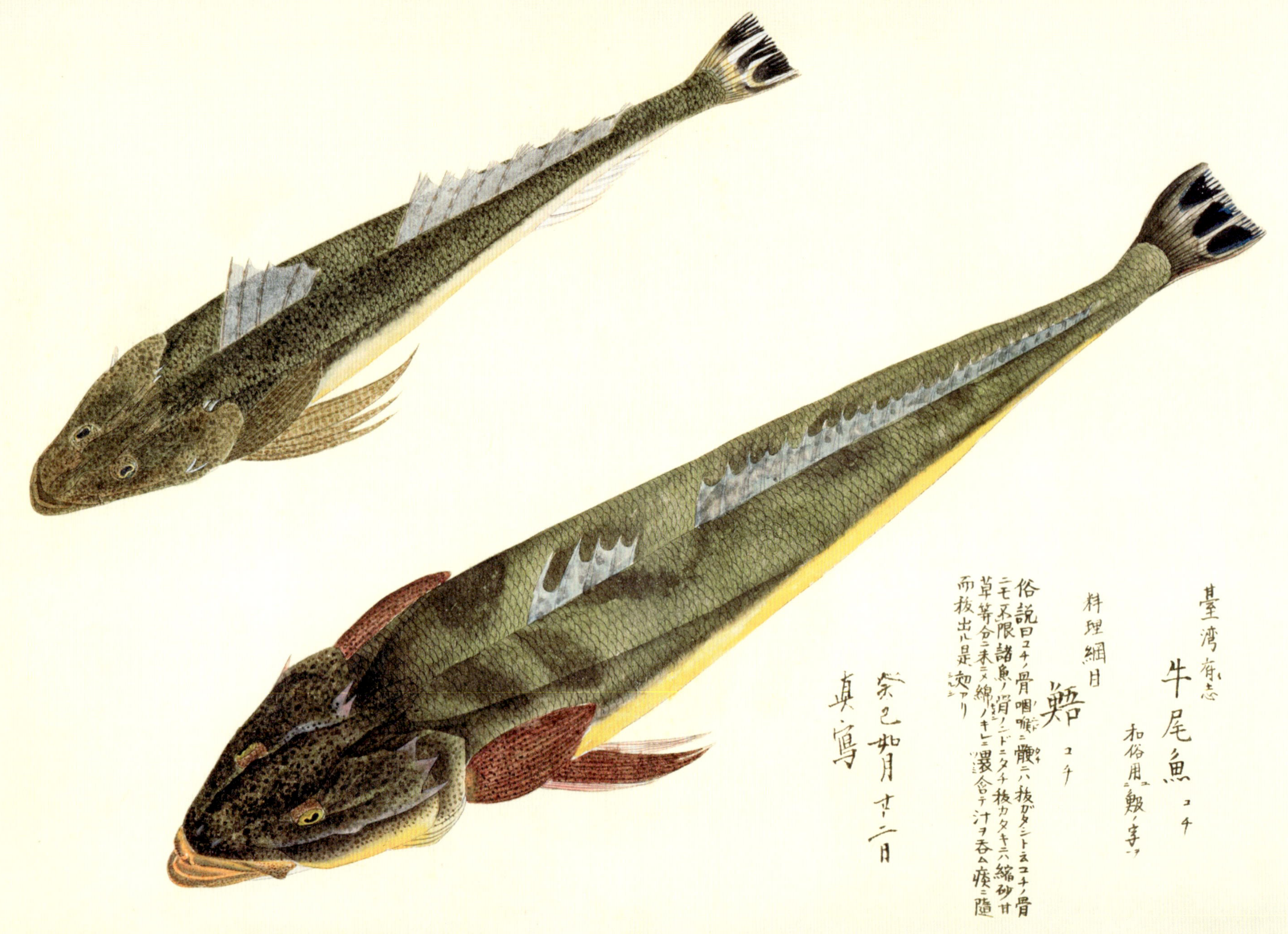

臺灣府志
牛尾魚 コチ
和俗用二鯹ノ字一
料理網目
鯇 コチ
俗説曰ユチノ骨咽喉ニ骾二八抜ガタシトヱコチノ骨
ニモ不限諸魚ノ骨ノ咽ニドニタチ抜カタキニ縮砂甘
草等合二未ニメ綿ノキレニ裹合テ汁ヲ吞ム癒ニ隨
而抜出ル是ヲ効アリ
癸巳貳月廿二日
真寫

真鯒
（Magochi）

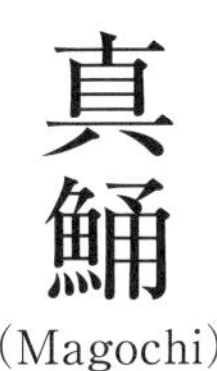

鯒 （Kochi）

鮲 （Kochi）

牛尾魚 （Kochi）

イソゴチ （Isogochi）

クロゴチ （Kurogochi）

ホンゴチ （Hongochi）

マゴチ

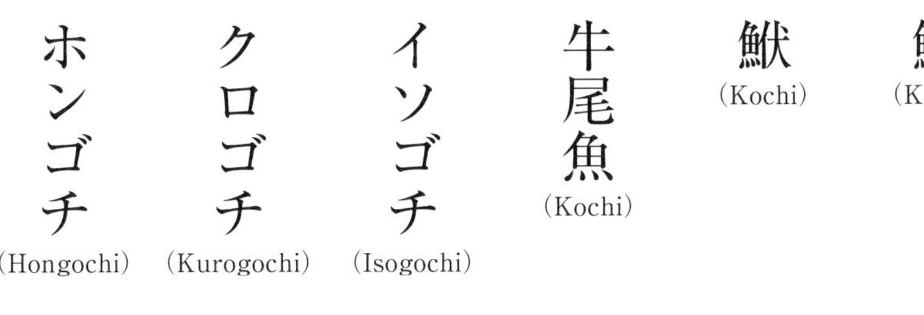

A flathead (no English name)

スズキ目コチ科コチ属。学名は *Platycephalus* sp.。北海道南部、宮城県から九州南岸までの太平洋沿岸、若狭湾から九州南岸までの日本海・東シナ海沿岸などに分布する。体長は40cm前後のものが多いが、70cmを超すものもいる。夏の日差しが照りつける時期が釣りの最盛期なことから「照りゴチ」と称されている。和名「マゴチ」の由来は、骨が硬いため「コツ（骨）」と呼ばれていたことに因るという説や、神官が持つ笏に形が似ており、笏は「コツ」とも呼ばれたことに因むという説などがある。現在では、刺身などにして食べられる。江戸時代の書物『魚鑑』にも「コチは江戸に多く、コイ、スズキに次いで酒の肴の逸品」と記されている。

Platycephalus sp. (Perciformes, Platycephalidae). This fish is found in southern Hokkaido, along the Pacific coast from Miyagi Prefecture to southern Kyushu, and along the coasts of the Sea of Japan and East China Sea from Wakasa Bay to southern Kyushu. They typically measure 40 cm in length. One theory is that their Japanese name, "magochi," comes from them being called "kotsu" ("bone") due to their hard bones. They are currently eaten as sashimi. The Edo era (1603–1867) book *Uo-kagami* says "there are many kochi in Edo, and they are second only to common carp and Japanese sea bass as an accompaniment to drinks."

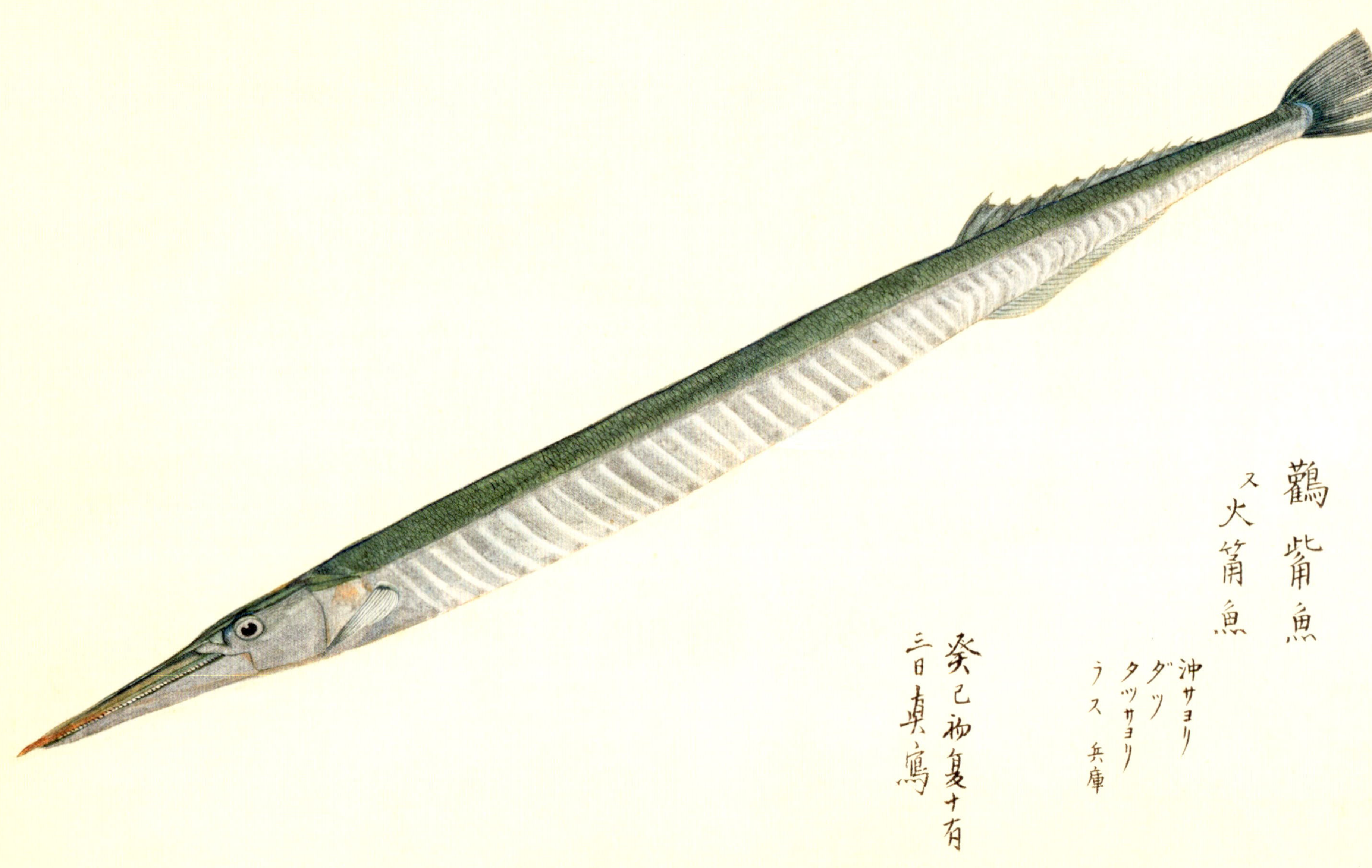

鸘觜魚
ス火箭魚
沖サヨリ
ダツ
タッサヨリ
ラス　兵庫
癸己初夏十有
三日真寫

駄津
(Datsu)

沖細魚
(Okisayori)　　啄長魚
(Dasu)

ダツ

ダツ目ダツ科ダツ属。学名は*Strongylura anastomella*。北海道から九州南岸までの各地沿岸、朝鮮半島南岸、南シナ海沿岸などに分布する。体長は70〜100㎝。一般的に食用とされていなかったようで、江戸時代の『和漢三才図会』には、味は良くないと書かれている。ただし、食用とする地方もあり、旬は夏。細長い体形と長く伸びた上下の顎が特徴的で、和名「ダツ」は口の大きい袋を意味する「駄簀」が語源。駄簀とは一般的に稲藁で作られた塩や石炭などを入れる口の大きい袋のことをいい、ダツの口がこの袋に似ていることから名付けられた。ダツには光に突進する習性があるため、夜釣りや夜間の潜水などでライトを持った人にダツが刺さって死傷する事故が起きている。

Strongylura anastomella (Beloniformes, Belonidae). This fish is found along the coasts from Hokkaido to southern Kyushu, along the southern coast of the Korean Peninsula, and in the South China Sea. They typically measure 70 to 100 cm in length. Generally, they have not been eaten, and the Edo era (1603–1867) encyclopedia *Wakan Sansai Zue* specifically states that they taste bad. Their Japanese name, "datsu," is said to come from "dasu," which means "large-mouthed bag." Dasu bags are wide-mouthed bags, usually made with straw and used to hold salt or coal, and the fish were named after dasu due to the resemblance of their mouths.

A needlefish (no English name)

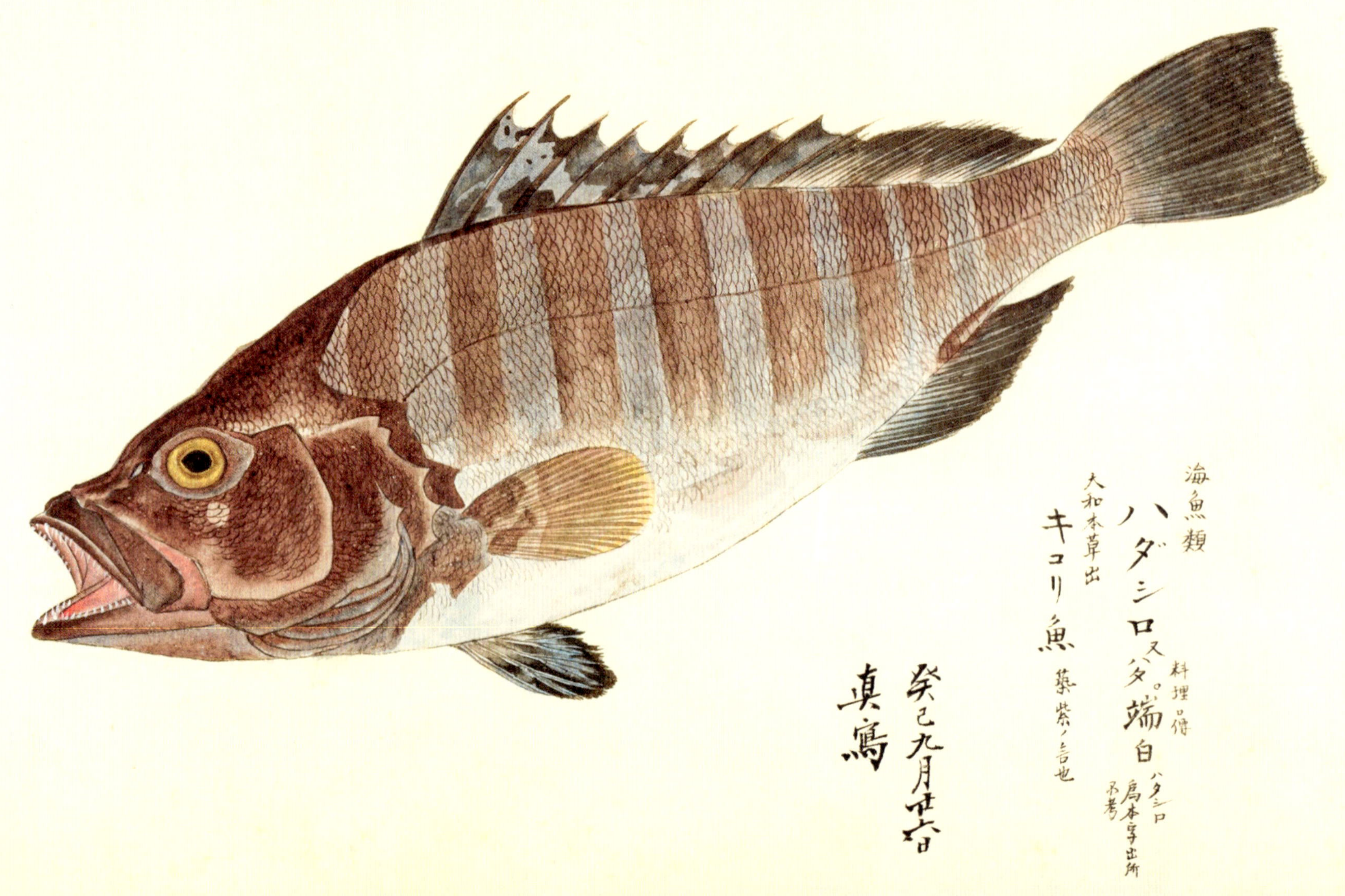

海魚類
ハダシロ又ハ多端白
大和本草出
キコリ魚
料理品偏
癸巳九月廿六
真寫

真羽太
（Mahata）

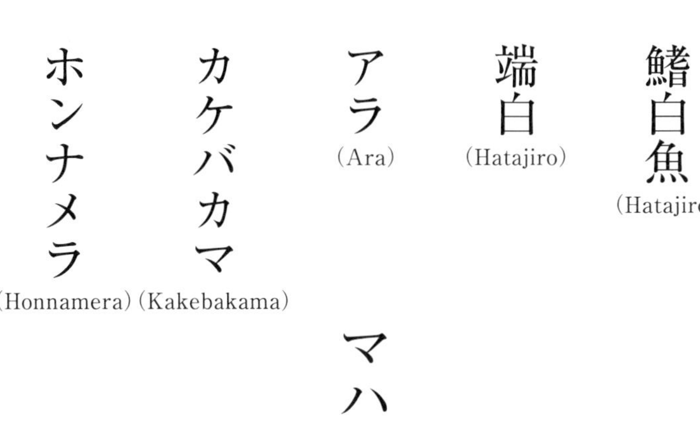

ホンナメラ（Honnamera）　カケバカマ（Kakebakama）　アラ（Ara）　端白（Hatajiro）　鰭白魚（Hatajiro）

マハタ

Convict grouper

スズキ目ハタ科マハタ属。学名は*Hyporthodus septemfasciatus*。北海道から九州南岸までの日本海・東シナ海沿岸、仙台湾から屋久島までの太平洋沿岸、瀬戸内海、伊豆-小笠原諸島などに分布する。体長は50〜60cmのものが多いが、大きいものは100cmを超える。食用とされ、白身で柔らかく美味。和名「マハタ」の由来は、背びれや尻びれに硬く太い棘があることから「羽根（ひれ）の太い魚」という意味で「ハタ」という説と、「ハダラ（斑。体の横縞から）」の「ラ」の脱落語に、ハタ類の代表品種であることを表す「マ」が付いたという説がある。『和漢三才図会』には「肉は脆白（淡甘）」、『魚鑑』には「種類多し。まはたを以て上とす」と記録がある。

Hyporthodus septemfasciatus (Perciformes, Epinephelidae). This fish is found along the coasts of the Sea of Japan and East China Sea, from Hokkaido to southern Kyushu, along the Pacific coast from Sendai Bay to Yakushima Island, in the Seto Inland Sea, and around the Izu and Ogasawara Islands. They typically measure 50 to 60 cm in length, but large ones exceed 100 cm in length. They are used in cooking, and their flesh is soft and delicious. Their Japanese name, "mahata," is said to come from "hata," meaning "fish with large wings," due to the large, hard spines of their dorsal and tail fins.

稲氏漢語抄云

銀口魚又細鱗魚アユ

雀鳥錫食経云貌似鯛
而小有白皮無鱗春
生甚長秋衰冬死故名
年魚也

〇元寿嘉永元年九月八日
出州多磨川ニ遊歴ス其
日漁父ノ言夜ハ香魚多
久竹籠ドリトスト云其具
箔ニ似タリ水中ニ沈メテ魚ヲ
獲ル竹ヲ割テ金ノ不開如
クニ造レリ其具
家々ニ多
ク見ヘタリ

細鱗魚アユ

日本記神功皇后記。平陽雁陰山志

雨航雑録

香魚

白鰷魚
魦魚

鰷魚アイ
白鰷魚
魦魚

香魚

一名記月魚

香魚鱗細不腥春初
生月長一寸至冬月
長盈則赴潮際生ス
子生已輒槁

搞ハ鱗ノサブルヲ云香魚
ハ香能故ニ名ク也鱗肉
亦子ノ醢トス俗ニ鮓腸ト云
子ノ醢ハ子ウルカト云雌
雄アリ雌ハ首小ニ而身廣
雄ハ首小ニ而身
色黄色雄ハ首小ニ而

莊子観魚ノ楽者
則ハ此魚ノ朝。
鮓魚出游従容以
為魚楽

漳州府志
渓鰡魚

真寫

癸巳六月廿七日

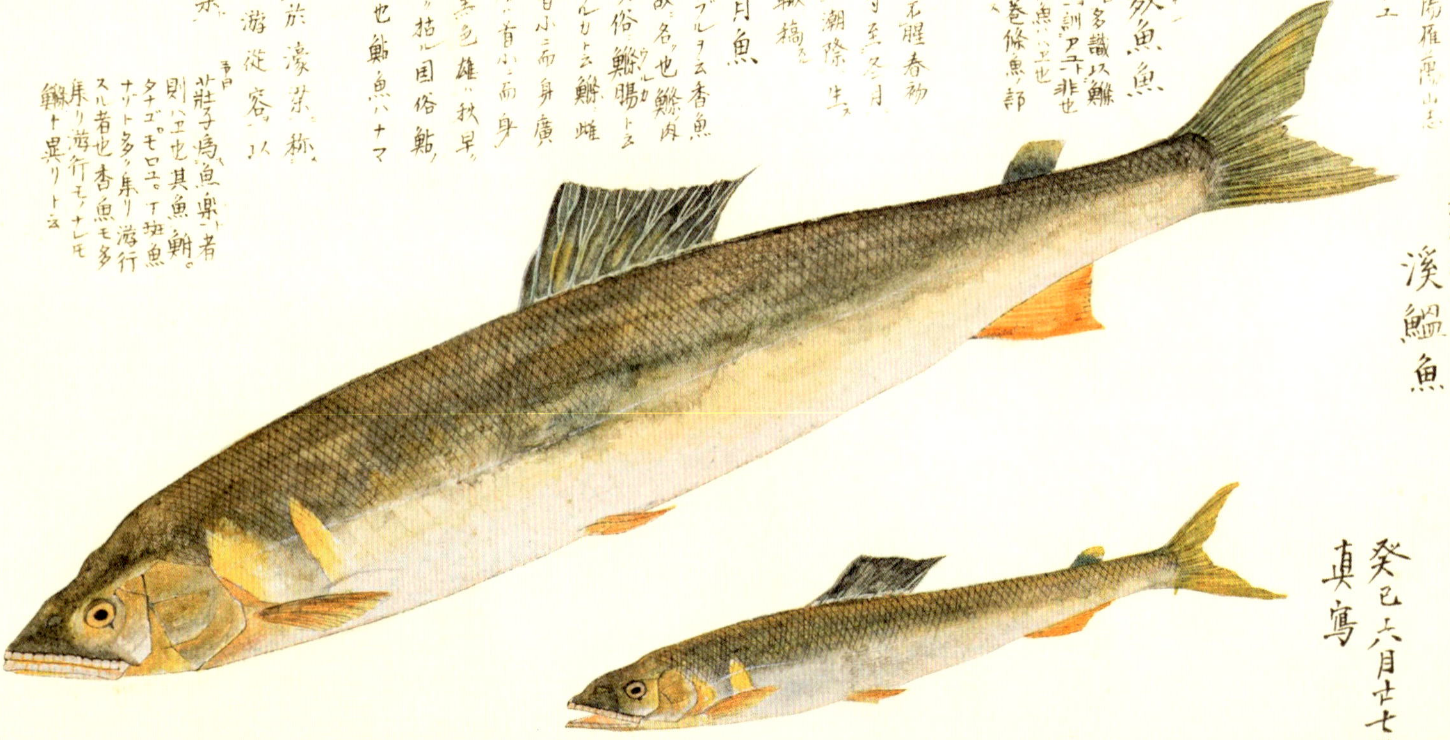

鮎
（Ayu）

香魚
（Kogyo）

年魚
（Nengyo）

アイ
（Ai）

アユ

アイノイオ
（Ainoio）

アイノヨ
（Ainoyo）

Ayu sweetfish

サケ目アユ科アユ属。学名は*Plecoglossus altivelis altivelis*。北海道西部から九州までの各地、朝鮮半島、済州島、ベトナム北部などに分布する。体長は約30cm。「アユ」の名前は、秋になると産卵のために川を降りる（落ちる）ことを意味する古語の「アユル」が語源という説や、「愛らしい魚」「味佳き魚」を語源とする説など、諸説ある。釣り人の間では、釣って良し、食べて良しの人気の種であるため「清流の女王」と呼ばれる。『日本書紀』によると、神功皇后が「戦に勝利できるなら魚が釣れますように」と祈りながら米粒を投げたところアユが釣れたという言い伝えがあり、ここから「祝賀の魚」「占いの魚」として用いられたことから「鮎」と表記するようになったという。

Plecoglossus altivelis altivelis (Salmoniformes, Plecoglossidae). This fish is found from western Hokkaido to Kyushu, the Korean Peninsula, around Jeju Island, and northern Vietnam. They typically measure 30 cm in length. The name "ayu" is said to come from the ancient word "ayuru," which means to swim down a river in autumn to spawn. According to the *Nihon Shoki* (completed in 720), there is a legend that Empress Jingu prayed, "If I am to win the battle, may I catch a fish" and cast grains of rice into the water as bait. She then caught an ayu. Because of this, the Japanese symbol for "ayu" is made up of symbols for "fortune-telling" and "fish."

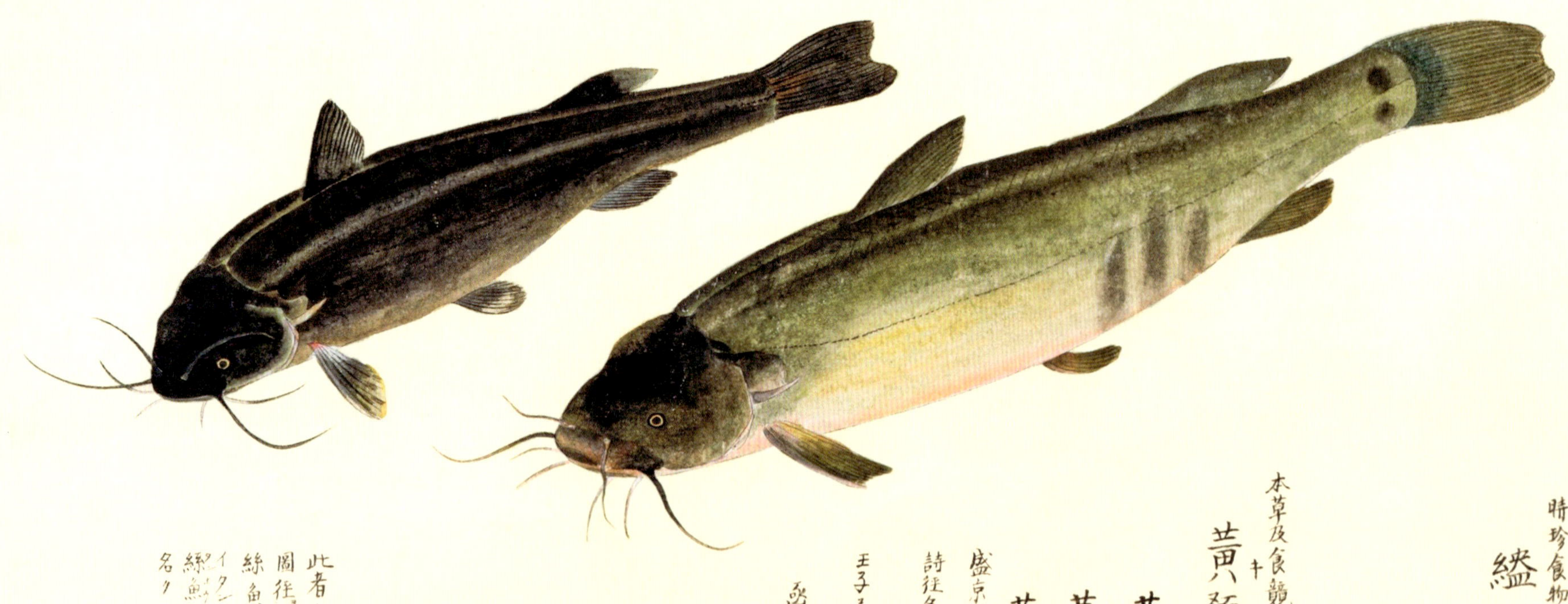

時珍食物本草載無鱗魚
緇絲魚　ギヽ　二種
キヽ八千　江戸
ヱコ魚　山州
ハヽアリ
蜂振　筑紫
ヒレニ刺アリテ
今撒故ニ方言
トス
本草及食物競出ヽ十ニ
黄頰魚　鮫魜
黄魜
黄鱨魚　名ヒ
黄頰魚　註詩
盛京通志
詩往名物圖説
昂思
王子通
剛腮魚
函史
鮫魚
燕頭魚
此者太羅ト訓ス甚誤也考フ本草
圖往ニ可知時珍食物本草載緇
絲魚與此者異名相同ニ生海ザ
イクヽホウト云生河ニギヽハチヽ云海ニ緇
絲鯐形狀相同キヽハ其鳴声ヲ以
名ク
甲午五月廿四日於
戸川蝶真庵

義蜂

（Gibachi）

ゲバチ
（Gebachi）

ギンギロ
（Gingiro）

ギュウタ
（Gyuta）

カバチ
（Kabachi）

ギバチ

Cut-tailed bullhead

ナマズ目ギギ科ギバチ属。学名は *Tachysurus tokiensis*。神奈川県・富山県以北の本州に分布する。体長は約20cm。ナマズに似て体は細長く、口部に四対のひげがある。体色は茶褐色から青みのある暗褐色。背びれと胸びれには有毒の棘がある。和名「ギバチ」の由来は「ギーギー」という音を出すこと、棘で刺されたときの蜂に刺されたような痛みから「ギバチ」と名付けられたと考えられているが定かではない。「ゲバチ」などの地方名も多数ある。江戸時代の怪談話「本所七不思議」に出てくる「置いてけ堀」の話は、ギバチの発した音に驚いたのではないかと推測する研究者もいる。近年は生息数の減少が著しく、環境省のレッドリストでは絶滅危惧II類に指定されている。

Tachysurus tokiensis (Siluriformes, Bagridae). This fish is found in Honshu by Kanagawa Prefecture and from Toyama Prefecture northward. They typically measure 20 cm in length. Cut-tailed bullhead have poisonous dorsal and pectoral fin spines. Their Japanese name, "gibachi," is believed to come from the "gi-gi" sound they make and the fact that their sting is as painful as that of a bee "bachi," but this etymology is uncertain. Some researchers believe that the voice in the story of *"Oiteke-bori,"* recounted in *Honjo Nanafushigi*, a book of supernatural tales from the Edo era (1603–1867), was the sound of a cut-tailed bullhead.

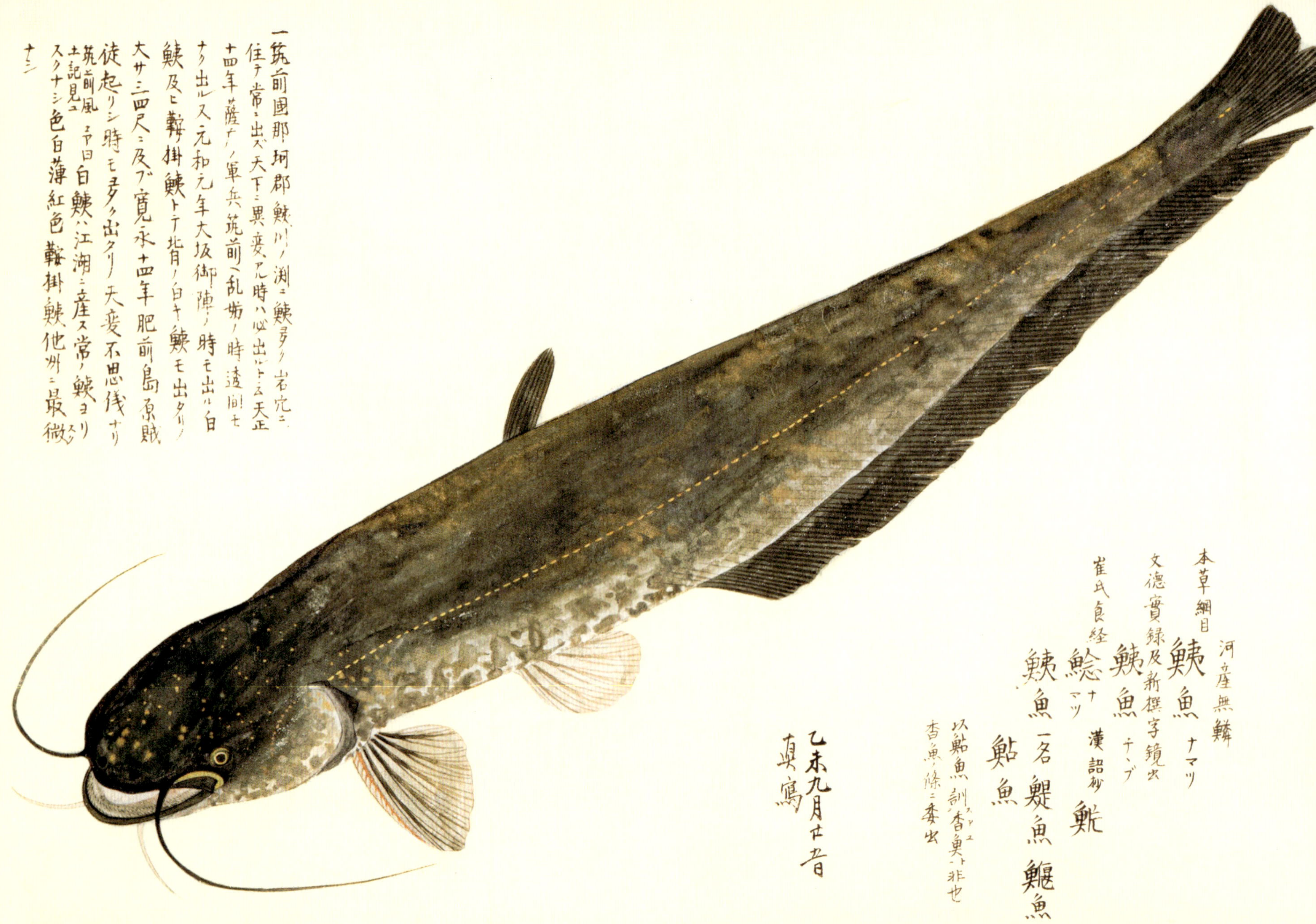
本草綱目　河産無鱗
文德實錄及新撰字鏡出　鯷魚　ナマツ
鰋魚　ナ、ブ
崔氏良経　鯰十マツ　漢詔抄　鮧
鯷魚
鯷魚一名鰋魚鯷魚
一筑前國那珂郡鯷川ノ淵ニ鯷多ク岩穴ニ
住テ常ニ出ズ天下ニ異変アル時ハ必ズ出ヅトイフ天正
十四年薩广ノ軍兵筑前ヘ乱妨ノ時遠間ヒ
ナク出ル又元和元年大坂御陣ノ時モ出ル白
鯷及ヒ鞍掛鯷トテ北肯ノ白キ鯷モ出タリ
大サ三四尺ニ及ブ寛永十四年肥前島原賊
徒起リシ時モ多ク出タリ天変不思後ナリ
筑前風土記見ユ白鯷ハ江湖ニ産ス常ノ鯷ヨリ
スクナシ色白薄紅色鞍掛鯷他州ニ最微
十三
乙未九月廿音　真寫

鯰
（Namazu）

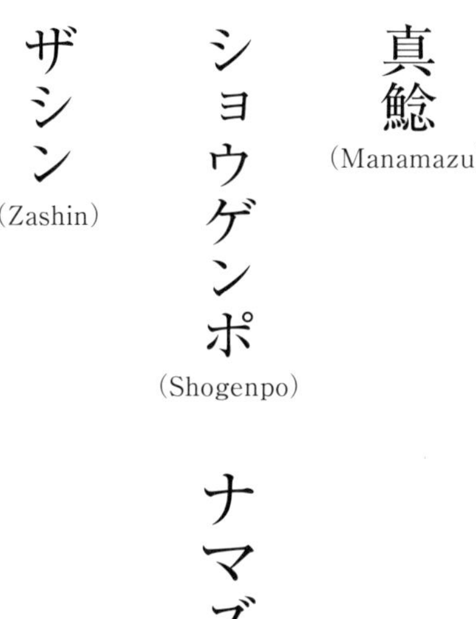

真鯰
（Manamazu）

ショウゲンポ
（Shogenpo）

ザシン
（Zashin）

ナマズ

Amur catfish

ナマズ目ナマズ科ナマズ属。学名は*Silurus asotus*。北海道南部から九州、朝鮮半島西岸、台湾、中国東部などに分布する。日本ではかつては東海地方以西の本州、四国、九州に分布していたが、江戸時代頃に関東地方に人為的に導入されて以来、北海道まで分布が広まったといわれている。体長は60〜70cm。「ナマズ」の名前の由来は、「滑らかな頭」を語源とする説、「ナマツ（魚不味）」の意という説など諸説ある。ナマズは平安時代の説話集『今昔物語集』や、江戸時代の浮世絵に描かれているように、古くから日本人にとって身近な種であった。ナマズは地震とともに語られることが多く、室町時代や江戸時代には、地震はナマズが地中で暴れているために起こると考えられていた。

Silurus asotus (Siluriformes, Siluridae). This fish is found from southern Hokkaido to Kyushu, in the west of Korean Peninsula, in Taiwan, and in eastern China. They typically measure 60 to 70 cm in length. One of the theories behind their Japanese name, "namazu," is that it came from having a smooth ("nameraka") head ("zu"). Amur catfish have long been well-known among the Japanese people, appearing in woodblock printes from the Edo era (1603–1867). Amur catfish are often spoken of in the same breath as earthquakes. During the Muromachi era (1336–1573) and Edo era, earthquakes were believed to be caused by Amur catfish thrashing underground.

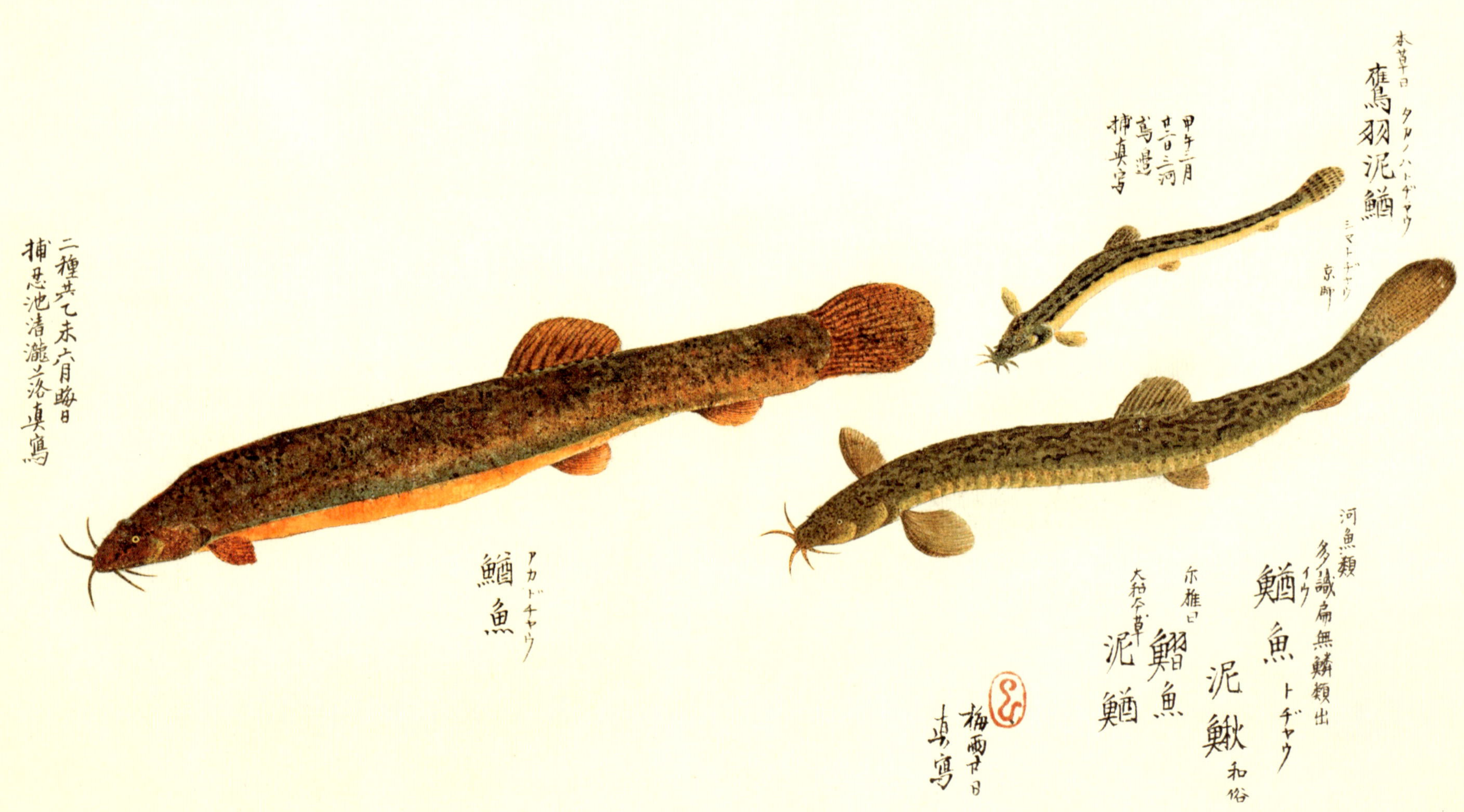
鳶羽泥鰌
二種共乙未六月晦日
捕恶池清瀧之落真寫
鰌魚
泥鰌

東縞泥鰌

（Higashishimadojo）

ヒガシシマドジョウ

コイ目ドジョウ科シマドジョウ属（図の右上の個体）。学名は *Cobitis* sp.。中部以東の本州と佐渡島に分布する。体長は約10cm。従来はシマドジョウとされていたが、遺伝的、形態的に本種とオオシマドジョウ、ニシシマドジョウ、トサシマドジョウの4種に区別された。「シマドジョウ」の名前の由来は黒い縞のような斑紋があることから、また分布する地域から「ヒガシシマドジョウ」と呼ばれるようになった。一般的に食用とされない。別種のドジョウは古くから食用とされており、ドジョウ鍋は1804年に浅草駒形にある越後屋が始めたものが最初だといわれている。漢字では「泥鰌」や「鰌」と書くが、「酋」は壺から酒が上がってくる形を表し、「暴れるので酒を飲ませて料理する魚」を意味しているという。

Cobitis sp. (Cypriniformes, Cobitidae). This fish is found in Honshu, from central Honshu eastward, and around Sado Island. They typically measure 10 cm in length. Their Japanese name, "shimadojo," comes from the fact that they have black stripes ("shima"). Also, due to where they can be found, they have come to be called "higashi shimadojo" ("eastern striped loaches"). Generally speaking, they are not eaten. Another species of loach (pond loach *Misgurnus anguillicaudatus*) has been eaten since antiquity, and the loach hotpot is said to have been created in 1804, during the Edo era, by Echigoya, in Asakusa Komagata.

Eastern striped loach

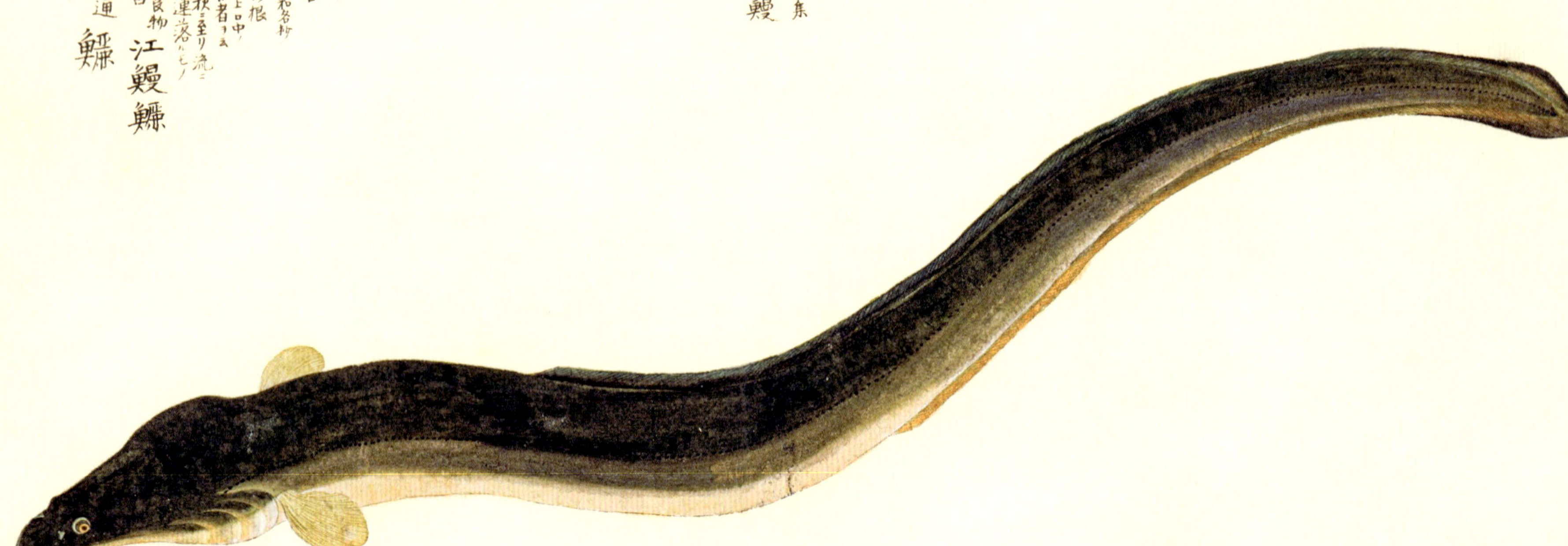

河魚類

多識扁無鱗類出

鰻鱺魚、ウナギ 古名

本草綱目曰釋名
白鱓 蛇魚 乾者爲風鰻

萬葉集

輪ノ内筑地両国川
及神田川筋ニテ釣
ル者ヲ江戸前トス又
本所千住高輪前
ニテ釣ル河魚ノ味最
上品トス

萬葉集第十六巻大伴ノ家持
石麻呂ニソレ物申ス夏ヤセニ

本綱口 鰻鱺魚

通志畧

鰻狖魚 鰻魚上 時珍曰食物
異魚圖賛及出 本草曰 江鰻
海鹽縣圖径 正字通 鱺

元曰
和名鈔ニ以鰻鱺魚訓ス
波之加畝伊乎以鱧魚
訓ス無奈木以鱓魚
訓ス鱧ニ鱓魚トス固
俗宇太奈岐ト云誤此宇太奈岐
鰻鱺也鱧魚ハ不加トス鮫
之類也又和各抄ニ鱓魚ス
訓衣比此ハ鰻鱺
海中ニ産ス水蛇ト云湖中産
物ニ詳也

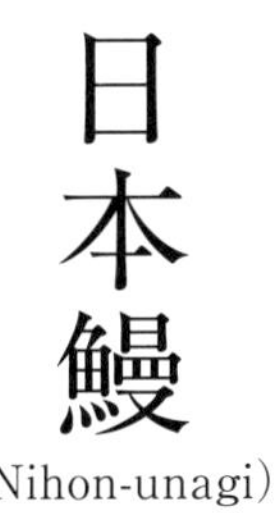

日本鰻
(Nihon-unagi)

鰻鱺魚
(Unagi)

無奈木
(Unagi)

武奈伎
(Munagi)

江戸前
(Edomae)

カヨコ
(Kayoko)

ニホンウナギ

Japanese eel

ウナギ目ウナギ科ウナギ属。学名は*Anguilla japonica*。日本、韓国、中国、台湾などの河川、湖沼、河口から沿岸域まで広く生息する。体長は50cm〜1m。「ウナギ」という名前の由来は家屋の屋根に使われる部材「棟木（むなぎ）」が語源で、ウナギの体が棟木のように細長いことに由来するという説や、胸が黄色いことから「胸黄（むなぎ）」が転訛したという説など諸説ある。日本では『万葉集』に夏バテ防止にウナギを勧める歌が残っているほど、古くから食用とされてきた。現代でも土用の丑の日にウナギを食べる習慣があるが、これは一説によると江戸時代の本草学者である平賀源内が馴染みのウナギ屋に頼まれて看板を出したのが定着したといわれている。

Anguilla japonica (Anguilliformes, Anguillidae). This fish is found over a wide area, from the rivers, lakes, and estuaries to the coastal areas of Japan, Korea, China, and Taiwan. They typically measure 50 to 100 cm in length. Their Japanese name, "unagi," is said to come from "munagi" ("ridge beams") which are used in building roofs. It is currently customary to eat Japanese eel on a day called Doyo-no Ushi-no Hi (a midsummer day of the ox). This is said to date back to the Edo era (1603–1867), when a herbalist named Hiraga Gennai put out a sign at the request of an eel restaurant owner Hiraga knew.

金魚
(Kingyo)

キンギョ

Goldfish

コイ科フナ属の淡水魚で、学名は*Carassius auratus*。キンギョはフナ類を人工的に改良してつくられた品種で、祖先は中国南部のフナ類とされる。体色は主に赤で、白や黒もいる。「金の魚」という意味で「金魚」と名付けられた。日本へは1502年頃に渡来し、江戸時代に観賞用として多くの品種がつくられたといわれている。江戸前期の俳諧師・井原西鶴による『西鶴置土産』には、当時すでに金魚売りがいて、大名や富豪たちに売っていたと記されている。「生類憐みの令」の一環で金魚は没収され遊行寺の泉水に放されたが、繁殖しやすい魚であったために大衆へと広まったと考えられている。祭りや縁日で見られる金魚すくいの屋台は大正時代に始まったものといわれている。

Carassius auratus (Cypriniformes, Cyprinidae). These fish are selectively bred varieties of crucian carps. Their ancestors are believed to be crucian carps from southern China. Their bodies are primarily red, though there are also black and white goldfish. They are called goldfish due to their reddish golden color. Goldfish were brought to Japan in roughly 1502, and during the Edo era (1603–1867) many varieties were created for decorative use. *Saikaku Okimiyage*, by early Edo era haiku poet Ihara Saikaku, indicates that there were already goldfish sellers at the time, and goldfish were sold to feudal daimyo and wealthy families.

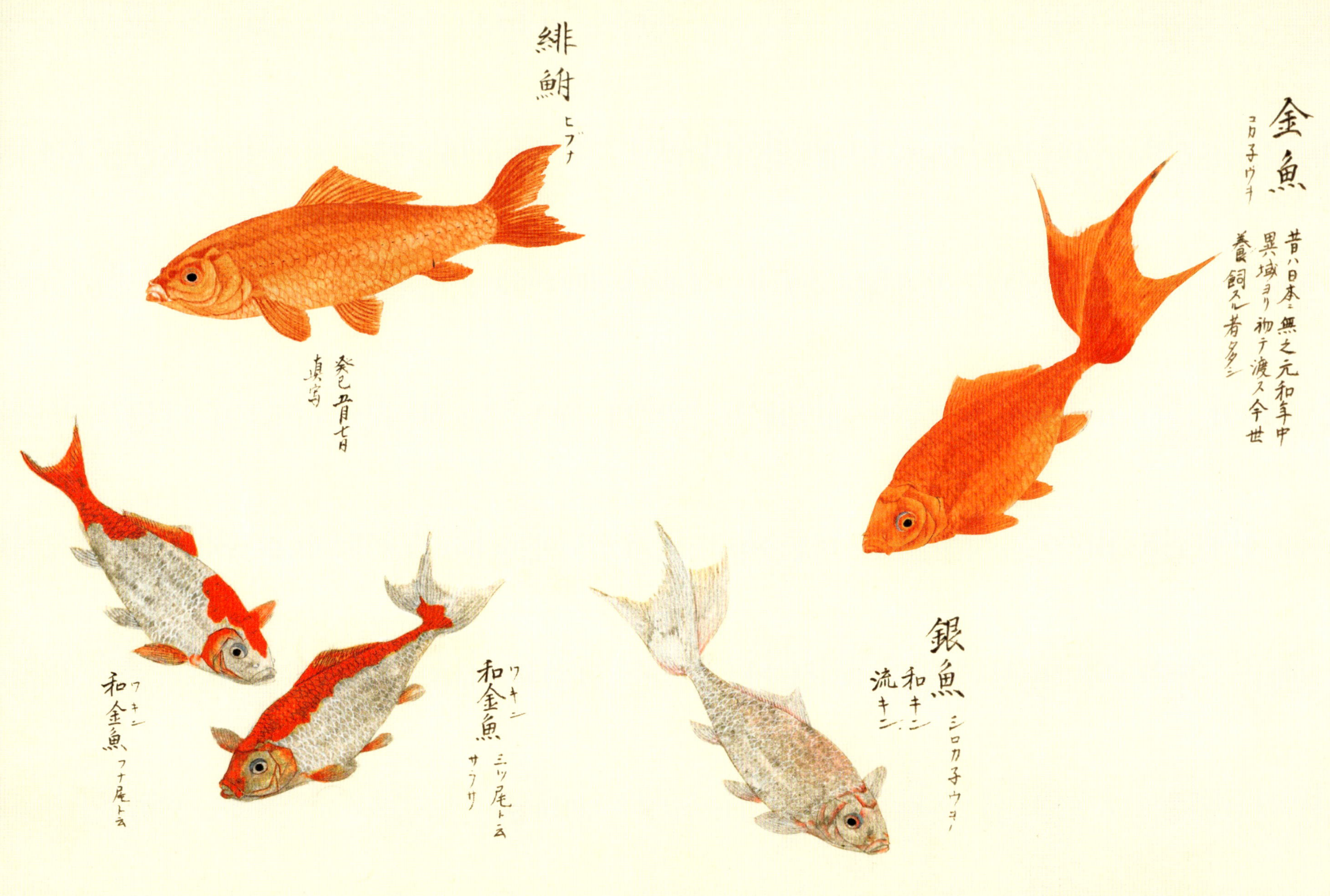

緋鮒
ヒブナ

金魚
コガ子ウヲ

昔ハ日本ニ無之元和年中
異域ヨリ初テ渡ス今世
養飼スル者多シ

癸巳五月七日
貞寫

銀魚
和キン
流キン
シロカ子ウヲノ

ワキン
和金魚 フナ尾ト云

ワキン
和金魚 三ツ尾ト云
サフサ

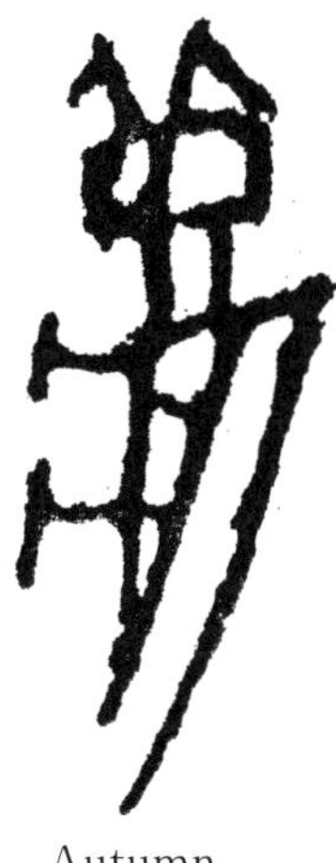

Autumn

海魚類
サンマ

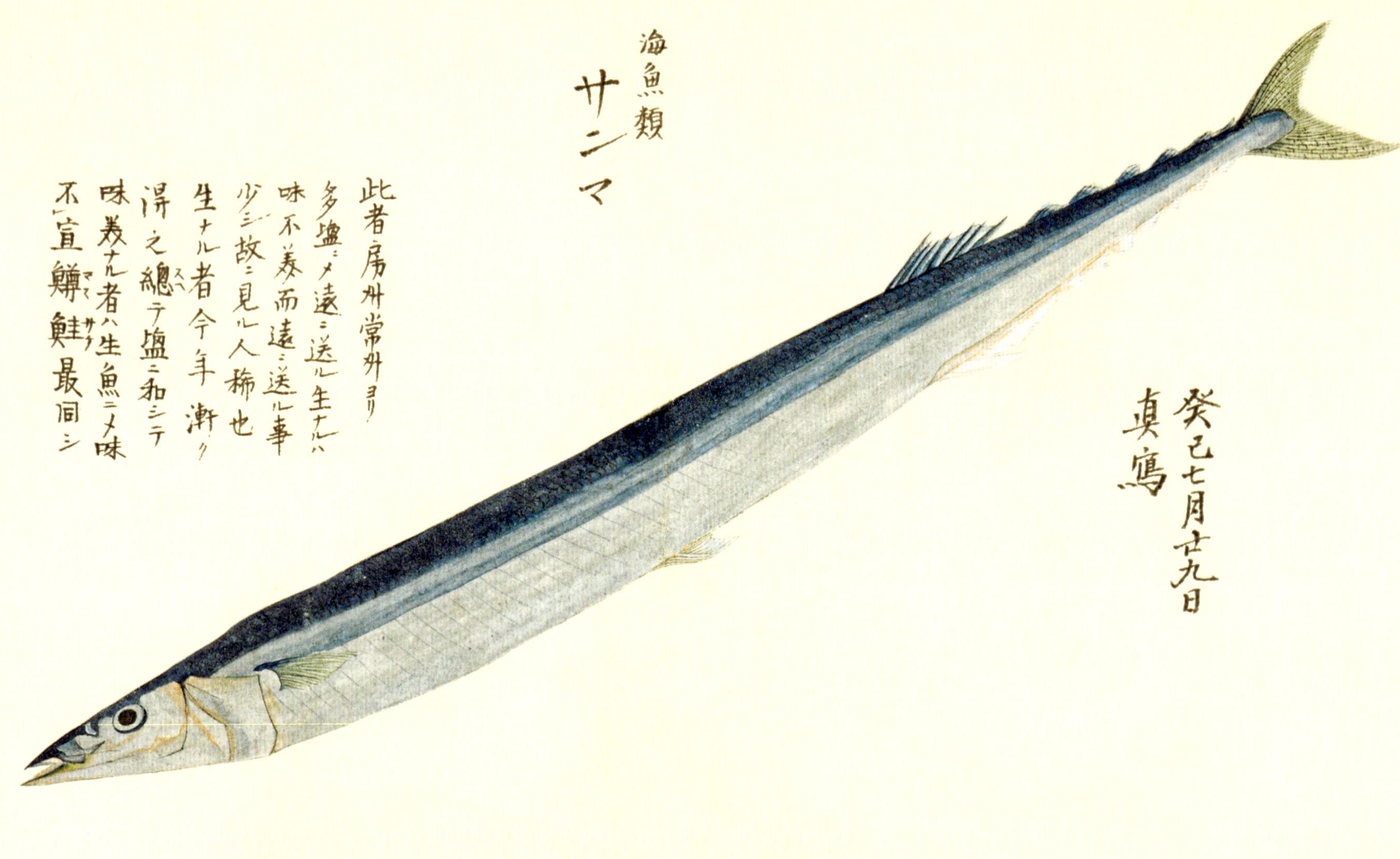
此者房州常州ヨリ
多ク盬ニ〆遠ニ送ル生ナルハ
味不美而遠ニ送ル事
少シ故ニ見ル人稀也
生ナル者今年漸ク
得之總テ盬ニ和シテ
味美ナル者ハ生魚ニ〆味
不宜鱐鮭最同シ
癸巳七月廿九日
真寫

秋刀魚
(Sanma)

三摩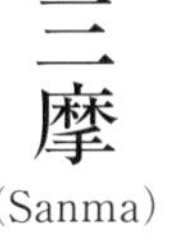
(Sanma)

三馬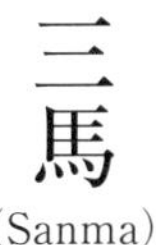
(Sanma)

狭真魚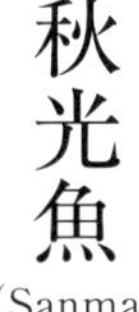
(Samana)

秋光魚
(Sanma)

サンマ

Pacific saury

ダツ目ダツ科（またはサンマ科）サンマ属。学名は*Cololabis saira*。北太平洋全域の温帯・亜寒帯に分布し、日本近海では千島列島から屋久島付近まで季節回遊する。体長は約30cmのものが多いが、最大で約40cmになる。和名「サンマ」の由来は、体が細長いところから「狭真魚（サマナ）」が転訛したという説、「サンマ」は「たくさん」「うまい」という意味を持つ言葉で「うまさがたくさん」と称賛して付けた名前という説など諸説ある。昔はサンマの塩漬けをサヨリと偽って売るほど人気ではなかった。一般的に食べられるようになったのは江戸時代からで、ある大名が目黒で食べたサンマのうまさに感動したという落語「目黒の秋刀魚」にもなるほど、親しまれる魚となった。

Cololabis saira (Beloniformes, Belonidae (or Scomberesocidae)). This fish is found in the temperate and subpolar zones of the entire northern Pacific Ocean. Near Japan, they seasonally migrate to the area between the Kuril Islands and Yakushima Island. They typically measure 30 cm in length. One theory behind their Japanese name, "sanma," is that it comes from "samana" (meaning "narrow fish"). They came to be widely eaten in the Edo era (1603–1867), and they have become such a beloved fish that there is even a rakugo story, "Meguro no Sanma," about a feudal daimyo that was moved by a Pacific saury he ate in Meguro.

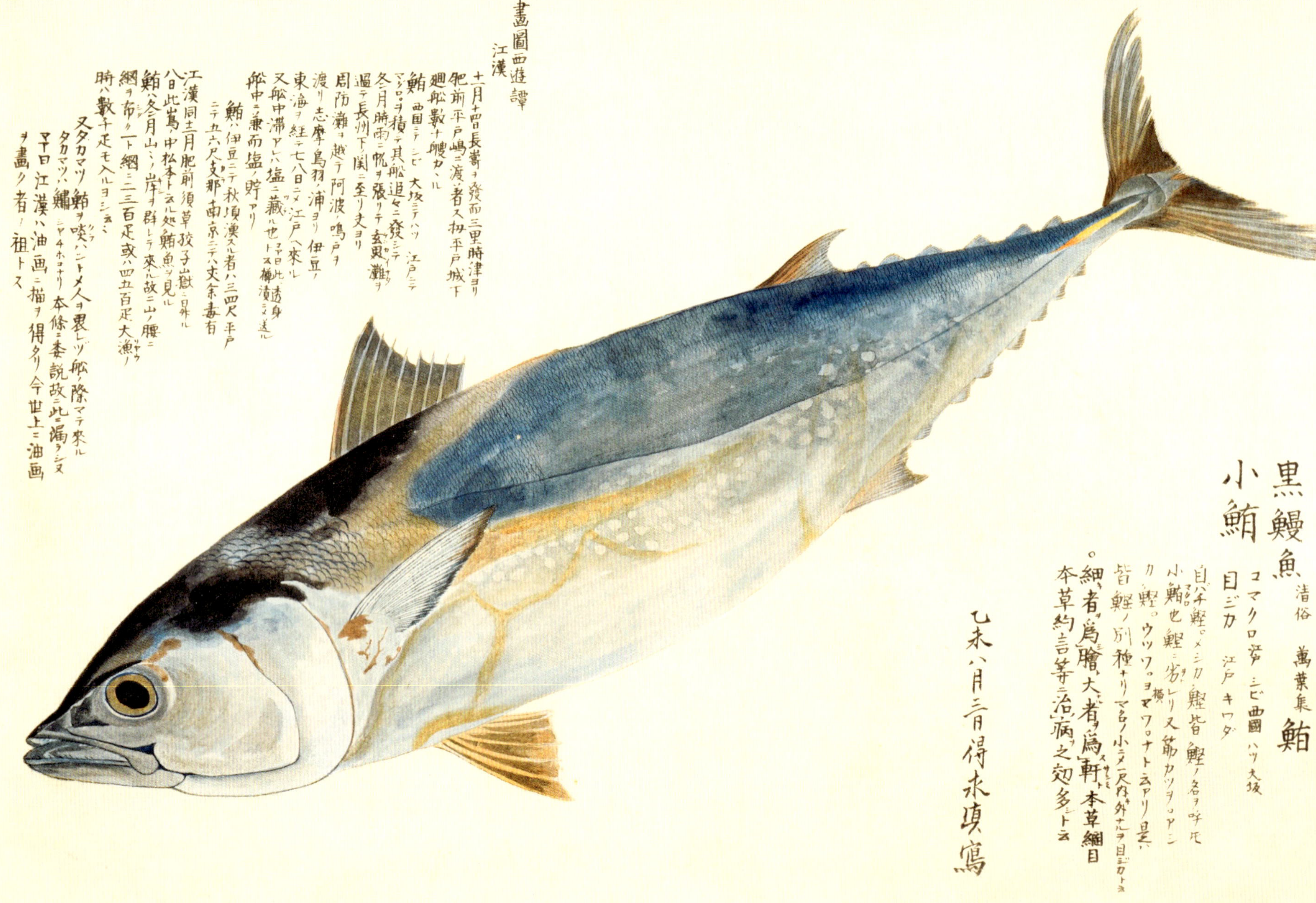

黒鰻魚　清俗　萬葉集　鮪
小鮪
畫圖西遊譚
江漢
乙未八月二十日得永頃寫

黒鮪

（Kuromaguro）

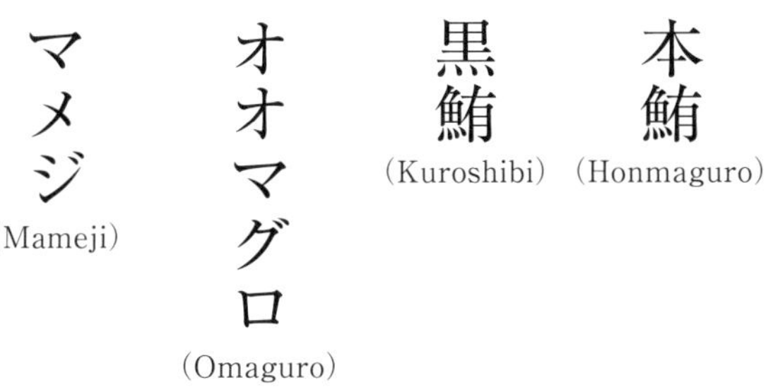

マメジ
（Mameji）

オオマグロ
（Omaguro）

黒鮪
（Kuroshibi）

本鮪
（Honmaguro）

クロマグロ

Pacific bluefin tuna

スズキ目サバ科マグロ属。学名は *Thunnus orientalis*。主に太平洋の北半球亜熱帯～温帯域に生息するが、太平洋の南半球側にも生息する。日本近海が主な産卵場。体長は最大で約3m、体重は450kg超に達するものもいる大型のマグロ類。高級食材として知られ、刺身や寿司が特に美味。和名の由来は眼が黒いので「眼黒」、泳ぐ姿が黒いことから「真黒」など、諸説ある。太古から人はマグロ漁をしていたようで、縄文・弥生時代の貝塚から釣針や骨が出土している。江戸時代には、熊野灘にある湾にマグロの大群が押し寄せてきたため約3,000尾を捕獲し、付近の住人が飢饉から救われた。人々は「支毘大命神」としてマグロを崇め、供養塔を建立したという記録もある。

Thunnus orientalis (Perciformes, Scombridae). This fish primarily lives in the semi-tropical to temperate parts of the Pacific Ocean in the northern hemisphere, but they also live in the southern hemisphere. They can grow as large as 300 cm in length and weigh over 450 kg. One theory holds that their Japanese name, "maguro," comes from the fact that their eyes ("me") are black ("kuro"). During the Edo era (1603–1867), Pacific bluefin tuna swam into a bay of the Kumano Sea and roughly 3,000 were caught, saving nearby residents from famine. Records state the tuna was worshiped as Shibi Daimyojin, and a memorial tower was erected.

海産
赤魚
ヒメチ
ヒメギス
ヲキノ魚

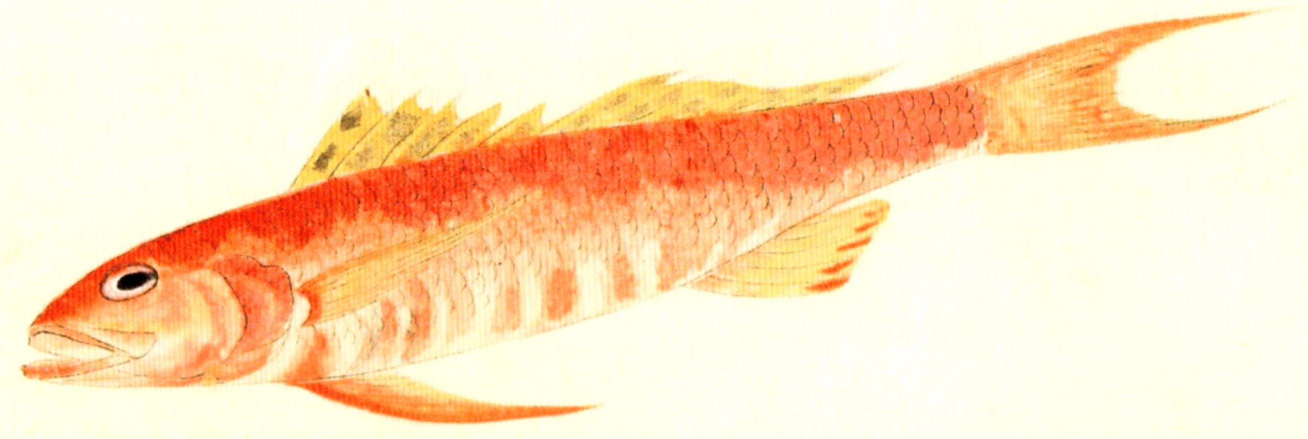

西魚
丙申十月廿三日
真写

姫小鯛

（Himekodai）

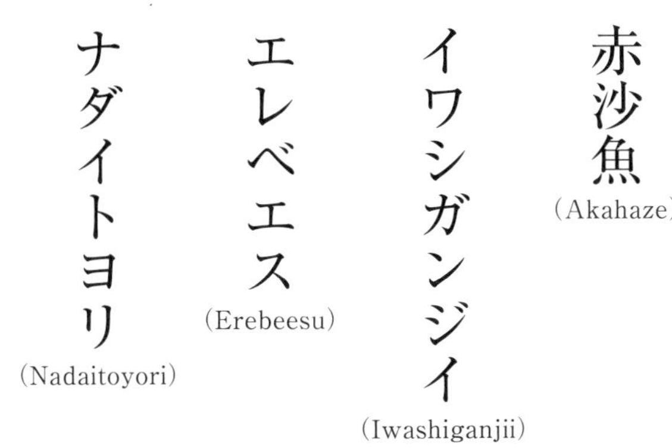

赤沙魚
（Akahaze）

イワシガンジイ
（Iwashiganjii）

エレベエス
（Erebeesu）

ナダイトヨリ
（Nadaitoyori）

ヒメコダイ

Red blotch perchlet

スズキ目ハタ科（またはハナダイ科）ヒメコダイ属。学名は *Chelidoperca hirundinacea*。若狭湾から九州南岸までの日本海・東シナ海沿岸、相模湾から九州南岸までの太平洋沿岸、朝鮮半島、台湾南部などに分布する。体長は約20cm。体は円筒形で赤色、胸びれの上方の側面に濃赤色の斑紋がある。アマダイやマダイ釣りの外道とされるが、味は良い。底引網で漁獲され、刺身や天ぷら種、練り製品の材料としても利用される。和名「ヒメコダイ」の由来は不明。地方名には「アカハゼ」などがあり、赤色の体色を連想させる名で呼ばれることもある。よく似た種にホシヒメコダイがあるが、ホシヒメコダイは体側に5つの黒斑があることや尾びれの形の違いから本種と区別できる。

Chelidoperca hirundinacea (Perciformes, Serranidae). This fish is found along the coasts of the Sea of Japan and the East China Sea from Wakasa Bay to southern Kyushu, the Pacific coast from Sagami Bay to southern Kyushu, the Korean Peninsula, and southern Taiwan. They typically measure 20 cm in length. They are commonly accidentally caught by those trying to catch tilefish or red seabream, but they are delicious. They are caught by bottom trawling and used in sashimi, tempura, and fish-paste products. The origin of their Japanese name, "himekodai," is unknown.

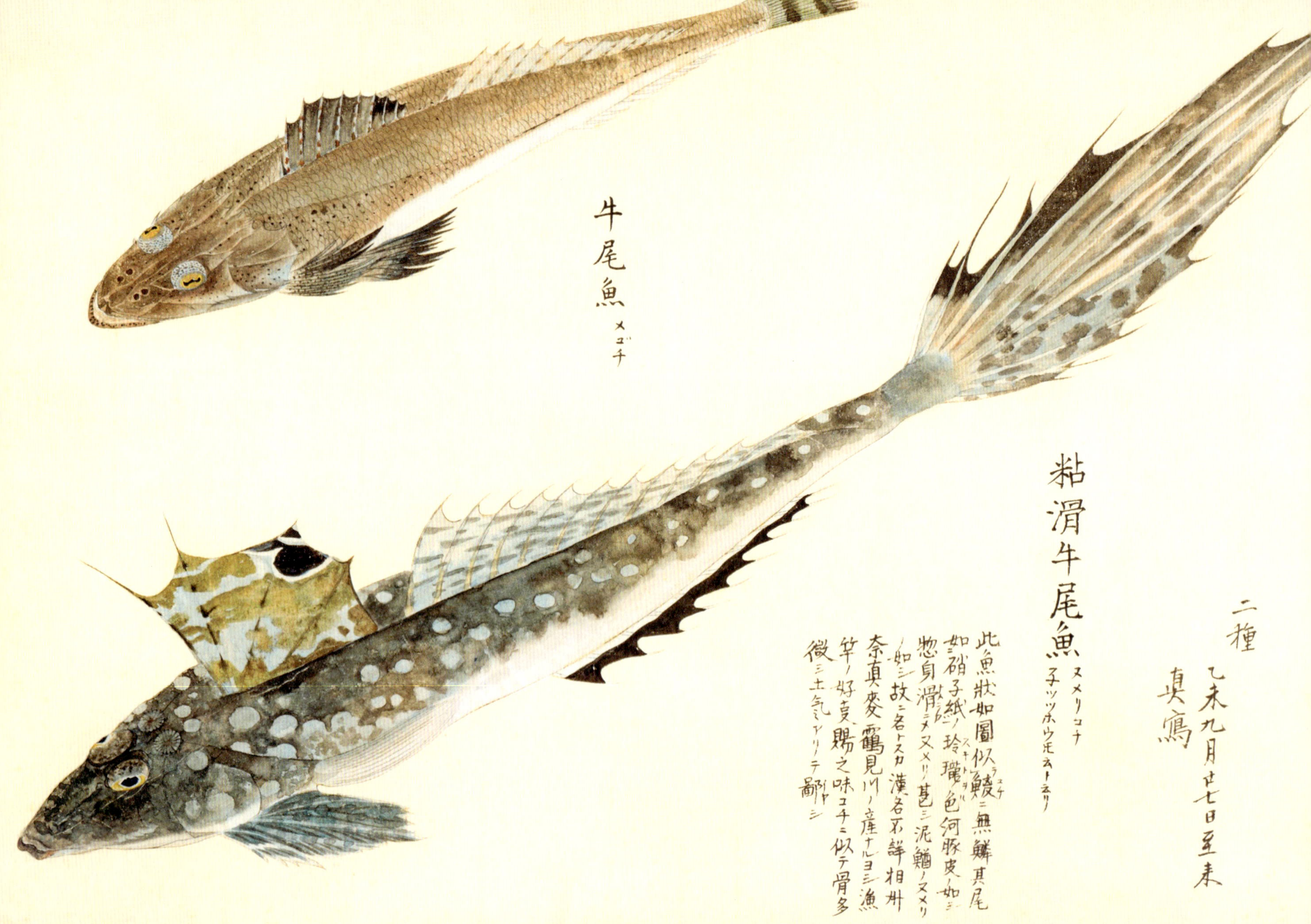
牛尾魚　メゴチ
粘滑牛尾魚　ヌメリコチ
チヽツホウモエトヽネリ
二種
乙未九月廿七日至末
真寫
此魚狀如圖似鯰ニ無鱗其尾
如硝子紙ノ玲瓏色河豚皮ノ如ク
惣身滑ニメヌメリ甚シ泥鰌ノヌメリ
如シ故ニ名トスカ漢名不詳相州
奈真麥鶴見川ノ産ナルヲ三漁
竿ノ好夏賜之味ユチニ似テ骨多
微ニ土氣アリテ劣レリ

眼鯒
（Megochi）

メゴチ

図の上はメゴチで下はヨメゴチである。メゴチはスズキ目コチ科メゴチ属。学名は*Insidiator meerdervoortii*。青森県から九州南岸までの各沿岸、東シナ海大陸棚域、朝鮮半島西岸・南岸などに分布する。体長は約20cm。体は縦扁し、鱗に覆われている。体色は黒褐色。関東地方ではネズッポ科の魚類を「メゴチ」と呼ぶが、本種とは鱗の有無等で区別できる。他のコチ類と同様に、先に雄として成熟する雄性先熟型の性転換をする種で、全長が14cm以下では雄が多く、19cmを超える頃にはほとんどが雌となる。ヨメゴチはスズキ目ネズッポ科ヨメゴチ属。学名は*Calliurichthys japonicus*。和名「メゴチ」「ヨメゴチ」の由来はともに不詳。「ヨメゴチ」には「ネズミゴチ」「セキレン」などの地方名がある。

Insidiator meerdervoortii (above; Perciformes, Platycephalidae) and *Calliurichthys japonicus* (below; Perciformes, Callionymidae). This fish (above) is found along the coasts from Aomori Prefecture to southern Kyushu, the East China Sea continental shelf, and the western and southern coasts of the Korean Peninsula. They typically measure 20 cm in length. They are hermaphroditic fish, first maturing as males before changing sexes. Most measuring 14 cm or under are males, while almost all over 19 cm are females. The origin of Japanese names of big-eyed flathead and Japanese longtail dragonet, "megochi" and "yomegochi," respectively, are unknown.

Big-eyed flathead

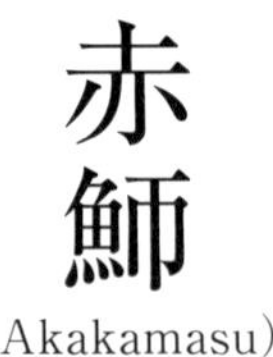

赤鯎
（Akakamasu）

磯鯎　尺八　赤挍魚　叭子
（Isokamasu）（Shakuhachi）（Akakamasu）（Kamasugo）

アカカマス

Red barracuda

スズキ目カマス科カマス属。学名は*Sphyraena pinguis*。北海道から九州南岸までの各沿岸、沖縄島、渤海、黄海などに分布する。体長は30〜40cmで、最大で50cmになるものもいる。日本の沿岸ではヤマトカマスもみられるが、本種の方が漁獲量の多い地域が多く、一般的に「カマス」といえば本種を指し「カマス」「ホンカマス」とも呼ばれる。「カマス」の名前は石炭などを入れる袋の叭（カマス）が語源で、本種の大きく開く口が似ていることから。特に脂がのったものは「霜降りカマス」と呼ばれる。現在では塩焼きやフライにして食べられているが、特に干物が美味。江戸時代でも干物を食していたようで、『和漢三才図会』には「備前から多くひものとして出荷している」と記されている。

Sphyraena pinguis (Perciformes, Sphyraenidae). This fish is found along coasts from Hokkaido to southern Kyushu, around Okinawa-jima Island, the Bohai Sea, and the Yellow Sea. They typically measure 30 to 40 cm in length. The Japanese name "kamasu" comes from a straw bag used to hold coal called a "kamasu," and it was given to them because of the resemblance of their wide open mouths. They are currently generally eaten salt-grilled or deep-fried, but dried red barracuda are especially tasty. They were eaten dried even during the Edo era (1603–1867), and the *Wakan Sansai Zue* states that "many dried red barracuda were shipped from the Bizen area."

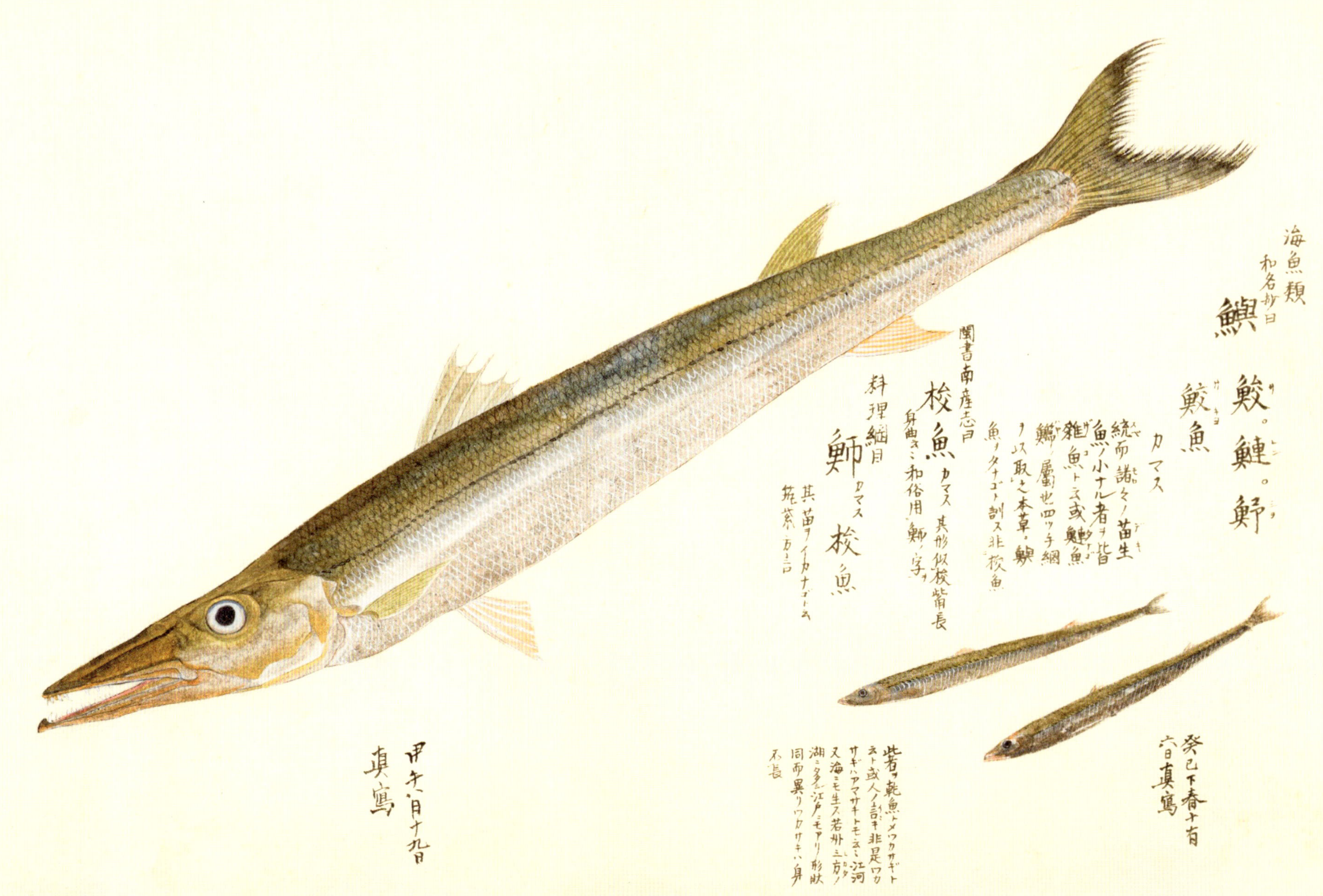

海魚類
和名抄曰
鱴　鮻・鰊・鰰
鮻魚
カマス

閩書南産志曰
校魚　カマス
身曲キミ和俗用鮖字
料理綱目
鮖　カマス
校ノ魚

甲午八月十九日
眞寫

癸巳下春十有
六日眞寫

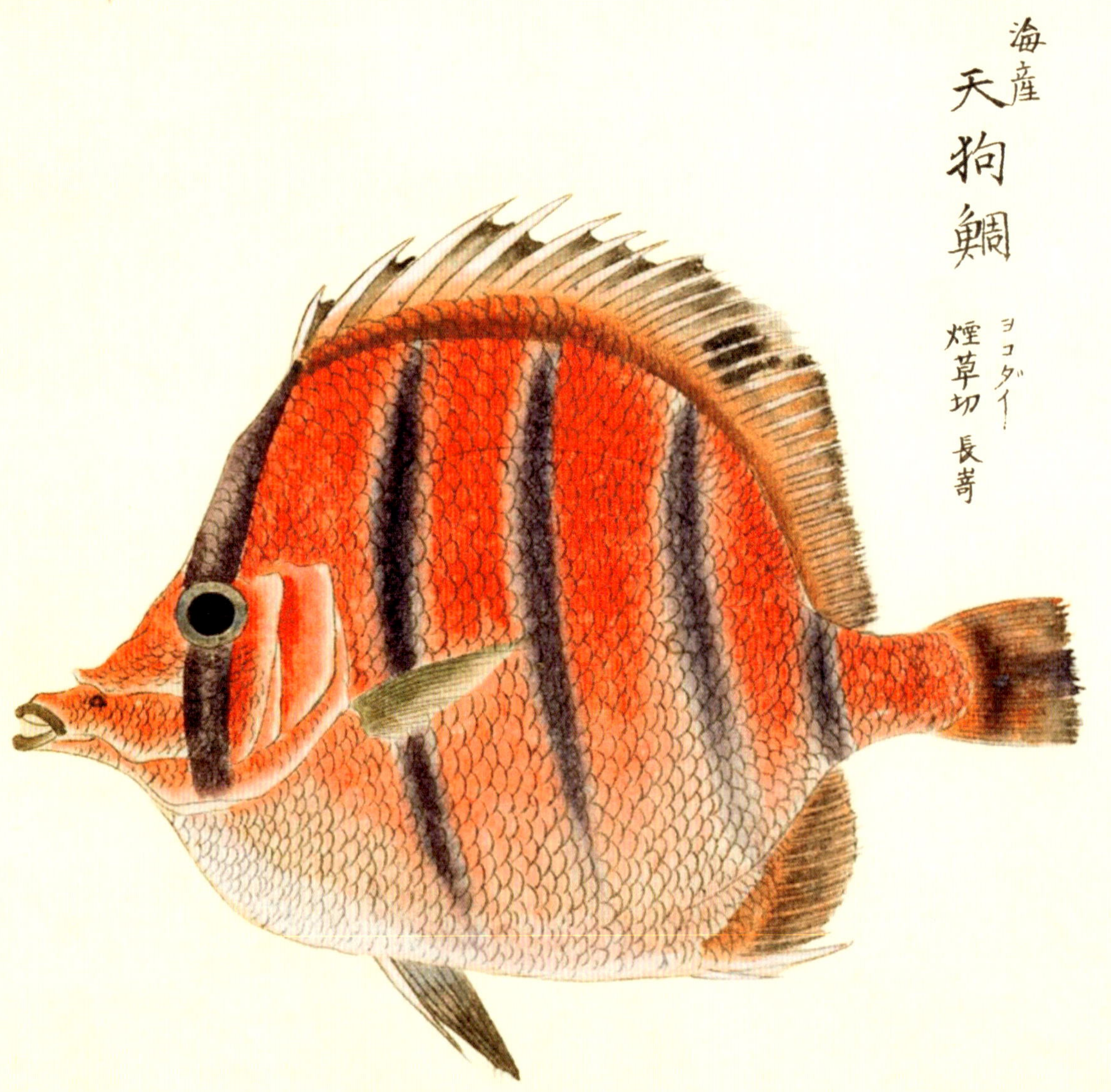

海産
天狗鯛　ヲコダイ
煙草切　長嵜
長嵜産戊戌四月九日送
尚勝公羽之真寫

元禄鯛

(Genrokudai)

縞鯛 鏡魚 胡盧鯛

(Shimadai) (Kagamiuo)

(Korodai)

ゲンロクダイ

Brown-banded butterflyfish

図は実物と色彩が異なるが、吻の状態や体の斑紋のパターンなどからハシナガチョウチョウウオ、またはゲンロクダイの可能性が高い。ハシナガチョウチョウウオは日本での確からしい記録は数例であることから、ここではゲンロクダイとして扱う。スズキ目チョウチョウウオ科ゲンロクダイ属。学名は*Roa modesta*。日本では津軽海峡から九州南岸までの日本海・東シナ海沿岸、宮城県から九州南岸までの太平洋沿岸、沖縄島などに分布する。体長は約15cm。体には2本の幅広い褐色横帯があり、それを縁取る暗褐色帯もある。図では、この暗色帯を4本の横帯として描き、保存により薄れた体色を赤色で補ったと解釈される。「ゲンロクダイ」の名前の由来は、元禄袖を連想させることから。

Roa modesta (Perciformes, Chaetodontidae). This fish is found along the coasts of the Sea of Japan and East China Sea from the Tsugaru Straits to southern Kyushu, on the Pacific coast from Miyagi Prefecture to southern Kyushu, and around Okinawa-jima Island. They typically measure 15 cm in length. In the figure, the two dark bands are depicted as four transverse bands, and the body color can be interpreted as having been supplemented using red to compensate for the fading that occurred as a result of preservation. Their Japanese name, "genrokudai," comes from their resemblance to "genrokusode," the short and round sleeves of a kimono.

車鯛

（Kurumadai）

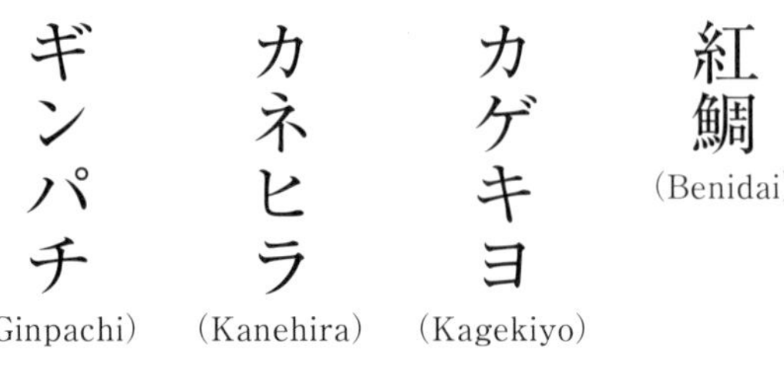

紅鯛
（Benidai）

カゲキヨ
（Kagekiyo）

カネヒラ
（Kanehira）

ギンパチ
（Ginpachi）

クルマダイ

Japanese big-eye

スズキ目キントキダイ科クルマダイ属。学名は*Pristigenys niphonia*。相模湾から九州南岸までの太平洋沿岸、新潟県から九州北西岸までの日本海沿岸、東シナ海、南シナ海南部、インド-西太平洋に分布する。体長は約20cm。体は鮮紅色、体側に4本の赤い横帯がある。この横帯は成長するにつれて薄くなるため、老成魚では横帯が見られないものもいる。和名「クルマダイ」は新潟県寺泊地方の名前で、幼魚の赤い縞模様が車の車輪のように見えることから名付けられた。他にも千葉県房州、神奈川県江ノ島では「カゲキヨ」、富山県では「ギンパチ」、高知市では「カネヒラ」などと呼ばれる。眼が大きいことから、英名には「Japanese big-eye」などがある。

Pristigenys niphonia (Perciformes, Priacanthidae). This fish is found along the Pacific coast from Sagami Bay to southern Kyushu, on the coast of the Sea of Japan from Niigata Prefecture to northwestern Kyushu, the East China Sea, the southern South China Sea, and the western Indo-Pacific. They typically measure 20 cm in length. Their bodies are a bright red, and they have four red bands on their sides. These bands lighten as they age, so older Japanese big-eye sometimes do not have visible bands. Their Japanese name, "kurumadai," comes from the resemblance of the red stripes on young fish and the spokes of a wheel ("kuruma").

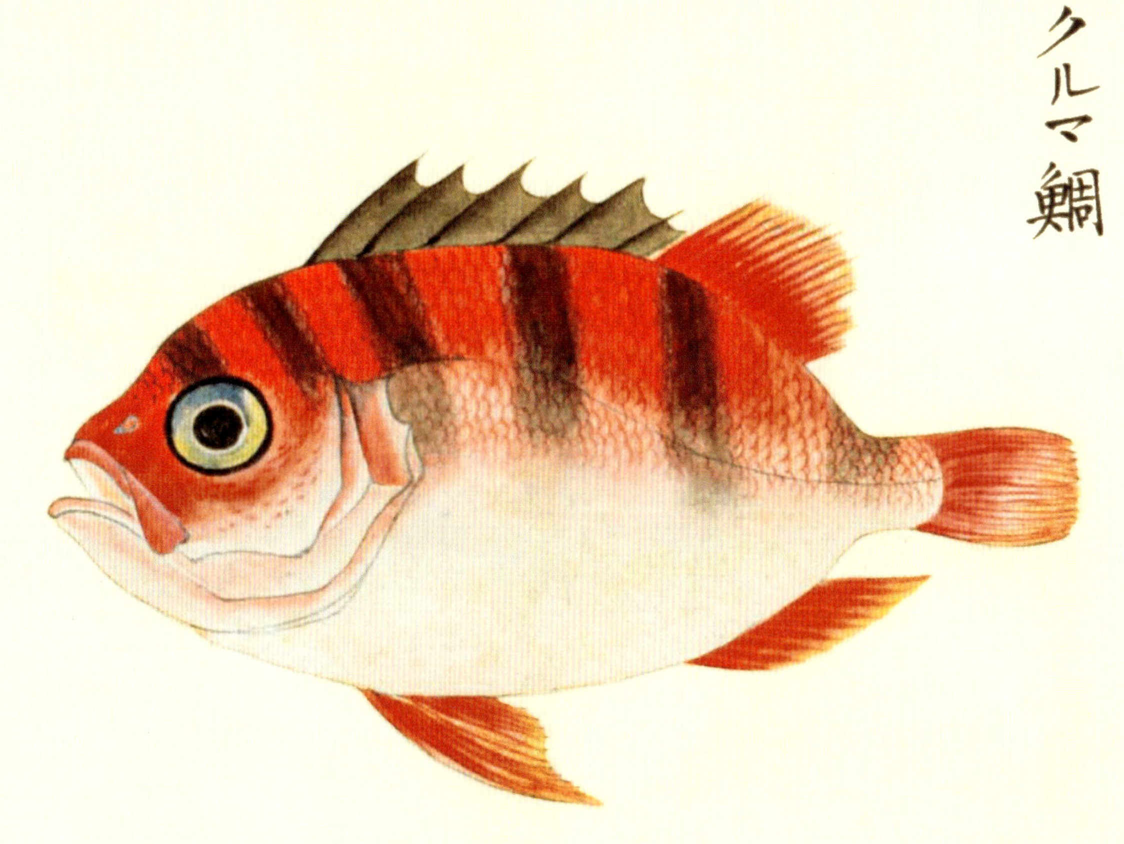

形狀小ニ而食ニ不過故
肉味佳ナランヲ不知

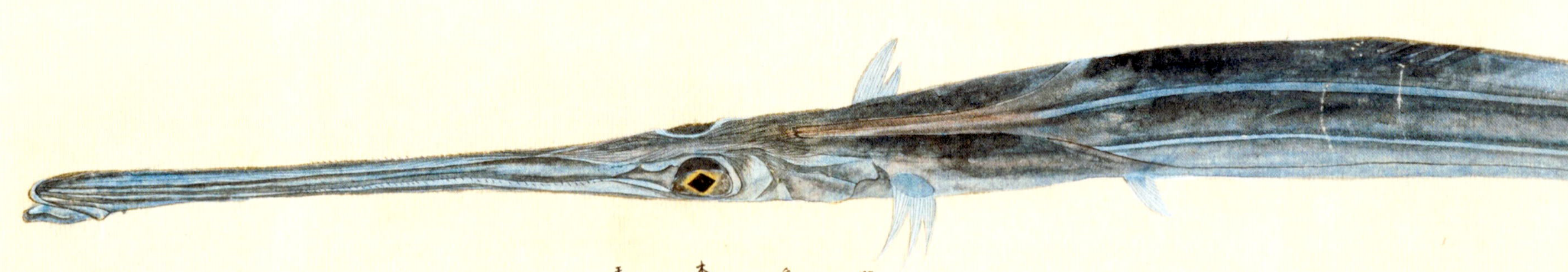

遊園魚品　海産無鱗

魚品

幹魚

本草綱目出　海魚

火笛箭筒　ヤガラ

王氏彙苑曰

鮹魚　ヤガラ

戴帽魚　タイ　ホウギヨ

西國ニ笛吹魚トス西州ニ多ク産關東稀ニ有之其形圖スル如クニメ目ヨリ口近立六寸其端甲不圓口ハ筒ノ先ニアリ目ヨリ口近ノ長サ七身ト同シ竹筒矢幹ニ似タル故矢カラトス無鱗黒ニメ味ユキニ似テ害ヒリ鮹魚ヲ國俗タコト通ス タコハ章魚也本草ニ膈噎ノ病ヲ治ス妙也トス

乙未八月二日送鷹喜子之真寫

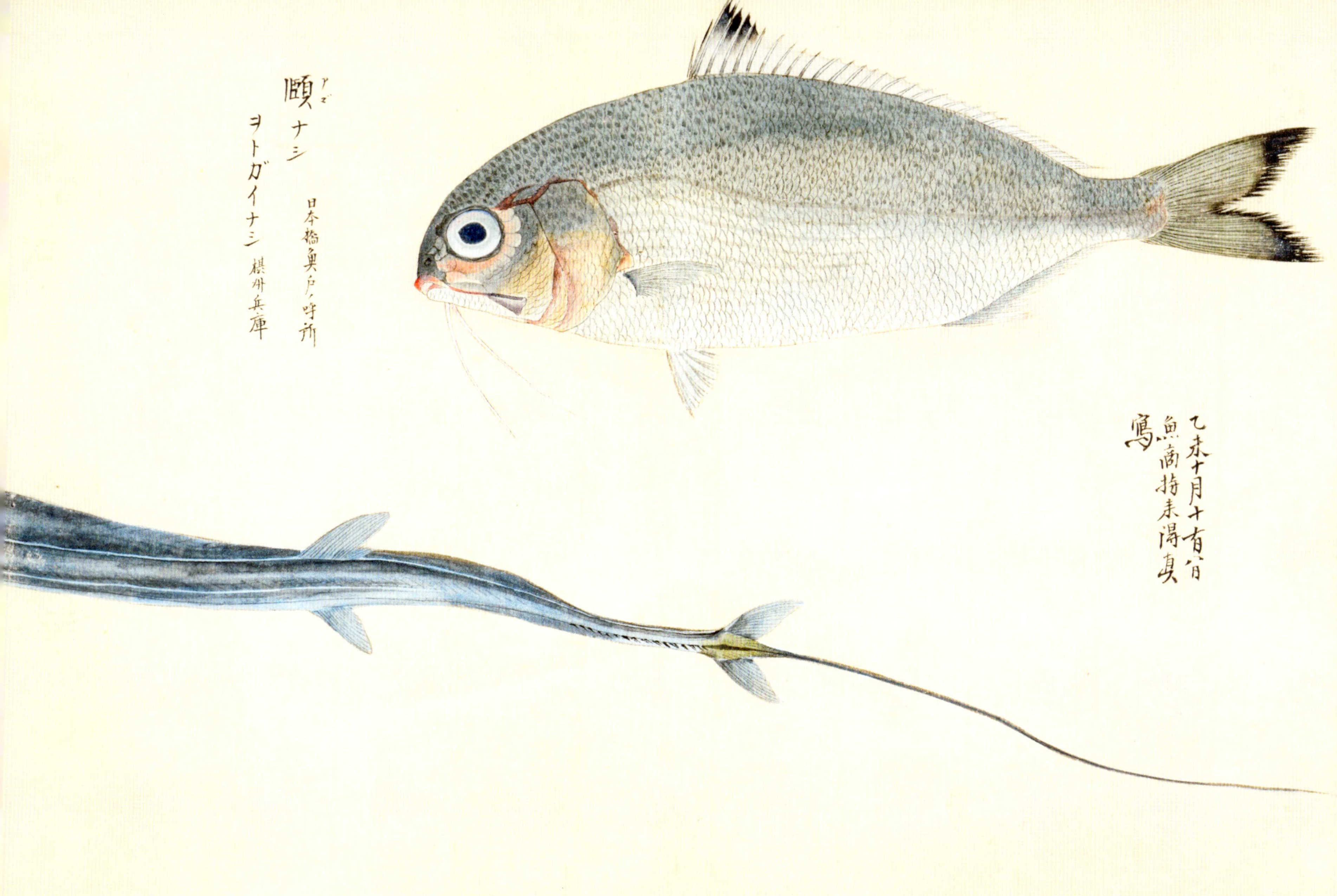

頤ナシ　日本橋奥戸ノ呼所
ヲトガイナシ　槙丹兵庫
乙未十月十有冒日
魚商持来未得真
寫

青矢柄
（Aoyagara）

笛吹
（Fuefuki）

青簳
（Aoyagara）

青矢幹
（Aoyagara）

アオヤガラ

Bluespotted cornetfish

トゲウオ目ヤガラ科ヤガラ属。学名は*Fistularia commersonii*。北海道から九州南岸までの各沿岸、琉球列島、山東省から広東省までの中国沿岸など、インド-汎太平洋に分布する。体長は約150cm。体は細長く、尾びれの中央軟条が長く伸びるのが特徴。和名「アオヤガラ」は、「青みがかったヤガラ」という意味で付けられた。「ヤガラ」の名前は、細長い体が矢柄の形に似ていることから。能登守平教経が射った矢がヤガラに変身したという俗説もある。高級魚のアカヤガラに比べて味が良くないため、食用とされることは少ない。口先の形から外国名には楽器にちなんだものが多く、英名には「Bluespotted cornetfish」などがある。

Fistularia commersonii (Gasterosteiformes, Fistulariidae). This fish is found on Japanese coasts from Hokkaido to southern Kyushu, around the Ryukyu Islands, along the Chinese coast from Shandong Province to Guangdong Province, and across the Indian and Pacific Oceans. They typically measure 150 cm in length. Their Japanese name, "aoyagara," means "bluish yagara." The name "yagara" comes from the fact that the shape of their body resembles the shaft of an arrow ("yagara") . There is a legend that Taira no Noritsune, protector of Noto Province, shot an arrow that turned into a bluespotted cornetfish.

銀目鯛

（Ginmedai）

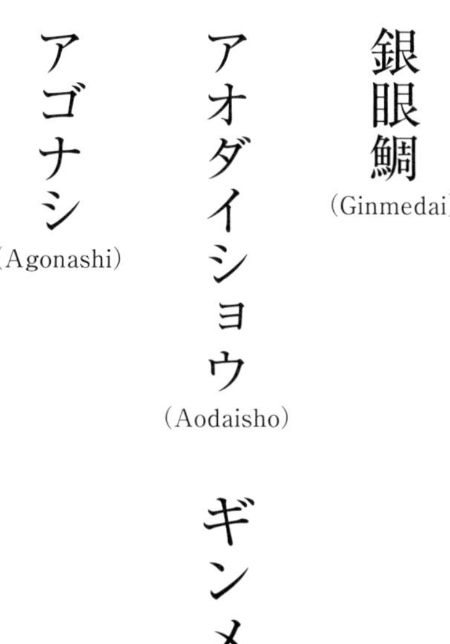

銀眼鯛
（Ginmedai）

アオダイショウ
（Aodaisho）

アゴナシ
（Agonashi）

ギンメダイ

Japanese beardfish

ギンメダイ目ギンメダイ科ギンメダイ属。学名は*Polymixia japonica*。福島県から九州南岸までの太平洋沿岸、東シナ海の大陸棚縁近域、九州-パラオ海嶺、台湾南部などに分布する。体長は20〜30cm。体は長卵形で側扁し、背側は青みがかった銀色、腹部は銀白色。眼と口が大きく、下顎に1対のひげがある。和名「ギンメダイ」は、光が当たると眼が銀色に輝くことに由来する。顎がないように見えることから「アゴナシ」、また高知市の周辺では、大正時代に入って漁法の発達とともに漁獲量が増えたこと、青みがかった体色から「青い大正魚」という意味で「アオダイショウ」と呼ばれる。英名には目の色から「Silver eye」「Beardfish」などがある。

Polymixia japonica (Polymixiiformes, Polymixiidae). This fish is found along the Pacific coast from Fukushima Prefecture to southern Kyushu, near the East China Sea continental shelf, Kyushu-Palau Ridge, and southern Taiwan. They typically measure 20 to 30 cm in length. Their bodies are long, oval, and flat, with bluish-silver dorsal areas and whitish-silver ventral areas. They have large eyes and mouths, and they have a pair of barbels on their lower jaws. Their Japanese name, "ginmedai," comes from the fact that their eyes ("me") glitter silver ("gin") in the light.

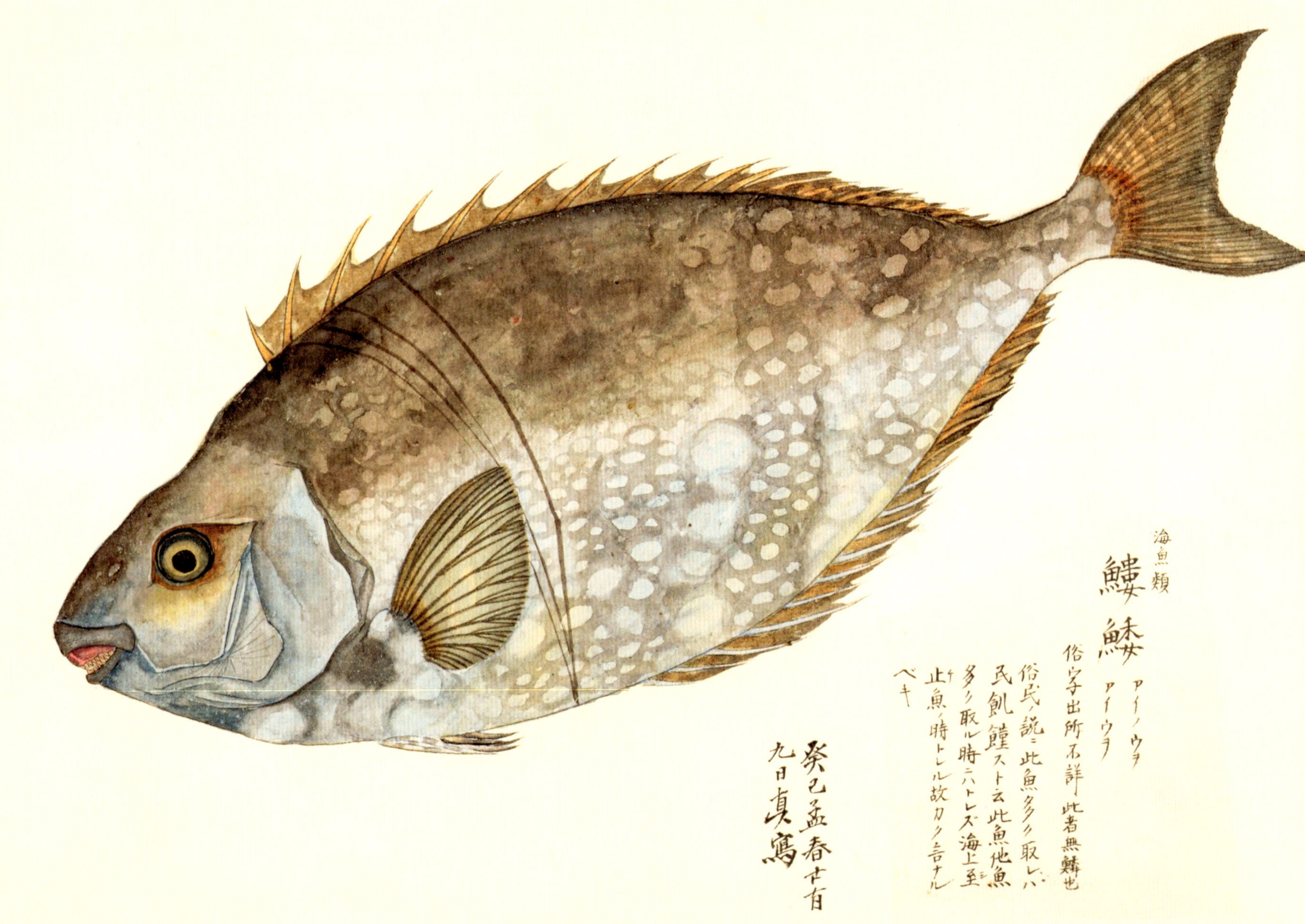

海魚類
鱫鱜　アイノウヲ　アイウヲ
俗字出所不詳　此者無鱗也
俗民ノ説ニ此魚多々取レハ
民飢饉スト云此魚他魚
多ク取ル時ニハトレズ海上至
此魚ノ時トレル故カク言ナル
ベキ
癸巳孟春中有
九日真寫

藍子
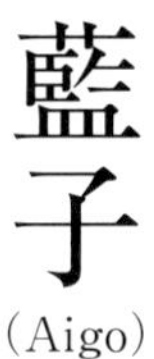
（Aigo）

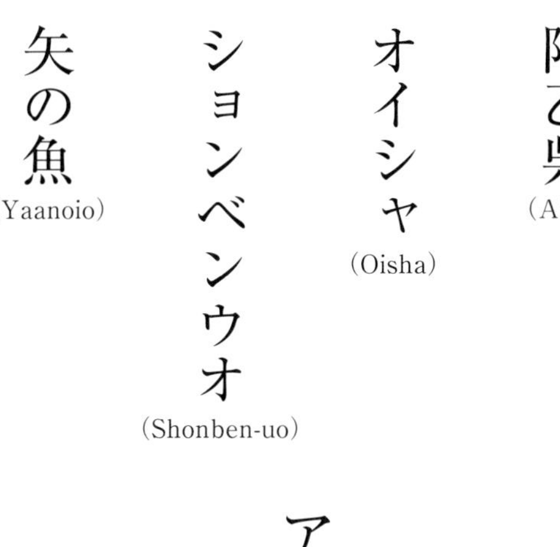

阿乙呉（Aigo）

オイシャ（Oisha）

ションベンウオ（Shonben-uo）

矢の魚（Yaanoio）

アイゴ

Mottled spinefoot

スズキ目アイゴ科アイゴ属。学名は*Siganus fuscescens*。青森県から九州南岸までの各沿岸、琉球列島、朝鮮半島南岸、済州島、台湾などに分布する。体長は約30cm。体は扁平した楕円形で、背部が褐色、腹部は淡褐色で、側面に白い斑点がある。背びれ、腹びれ、臀びれの鋭い棘に毒腺があり、刺されると激しく痛む。関東地方では「アイゴ」と呼ぶが、由来は不明。「藍子」は当て字で、アイヌの言葉で棘のあるものを「アイ」と呼ぶことから、「棘を持つ魚」という意味で「アイゴ」となったという説がある。地方名には棘を注射にたとえて「オイシャ」、肉が磯臭いため「ションベンウオ」などがある。他にも海藻を食べ尽くしてしまう様子から「磯の掃除屋」という異名もある。

Siganus fuscescens (Perciformes, Siganidae). This fish is found along the coasts from Aomori Prefecture to southern Kyushu, around the Ryukyu Islands, along the southern coast of the Korean Peninsula, around Jeju Island, and Taiwan. They typically measure 30 cm in length. They have poison glands along the sharp spines of their dorsal, ventral, and anal fins, and their stings are extremely painful. In the Kanto region they are called "aigo," but the etymology of the name is unknown. Other regional names include "oisha" ("doctor"), in reference to their needle-like spines, and "shonben-uo" ("urine fish") due to the rank odor of their flesh.

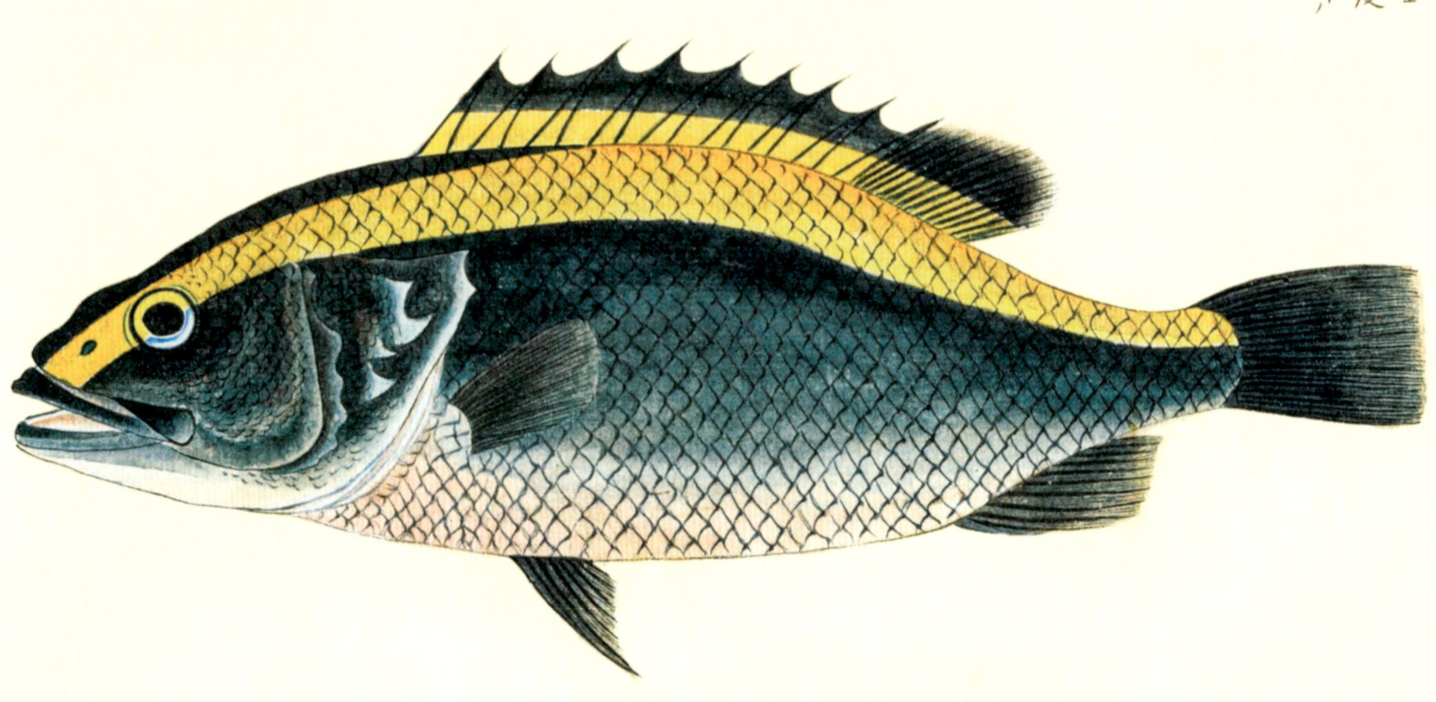

シマサキ　海魚

漢名不詳肉堅
硬リメ味不美皮
亦圭テ硬三鱗ノ
嶮起テ鋭利
肌不滑
冬月稀
ニ有リ

瑠璃羽太
（Rurihata）

ジョンサバッチ
（Jonsabatchi）

イシズミ
（Ishizumi）

油魚
（Aburauo）

アオハタ
（Aohata）

ルリハタ

Goldribbon soapfish

スズキ目ハタ科ルリハタ属。学名は*Aulacocephalus temminckii*。相模湾から高知県柏島までの太平洋沿岸、インド-西太平洋の局所的に分布する。体長は25～30cm。体はやや楕円形で側扁している。成魚の体色は瑠璃色から紫がかった紺色。吻端から眼、背中、尾びれの付け根まで黄色帯がある。幼魚は体が黄色で、鰓蓋の後端から側線に沿った体側上方が藍色。体表に毒腺を持ち、危険を感じると粘液毒を分泌する。「ルリハタ」の名前は、成魚の体色から「瑠璃色のハタ」の意で付けられた。「ルリハタ」は東京での呼称で、静岡県伊豆では「アオハタ」、三重県鳥羽では「イシズミ」、和歌山県田辺・周参見では「アブラウオ」、和歌山県雑賀崎では「ジョンサバッチ」と呼ばれる。

Aulacocephalus temminckii (Perciformes, Epinephelidae). This fish is found along the Pacific coast from Sagami Bay to Kochi Prefecture's Kashiwa-jima Island and scattered across the Indian and western Pacific Oceans. They typically measure 25 to 30 cm in length. Adult goldribbon soapfish have lapis lazuli or purplish blue bodies. A yellow band runs from their mouth past their eyes, back, and to the base of their caudal fin. Their body has poison glands that secrete poisonous mucus when they are threatened. Their Japanese name, "rurihata," comes from their lapis lazuli ("ruri") color.

鷺笛
（Sagifue）

鶯
（Uguisu）

角剝
（Tsunohage）

チュウチュウ
（Chuchu）

サギフエ

Longspine snipefish

トゲウオ目サギフエ科サギフエ属。学名は*Macroramphosus sagifue*。北海道南部から兵庫県浜坂までの日本海沿岸、相模湾から九州南岸までの太平洋沿岸、東シナ海大陸棚縁近域に分布する。体長は約15cm。500m以浅の砂れき底や砂泥底に生息し、小型動物を捕食する。頭をやや下に向けて泳いでいることが多いが、大きく移動するときなどは水平で泳ぐ。体色は鮮やかな薄紅色で、吻が管状に伸びているのが特徴。だが、生息する環境によって体型や体色の個体差が著しいといわれている。底曳網で大量に獲られるが、食用にされることはほとんどない。和名「サギフエ」の由来は不明。高知県の浦戸では「ウグイス」、御畳瀬では「チュウチュウ」、須崎では「ツノハゲ」などと呼ばれる。

Macroramphosus sagifue (Gasterosteiformes, Macroramphosidae). This fish is found along the coasts of the Sea of Japan from southern Hokkaido to Hyogo Prefecture's Hamasaka, along the Pacific coast from Sagami Bay to southern Kyushu, and around the East China Sea continental shelf. They typically measure 15 cm in length. Their bodies are a bright pink and their mouths extend like a tube. However, there are major differences in their body shape and color depending on where they live. Large numbers are caught by trawling nets, but they are rarely eaten. The origin of their Japanese name, "sagifue," is unknown.

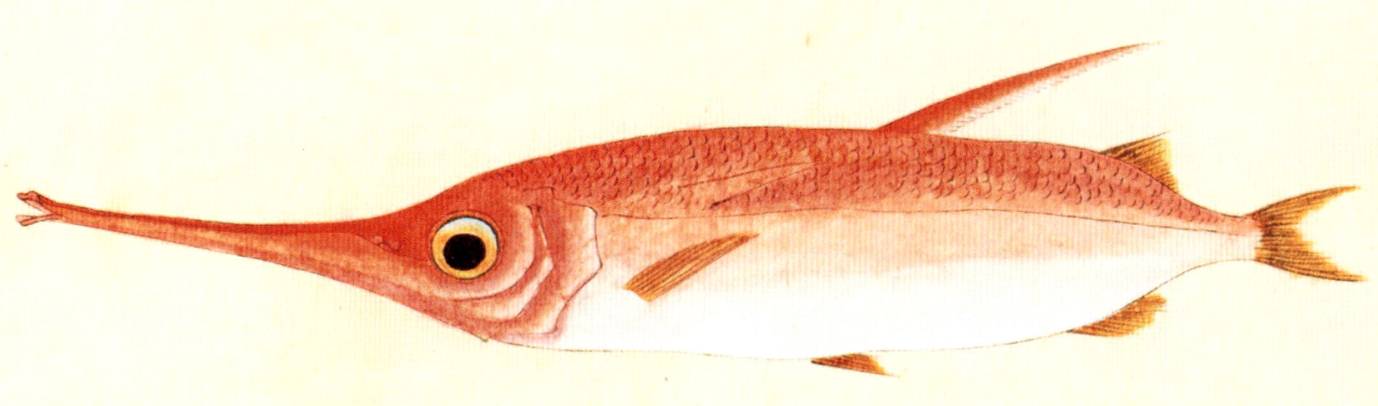

トウジン
カハセミ魚　海魚

元壽文受十二丑年十二月九日芝ノ高輪ノ
瀬ノ待合ニ云ル茶店ニ休息シ芝ノ朝河岸
ヨリ赤羽根魚市ニ鬻グ漁商輩ミニ其
中ニ魚ヲ荷擔エ此三魚ヲ鬻ギ牛尾魚ナゾノ
中ニ交ヱテ通リス又予眼ニ鯛タレハ僕ニ是ヲ
調ヒヲシム則茶店ノ於座稼小菜紙ニ寫
茶店ノ主如何ノ用ニナフニ予ト言リ予則多
年好ノ画筆ヲテ天下ニアラユル種品ヲ真寫セ
リヲ呑ノ主日ニ魚戸ノ運送ル者ノ中名モ
不知魚往々有之皆ハ毒アリトテ不買トヱリ
予晴々三田墓町寺院又泉岳寺ニ詣ズ故
芝河岸ニ八異魚ヲ鬻ク魚商ノ有ルヲヲ知
此三魚ハ往還先ナルハ不食ニマサキハ魚戸ノ食
ヒシト云ルヲ闘舌味ノ説其ハ代ニ記ス三魚トモ
何レノ産ナル乎不聞魚ハ皆ノ茶店ノ小兒ノモテ
㪅ニ置ニ今兹ニ其ハ小紙ヲ操出ニ著色清書
スルニテ時保十二己亥年十月九日

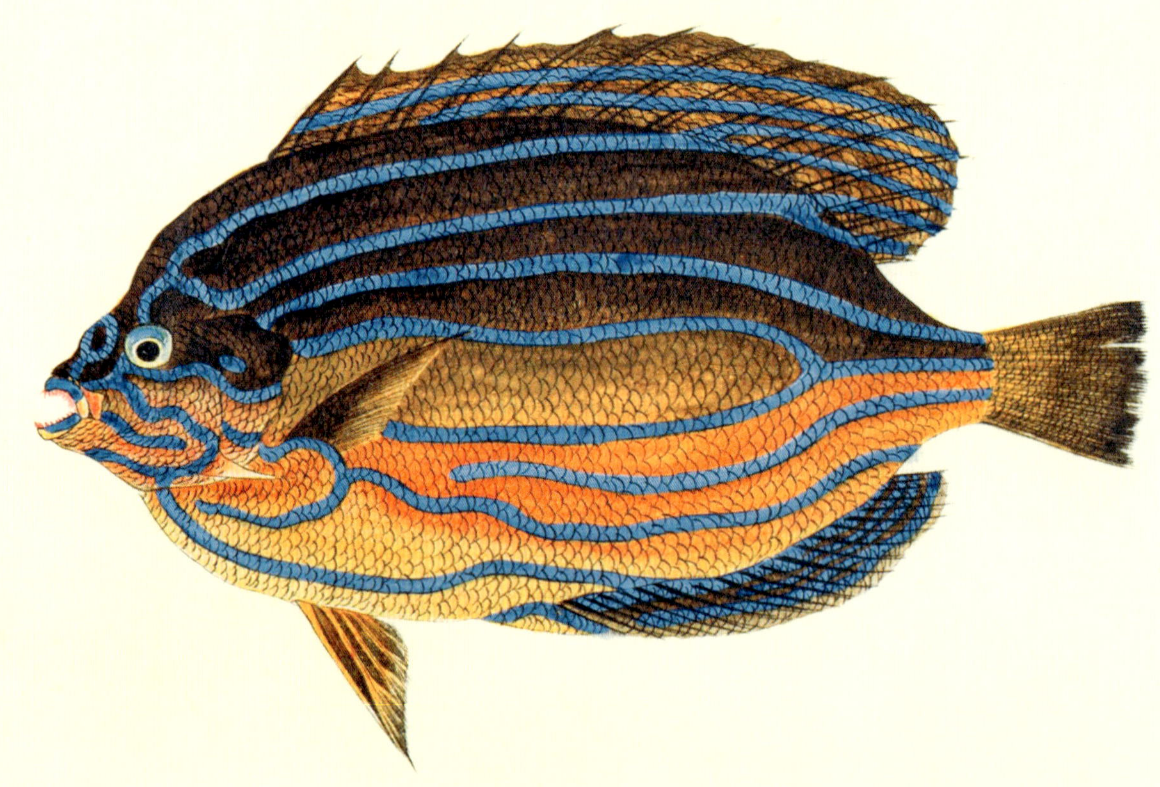

アユダ　魚戸ノ呼所

アユダ漢名不詳惣身扁ニメ海タナゴニ
似タリ鰓腹ヨリ脐ノヒレ脊ノ鬣ニ至ル
マテ細鱗アリ其體色如此骨硬肉白
メ赤硬ハシ皮ハ鱗ヲ去リカタシ厚而亦
硬シ味不ズ表トモ可食其肉青ク土臭
シ冬月稀ニ出ツ

保十七年初冬、
奥高特末水之寫

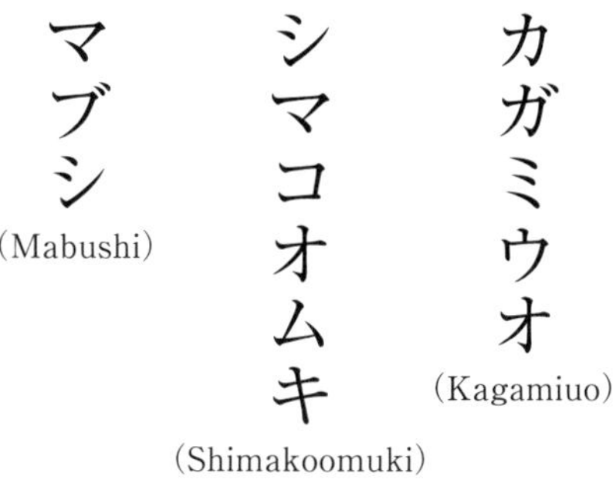

巾着鯛
（Kinchakudai）

キンチャクダイ

カガミウオ
（Kagamiuo）

シマコオムキ
（Shimakoomuki）

マブシ
（Mabushi）

Blue-striped angelfish

スズキ目キンチャクダイ科キンチャクダイ属。学名は *Chaetodontoplus septentrionalis*。山形県から九州南岸までの日本海・東シナ海沿岸、宮城県から九州南岸の太平洋沿岸、口永良部島、済州島、台湾などに分布する。体長は約20cm、最大で25cmほどになる。和名「キンチャクダイ」は手提げの袋の巾着の形に似ていることから、または巾着の模様を連想することに由来する。幼魚の体色は黒で黄色の横帯を持ち、成魚の体色は黄色、特に尾びれは鮮やかな色で、体側には青色の縦帯を持つ。キンチャクダイ科は美しい色と模様から観賞魚として人気が高い。英名は美しい色彩とひれの形状から「Blue-striped angelfish（青い線のある天使の魚）」。

Chaetodontoplus septentrionalis (Perciformes, Pomacanthidae). This fish is found along the coasts of the Sea of Japan and East China Sea from Yamagata Prefecture to southern Kyushu, along the Pacific coast from Miyagi Prefecture to southern Kyushu, around Kuchinoerabu Island, around Jeju Island, and Taiwan. They typically measure 20 cm in length, but can grow as large as 25 cm in length. Pomacanthids (angelfishes) are popular as pets due to their beautiful colors and patterns. Their Japanese name, "kinchakudai," comes from their resemblance to a handheld bag called a "kinchaku" and the designs used on kinchaku.

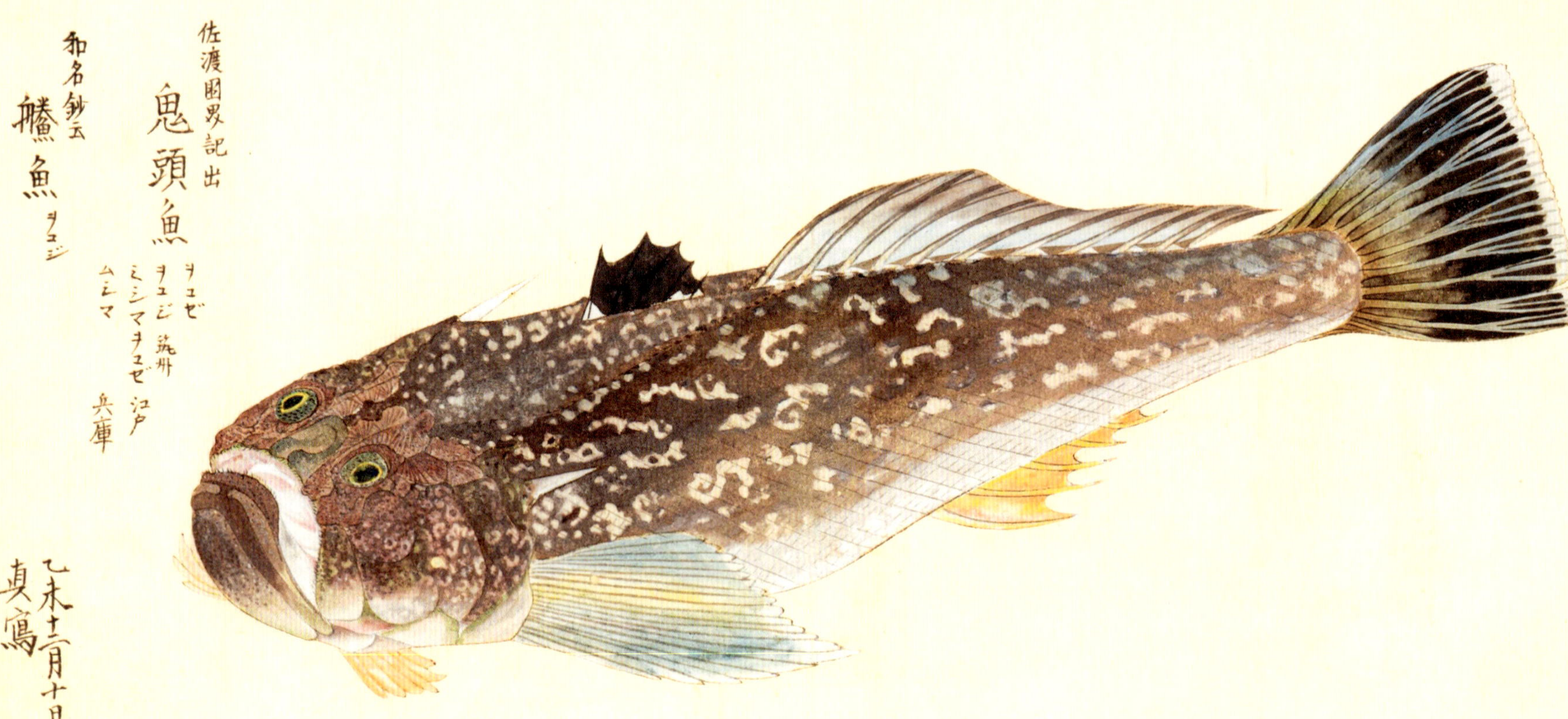
佐渡國界記出
鬼頭魚
ヲゼ
ヲコゼ 筑州
ミシマヲコゼ 江戸
ムシマ 兵庫
和名鈔云
鰧魚 ヲコジ
乙未十二月十日
真寫

三島䲛
（Mishimaokoze）

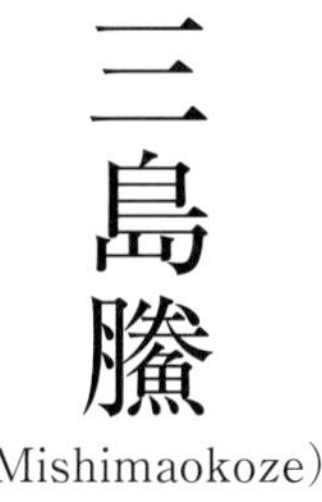

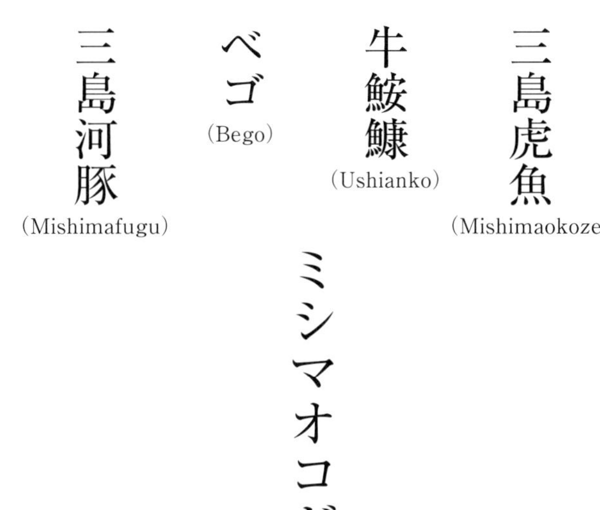

三島河豚
（Mishimafugu）

ベゴ
（Bego）

牛鮟鱇
（Ushianko）

三島虎魚
（Mishimaokoze）

ミシマオコゼ

Japanese stargazer

スズキ目ミシマオコゼ科ミシマオコゼ属。学名は *Uranoscopus japonicus*。北海道から九州南岸までの太平洋沿岸、青森県から九州南岸までの日本海・東シナ海沿岸などに分布する。体長は20〜30cm。体はオコゼに似て円筒形で、尾部はやや側扁している。和名「ミシマオコゼ」の由来は形がオコゼに似ていること、かつ三島焼きの陶器のような模様をしていることに因むという説、東海道の宿場名「ミシマ」の遊女に因んで「みだらで醜悪な」という意味からとする説など、諸説ある。属名の *Uranoscopus* はギリシャ語で「空を見るもの」の意味で、眼が上を向いているところから付けられた。英名の「stargazer」も「星を見つめるもの」という意味。

Uranoscopus japonicus (Perciformes, Uranoscopidae). This fish is found along the Pacific coast from Hokkaido to southern Kyushu and along the coasts of the Sea of Japan and East China Sea from Aomori Prefecture to southern Kyushu. They typically measure 20 to 30 cm in length. Their bodies are cylindrical, like stonefish, and their tails are slightly flat. Their Japanese name, "mishimaokoze," is said to come from the similarity of their body shapes to stonefish ("okoze") and their pattern, which resembles Mishima-yaki ceramics. It is also said to be in reference to the courtesans of the Mishima post station on the Tokaido route being "ugly and licentious."

現在ではどの魚を指すのか不明である。「金鯛」「アカハタ」と書いてあるが、下顎・尾びれの形状や鱗の大きさからアカハタとは同定しにくい。鱗の大きさや体形、尾びれの形はアカムツに似ているが鰓蓋の棘などが一致せず、フサカサゴの仲間にも見えるが特徴が一致する種はやはり見当たらない。

It is unclear what fish is shown in the figure. The figure states that it is a blacktip grouper (*Epinephelus fasciatus*), but based on the size of scales and shapes of the lower jaw and caudal fin, it does not appear to be a blacktip grouper.

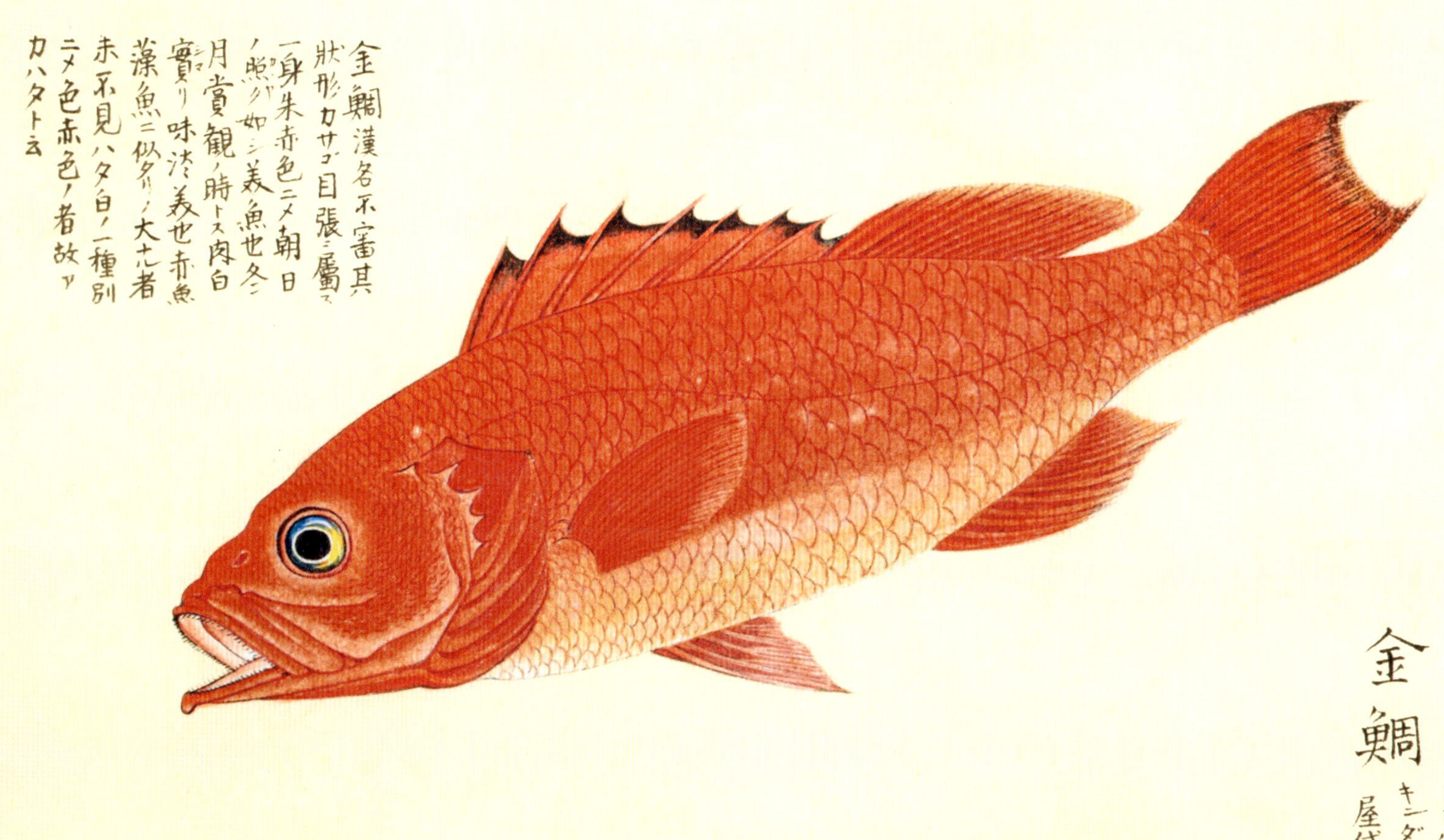

金鯛漢名不審其
狀形カサゴ目張ニ屬ス
一身朱赤色ニメ朝日
ノ照ガ如シ美魚也冬ニ
月賞観ノ時トス肉白
實リ味淡美也赤魚
藻魚ニ似タリノ大ナ者
未不見ハタ白ノ一種別
ニメ色赤色ノ者故ア
カハタトス

金鯛
キンダイ
アカハタ
屋代秘魚譜

虎雞魚　トラギス

虎キス肉白クメ味
鱚ニ勝レリ料理
方キス三同メヨシ

保十二辛丑年
八月廿日魚戸
華吉持朱永之
吉山写

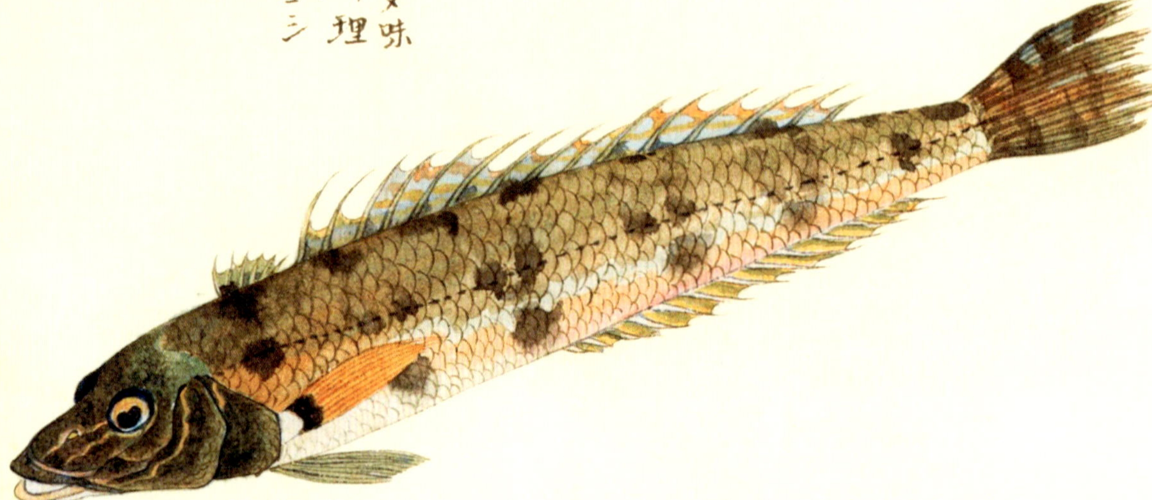

鞍掛虎鱚

（Kurakaketoragisu）

虎沙魚
（Torahaze）

イシブエ
（Ishibue）

クラカケトラギス

Grub fish

スズキ目トラギス科トラギス属。学名は*Parapercis sexfasciata*。青森県から九州南岸までの日本海沿岸、岩手県から九州南岸までの太平洋沿岸、東シナ海沿岸、朝鮮半島沿岸、台湾、ジャワ島南部などに分布する。体長は約20cm。体色は赤褐色で、背部から体側に4つのV字形の暗色斑がある。和名「クラカケトラギス」の由来は、このV字形の暗色斑が馬の背に鞍をかけた形に似ていることから「クラカケ」、さらに虎縞のように見えることから「トラギス」となったといわれている。底曳網で漁獲され、練り製品の原料や天ぷらの種として利用される。砂泥底での釣りの外道として掛かることが多く、以前は捨てられていたが、近年は味の評価が高まり、利用が増えつつある。

Parapercis sexfasciata (Perciformes, Pinguipedidae). This fish is found along the coast of the Sea of Japan from Aomori Prefecture to southern Kyushu, along the Pacific coast from Iwate Prefecture to southern Kyushu, on the coasts of the East China Sea, the Korean Peninsula, Taiwan, and southern Java. They typically measure 20 cm in length. They are reddish brown and have four V-shaped dark bands on the back and sides. Their Japanese name, "kurakaketoragisu," comes from the way the V-shaped dark bands look like a saddle ("kura") placed ("kake") on their back, and the similarity to tiger ("tora") stripes.

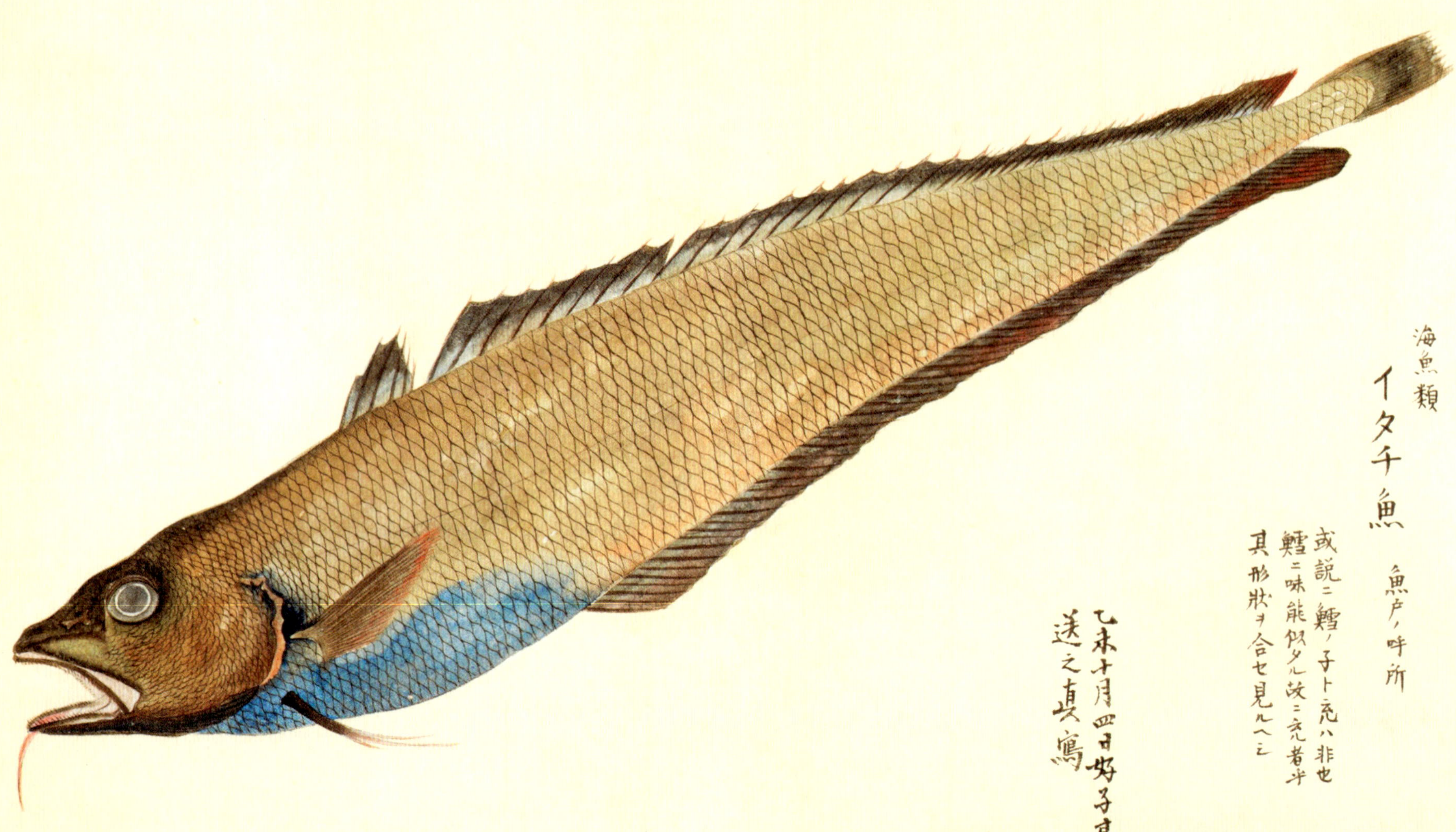

海魚類
イタチ魚　魚戸ノ呼所
或説ニ鱈ノ子ト云ハ非也
鱈ニ味能似タル故ニ云者半
其形状ヲ合セ見ルヘシ
乙未十月四日好子来
送之真写

稚児鱈

(Chigodara)

ノロマ
(Noroma)

ドンコ
(Donko)

オキナマズ
(Okinamazu)

ウミナマズ
(Uminamazu)

イタチ
(Itachi)

チゴダラ

Japanese codling

タラ目チゴダラ科チゴダラ属。学名は*Physiculus japonicus*。北海道から高知県までの太平洋岸、北海道から山口県までの日本海沿岸、東シナ海、済州島、台湾などに分布する。体長30〜40cm。体はやや長く、側扁している。体色は淡褐色。腹部に発光バクテリアによる丸い発光器があるのが特徴。漁獲量が少ないため鮮魚での流通はわずかで、主に練り製品の材料として利用される。和名「チゴダラ」の由来は不詳。地方名に「ドンコ」があるが、岩手県ではチゴダラを使った味噌汁（ドンコ汁）が郷土料理として親しまれている。他にも新潟県出雲崎の「イタチ」、茨城県水戸の「ノロマ」、和歌山県田辺の「ウミナマズ」、高知の「オキナマズ」などの地方名がある。

Physiculus japonicus (Gadiformes, Moridae). This fish is found along the Pacific coast from Hokkaido to Kochi Prefecture, along the coast of the Sea of Japan from Hokkaido to Yamaguchi Prefecture, the East China Sea, around Jeju Island, and Taiwan. They typically measure 30 to 40 cm in length. Their bodies are somewhat long and flat, and light brown in color. They have a light-producing organ that uses bioluminescent bacteria. While they are eaten, few are caught, so only a small amount of fresh Japanese codling are commercially available, and they are primarily used in fish paste products. The origin of their Japanese name, "chigodara," is unknown.

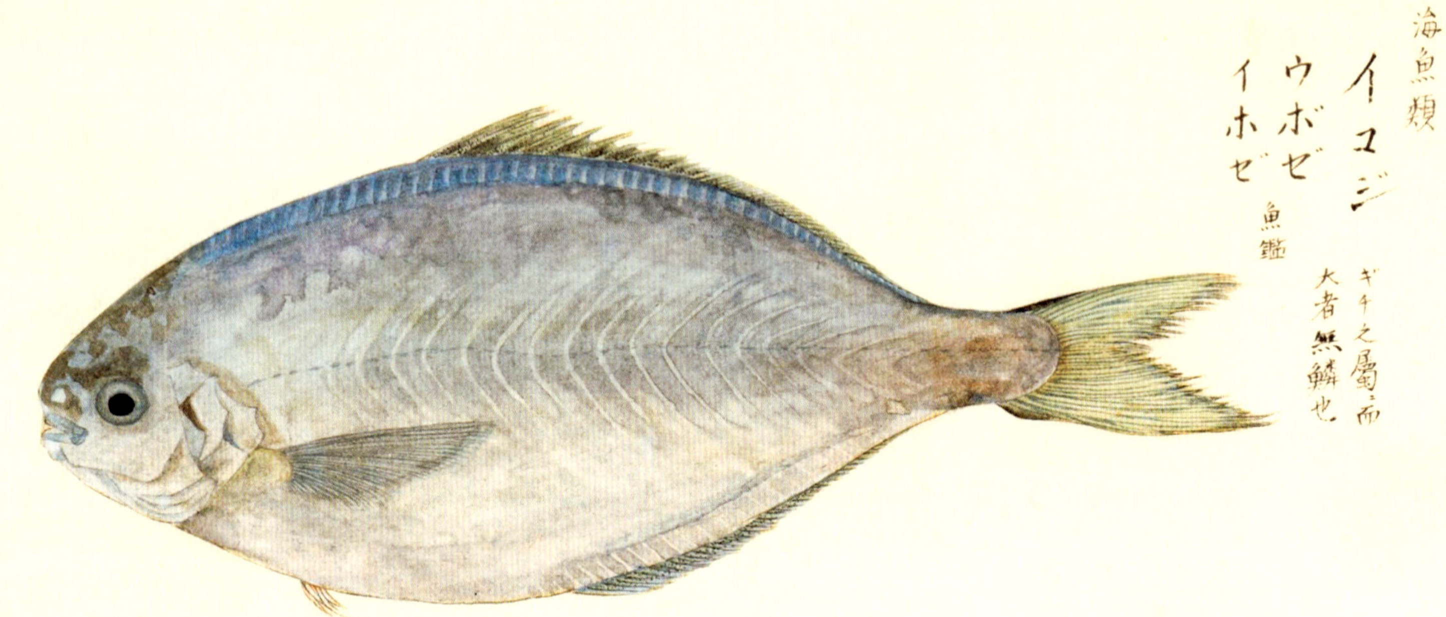

海魚類
イユジ ギギ之屬ニ而
ウボゼ 大者無鱗也
イホゼ 魚鑑
癸巳林鐘
四日真寫

疣鯛

（Ibodai）

嫗背魚

（Ubose）

イボダイ

Japanese butterfish

スズキ目イボダイ科イボダイ属。学名は*Psenopsis anomala*。北海道から九州南岸までの日本周辺海域、東シナ海大陸棚域、中国南シナ海沿岸などに分布する。体長は約20㎝。食用とされ、鮮魚として流通される他、干物に加工されることも多い。体表から粘液を多く出すのが特徴で、ぬめりがあるものほど鮮度が良いとされている。和名「イボダイ」は漢字では「疣鯛」と書き、背にいぼがあること（背びれ前方の棘がいぼを連想させたと考えられる）、褐色の斑点が「イボオ」というお灸の痕に似ていることなどが語源とされている。『和漢三才図会』には、「嫗背魚」という名称で記録されており、老女を意味する嫗の屈んだ背に似ていることから、この名が付けられたといわれている。

Psenopsis anomala (Perciformes, Centrolophidae). This fish is found in the seas around Japan, from Hokkaido to southern Kyushu, in the East China Sea continental shelf area, and along the coast of the South China Sea. They typically measure 20 cm in length. They secrete a large amount of mucus from their bodies, and the slipperier they are the fresher they are believed to be. Their Japanese name, "ibodai," is said to come from so-called bumps ("ibo") on their back or from the resemblance of their brown spots to moxibustion marks called "iboo."

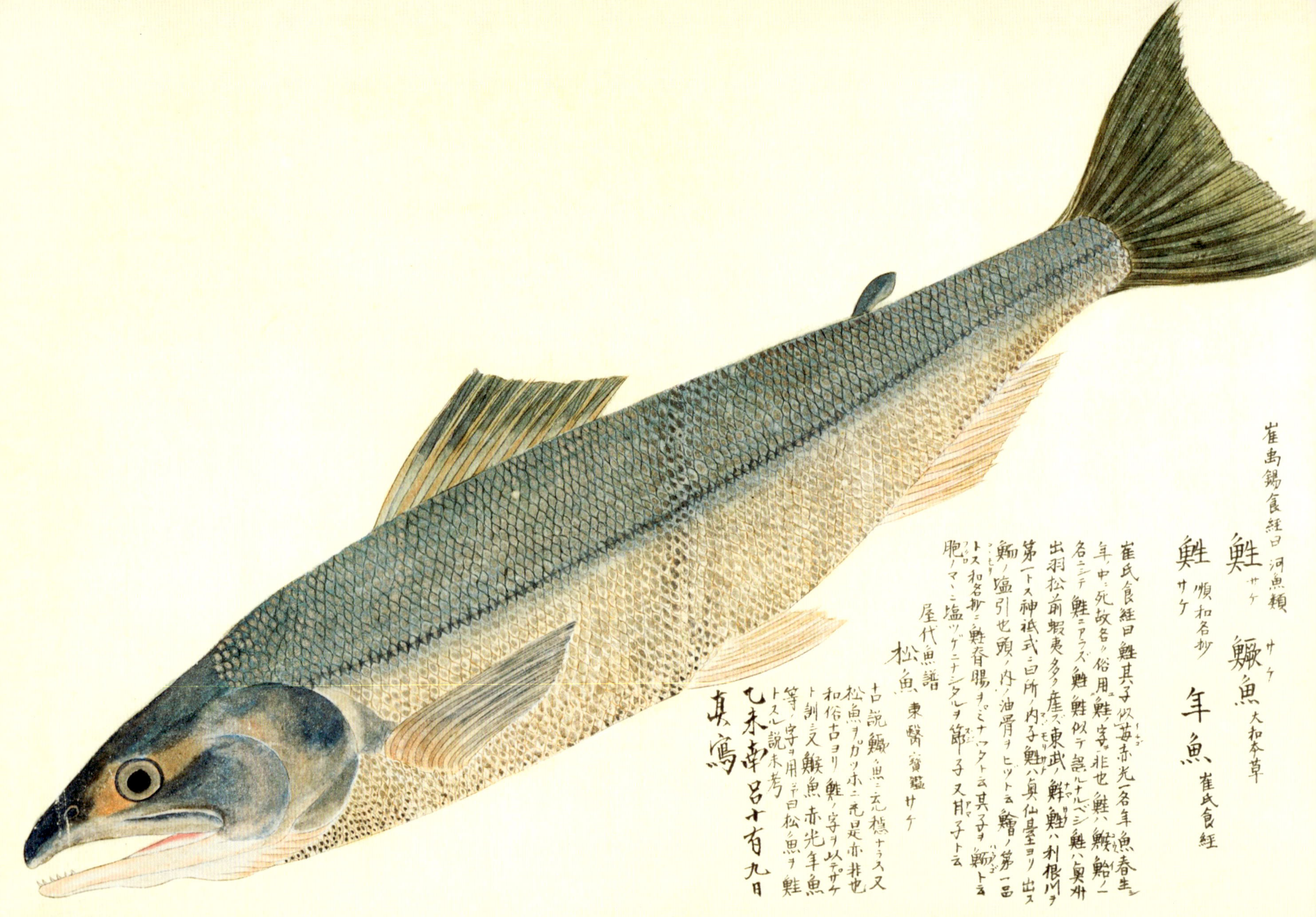

鮭
（Sake）

鮏
（Sake）

石桂魚
（Sake）

白鮭
（Shirozake）

秋味
（Akiaji）

カムイチェプ
（Kamuichepu）

トキシラズ
（Tokishirazu）

サケ

Chum salmon

サケ目サケ科サケ属。学名は*Oncorhynchus keta*。北海道から九州北部までの日本海沿岸の河川、利根川以北の太平洋岸の河川、朝鮮半島東部から北太平洋、北極海、カリフォルニア州北部の河川まで回帰する。体長は最大で約100cm。和名「サケ」の由来は、アイヌ語で「夏の食物」という意味の「サク・イペ」が転訛したという説、身が裂けやすいため「裂け」という説、瀬を遡上することから「瀬蹴」が転じたという説など、諸説ある。古くから食用とされてきた。平安時代に入ると乾物や塩引きが一般的となり、江戸時代の中期には現在でも歳暮で贈られる「新巻」が登場する。サケの塩物を荒むしろで巻いたことから「荒巻」と呼ばれ、進物用にしたのが起源といわれている。

Oncorhynchus keta (Salmoniformes, Salmonidae). This fish returns to rivers opening to the coast of the Sea of Japan from Hokkaido to northern Kyushu, on rivers opening to the Pacific coast from Tone River northward, from the eastern Korean Peninsula to the northern Pacific Ocean, the Arctic Ocean, and the rivers in northern California. They typically measure up to 100 cm in length. One theory about their Japanese name, "sake," is that it comes from an Ainu term, "saku ipe," meaning "summer food." The middle of the Edo era (1603–1867) saw the rise of salted salmon wrapped in a straw mat, which are still presented as a gift during the Seibo gift-giving season.

荔枝魚　マツカサウヲ
鯛ノ聲　源八
佐渡田以記

江府ノ魚戸ニテハ
エビス鯛ト云ス別
ニエビス鯛アリ與
此異リ
緋魚ハ食物本草
ニホサイセ大和本
草ニハスミメフシトス
雀フグ　マツカサ魚
一種也

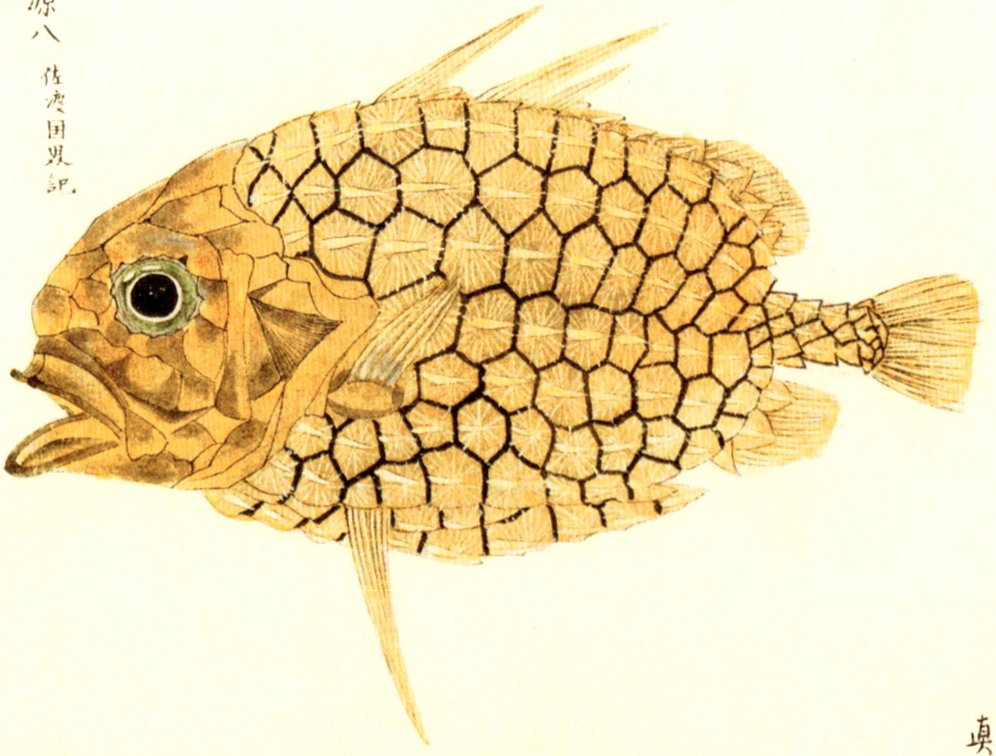

大和本草
緋魚　スヽメフグ　海產
スヾメウヲ

日本記齊明記出雲國言
北海濱魚死而横大如鰌
雀啄針鱗名曰雀魚

雀魚乾而送之
其生彩色チ不知只
其形狀ヲ許ニ圖ス
己

乙未十七月十日
真寫

松毬魚
（Matsukasauo）

鎧
（Yoroi）

鯱
（Shachihoko）

海雀
（Umisuzume）

恵比須魚
（Ebisuuo）

恵比須鯛
（Ebisudai）

荔枝魚
（Matsukasauo）

マツカサウオ

Pinecone fish

キンメダイ目マツカサウオ科マツカサウオ属。学名は*Monocentris japonica*。北海道から九州南岸までの日本海沿岸、青森県から九州南岸までの太平洋沿岸、フィリピン、インド洋、東アフリカにかけて広く分布する。体長は約15cm。和名「マツカサウオ」の由来は、黒で縁取られた黄色く大きな鱗が「松かさ」に似ていることから。ユニークな外観から観賞用として利用される。鱗に後ろ向きの鋭い棘が付いているのが特徴だが、これが魔力を持つと信じられていたのか、太平洋岸の地域では魔除けとして使われていたという。また、発光バクテリアを持つ発光魚として知られているが、このことが確認されたのは1914年、富山県の水族館での停電がきっかけだった。

Monocentris japonica (Beryciformes, Monocentridae). This fish is found along the coast of the Sea of Japan from Hokkaido to the southern coast of Kyushu, along the Pacific coast from Aomori Prefecture to the southern coast of Kyushu, the Philippines, the Indian Ocean, and eastern Africa. They typically measure 15 cm in length. Their Japanese name, "matsukasauo," comes from the fact that their large yellow scales, bordered with black, look like pinecones ("matsukasa"). They are kept as pets due to their unique appearance. They are also known for being bioluminescent due to the bioluminescent bacteria in their bodies.

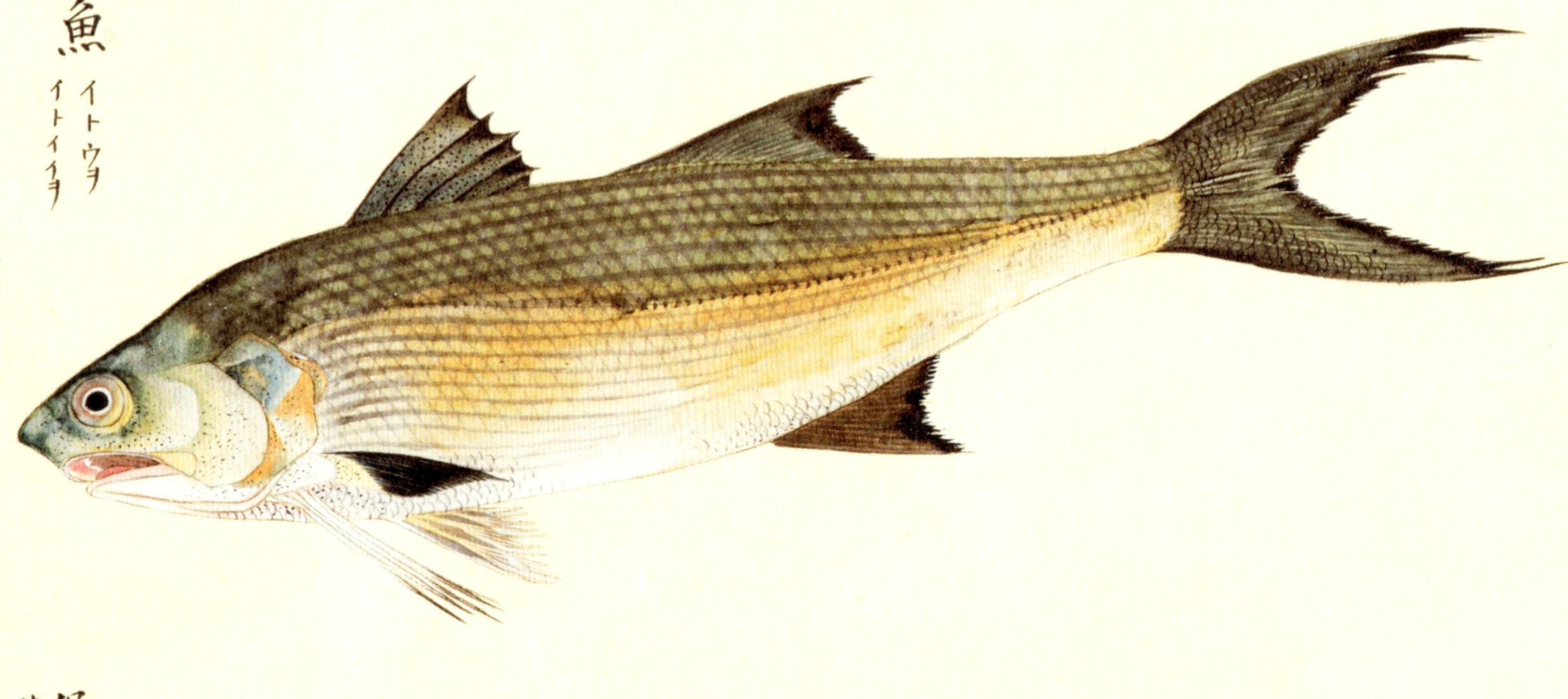

絲魚

イトウヲ
イトイラヲ

越後高田絲魚川
多ク此魚ヲ産ス故ニ川ニ名アリ漢名不詳其肉至テ少ク脆ク
味淡メ鱸セイゴニ似タリ魚戸ノ多商魚ニアラス

保十己亥年九月
廿三日魚商特来
永之真寫

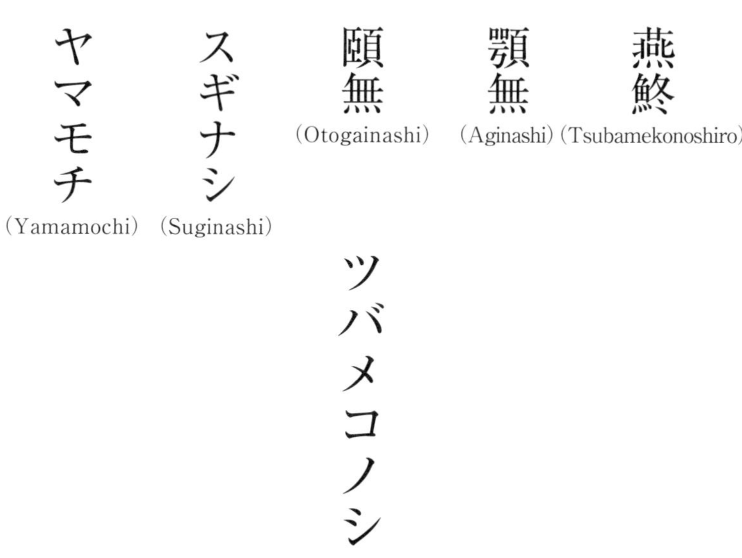

Striped threadfin

スズキ目ツバメコノシロ科ツバメコノシロ属。学名は *Polydactylus plebeius*。福島県から屋久島までの太平洋沿岸、若狭湾から長崎県までの日本海・東シナ海沿岸、伊豆-小笠原諸島、琉球列島、インド-太平洋に分布する。体長は約30cm。最大で50cmを超えるものもいる。和名「ツバメコノシロ」は、コノシロによく似ていること、尾びれの深い切り込みがツバメの尾羽に似ていることに由来する。胸びれは上下に分離し、下の部分は遊離軟条からなり、この遊離軟条で海底の餌を探す。この様子から英名は「糸のようなひれ」という意味の「Threadfin」、フランス名は「ひげのあるもの」という意味の「Barbure rayé」と名付けられている。

Polydactylus plebeius (Perciformes, Polynemidae). This fish is found along the Pacific coast from Fukushima Prefecture to Yakushima Island, along the coasts of the Sea of Japan and the East China Sea from Wakasa Bay to Nagasaki Prefecture, around the Izu and Ogasawara Islands, around the Ryukyu Islands, the Indian Ocean, and the Pacific Ocean. They typically measure 30 cm in length, but some exceed 50 cm in length. Their Japanese name, "Tsubame-konoshiro," comes from their resemblance to the dotted gizzard shad (*Konosirus punctatus*; "konoshiro") and the deep cuts in the tail fins resembling a swallow ("tsubame").

河魚類
ハゼ
蝦虎魚 産物志
彙苑詳註

鯊魚 ハゼ

沙溝魚 俗名
沙鰮魚 鮀魚 雅ニ
沙吹 璞郭
和俗呼ノ川波世。海波世ト
其藪ヲイサ・ト云三月四胃
ヨリ河ニ子ルユト野シ大和本
草鰌魚ノ別ニ録ス則
鯊魚ノ子也

壬辰閏二月
廿一日貞寫

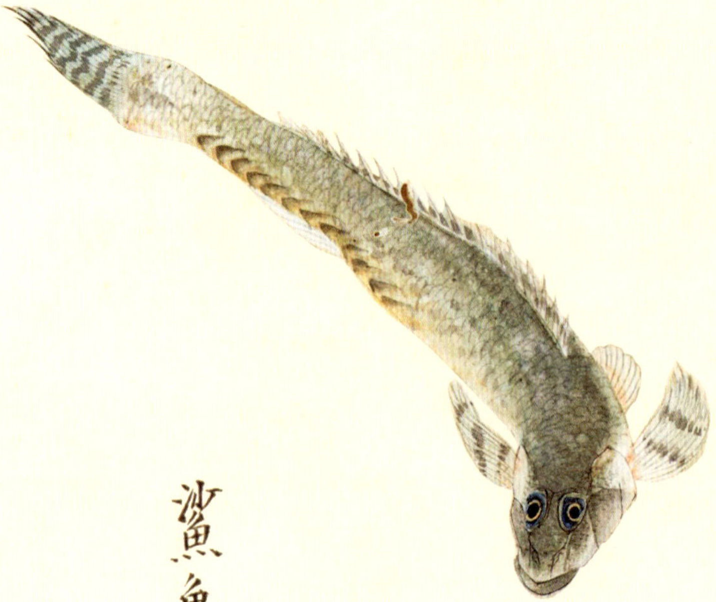

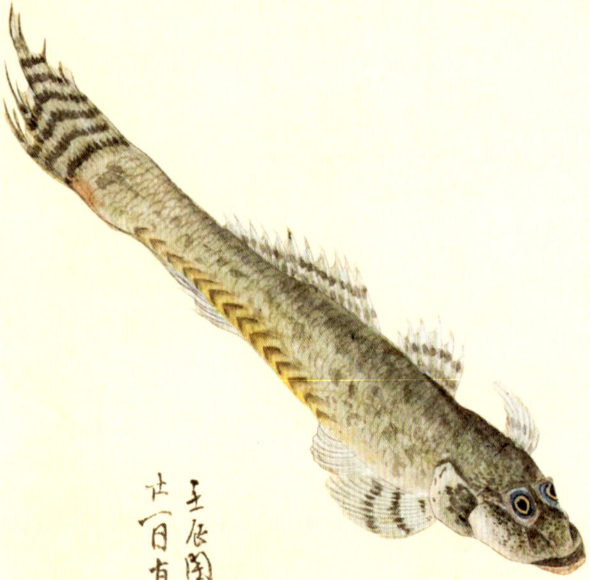

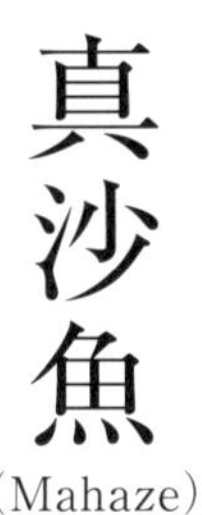

真沙魚
（Mahaze）

モミハゼ
（Momihaze）

グング
（Gungu）

カワギス
（Kawagisu）

カジカ
（Kajika）

蝦虎魚
（Haze）

真鯊
（Mahaze）

マハゼ

Yellowfin goby

スズキ目ハゼ科マハゼ属。学名は*Acanthogobius flavimanus*。北海道から九州南岸までの各沿岸、屋久島、朝鮮半島南西部、中国などに分布する。体長は20〜30cm。和名「マハゼ」は一説によれば、形が陰茎に似ており、陰茎を表す言葉が「ハセ（ハゼの古名）」だったことに由来するという。成長が早く、春に孵化したものが夏には6〜7cmになる。体長によって呼び名が変わり、6〜7cmのものは「デキハゼ」、彼岸の頃に10cmほどに成長したものは「彼岸ハゼ」、冬に20cm前後になると「ケタハゼ」などと呼ばれる。江戸では秋の行楽として、武士や遊び人たちが酒を飲みながらハゼ釣りを競ったという。現在でも東京湾はハゼ釣りの釣り場として知られている。

Acanthogobius flavimanus (Perciformes, Gobiidae). This fish is found along the coasts from Hokkaido to southern Kyushu, around Yakushima Island, the southwestern Korean Peninsula, and China. They typically measure 20 to 30 cm in length. According to one theory, their Japanese name, "mahaze," came from their resemblance to a penis, which was once called a "hase" (ancient word for "haze"). In Edo, one amusement people enjoyed in the autumn was for samurai and playboys to fish for yellowfin goby while drinking. Even now, Tokyo Bay is known as a yellowfin goby fishing spot.

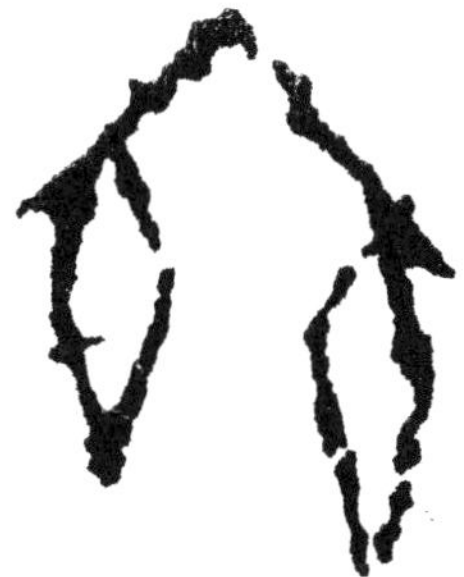

Winter

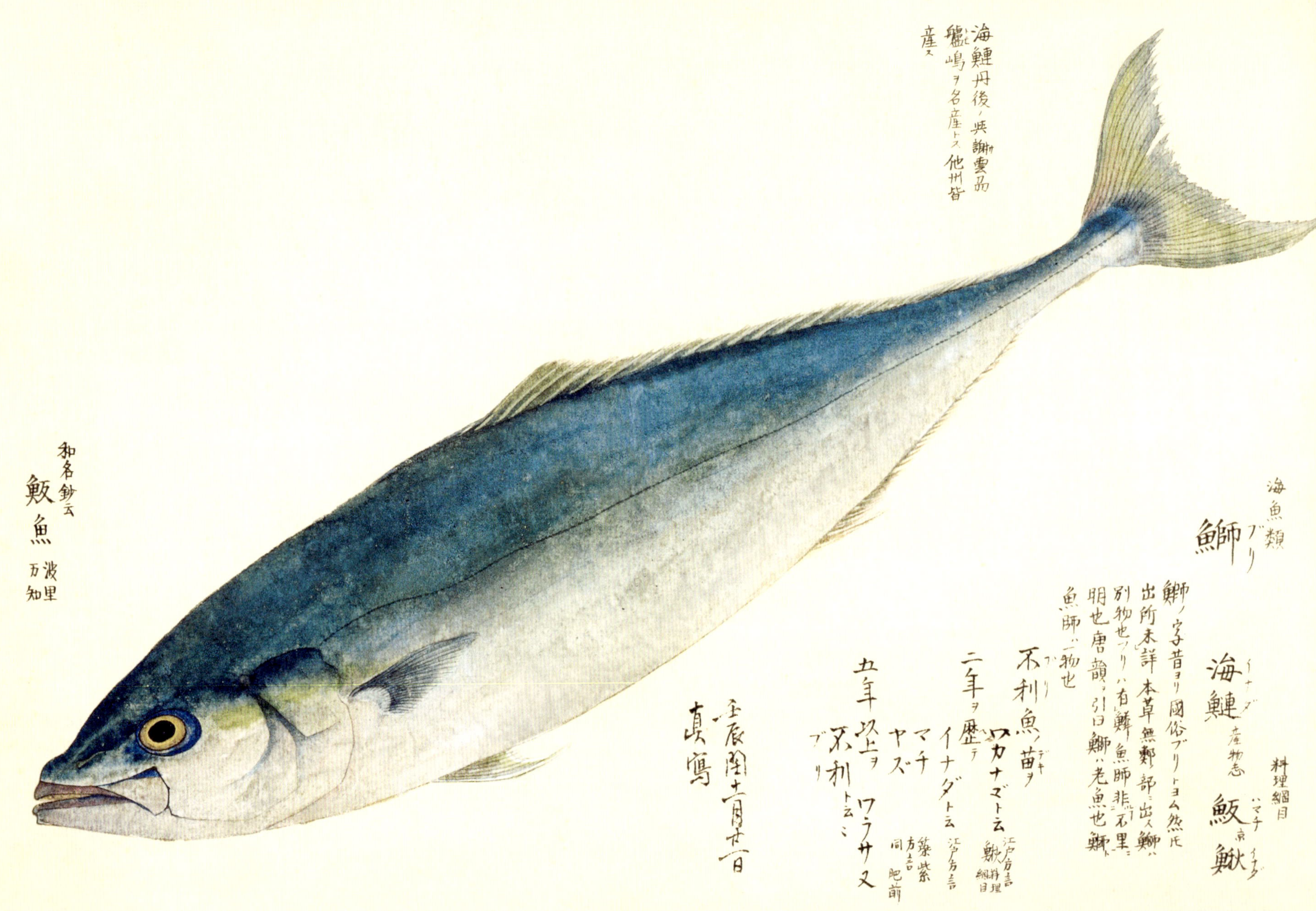

海魚類
ブリ
鰤
海鰤 産物志
料理綱目
鮫 鰍
鰤ノ字昔ヨリ國俗ブリトヨム然ドモ
出所未詳 本草無鄭部ニ出ス鰤ハ
別物也ブリハ有鱗魚師非石里ニ
明也唐韻ニ引曰鰤ハ老魚也鰤ト
魚師ハ一物也
不利魚ノ苗ヲ
二年ヲ歴テ ワカナゴト云
イナダトス マチ ヤズ
五年以上ヲ ワラサ又
海鰤丹後ノ與謝曇品
鑑嶋ヲ名産トス 他州皆
産ス
和名鈔云
鮫魚
万波里
知
壬辰閏十一月廿一日
眞寫

鰤
（Buri）

鰕（Hamachi）　鰍（Inada）　魚師（Buri）

ブリ

Japanese amberjack

スズキ目アジ科ブリ属。学名は*Seriola quinqueradiata*。日本では北海道から九州南岸までの各沿岸、屋久島などに分布する。体長は約100cm。和名の由来は、脂が適度に乗ったものがおいしいことから「アブラ」「ブラ」「ブリ」と転訛したといわれている。漢字の「鰤」は、旧暦の師走の頃に獲れたものが最もおいしいことから「魚」と「師」を組み合わせた、または老魚や大魚の総称である魚師に由来するなど、諸説ある。成長するにつれて名前が変わる出世魚で、東京ではワカシ、イナダ、ワラサ、ブリ、大阪ではツバス、ハマチ、メジロ、ブリと呼ばれる。タイと並んで祝儀魚とされ、尾やひれを板壁などに貼って残しておき、熨斗の代わりにしていた風習が日本各地であった。

Seriola quinqueradiata (Perciformes, Carangidae). This fish is found along the coasts from Hokkaido to southern Kyushu and Yakushima Island. They typically measure 100 cm in length. Their Japanese name, "buri," comes from the delicious flavor they have due to their fat content ("abura" means "fat," and the pronunciation later changed to "bura" and then "buri"). Like red seabream (*Pagrus major*), they are a fixture in congratulatory ceremonies, and in various parts of Japan, it was once customary to affix their tailfins to wooden walls to save them for use in place of noshi decorations on gifts.

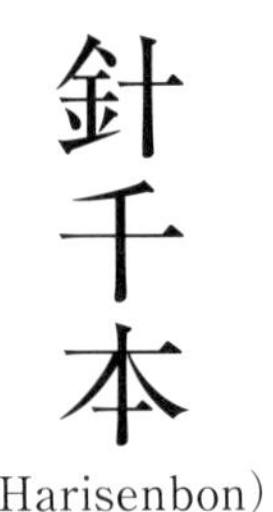

針千本
(Harisenbon)

針河豚
(Harifugu)

毬河豚
(Igafugu)

刺河豚
(Irabukuto)

ハリオ
(Hario)

ハリセンボン

Porcupine fish

フグ目ハリセンボン科ハリセンボン属。学名は*Diodon holocanthus*。世界中の熱帯から温帯域に分布し、日本では北海道から九州南岸までの各沿岸、屋久島、琉球列島などで見られる。体長は約30cm。和名「ハリセンボン」は、危険を察知すると体を膨らませ、たくさんの棘を逆立てることに由来する。漢字では「針千本」と書くが、実際の棘の数は350〜400本ほどといわれている。山陰や伊勢、志摩、三河地方には、魔除けとしてハリセンボンで作ったフグ提灯を戸口にかける風習がある。山陰・北陸地方では12月8日に海が荒れて大量のハリセンボンが海岸に打ち上げられたことから、この日をハリセンボンと呼ぶことがある。また、日本では地域によって12月8日を針供養の日としている。

Diodon holocanthus (Tetraodontiformes, Diodontidae). This fish is found around the world, from tropical to temperate areas. In Japan, they are found on coasts from Hokkaido to the southern coast of Kyushu, around Yakushima Island, and around the Ryukyu Islands. They typically measure 30 cm in length. Their Japanese name, "harisenbon" (literally "a thousand needles") , comes from the fact that when threatened, they puff up, causing their spines to radiate outward. Although their name means "a thousand needles," in reality they are said to have roughly 350 to 400 spines.

食物本草

䰶魚　一種　ハリセンボン　海産

佐渡國ニテ毎貝ニ記

針千本　ハリフグ

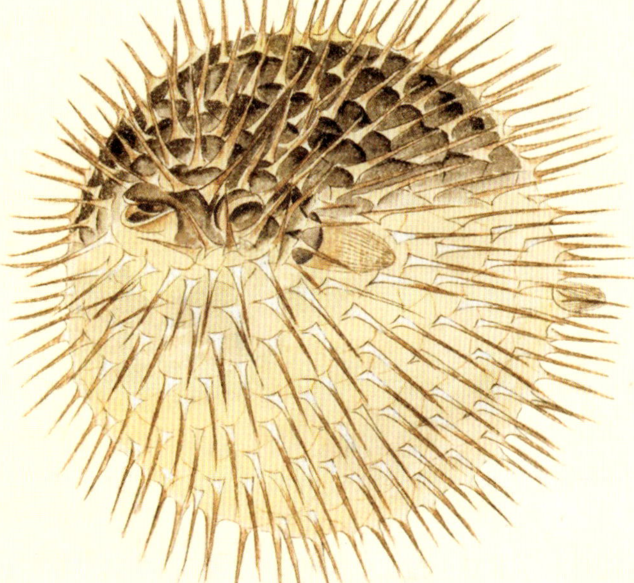

針千本漢名魚虎又鬼頭魚ナリト
云者アリ非也魚虎ハ簑カケフグナリ
針千本ニ似テ其刺伏シテ甚ヲ者タル
刀如ニ其刺直立スル者則針千本也
䰶魚ノ類猶多シ不可盡知佐
渡六三十種ノ異魚アリ大厦ニ記

針千本　箱フグ　鯛ノ智源ハ
禿骨畢列　龍宮ノ鶏
鉦敲魚　海馬
瘤鯛　此類三十首アリト跡ハ未詳

本多氏所藏　天保十
己亥年四月十日真寫

彼岸河豚

（Higanfugu）

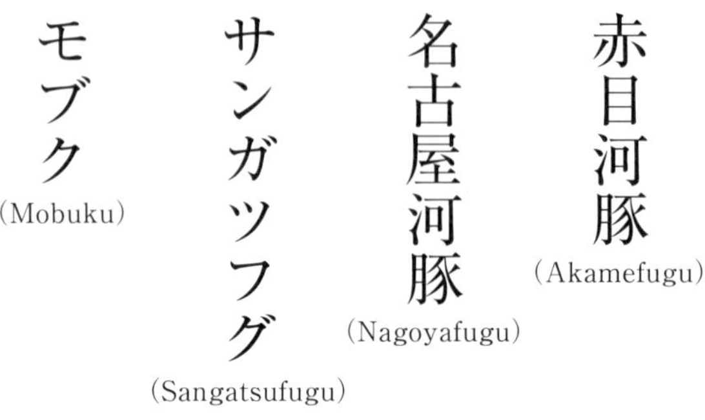

赤目河豚
（Akamefugu）

名古屋河豚
（Nagoyafugu）

サンガツフグ
（Sangatsufugu）

モブク
（Mobuku）

ヒガンフグ

Panther puffer

フグ目フグ科トラフグ属。学名は *Takifugu pardalis*。北海道から九州南岸までの各沿岸、朝鮮半島、東シナ海などに分布する。体長は20〜30cm。体表にいぼ状の小隆起がある。体の背側は褐色で黒色の斑点がある。基本的に筋肉は無毒とされるが、東北地方の一部地域では有毒個体も発見されている。特に肝臓と卵巣が猛毒。和名「ヒガンフグ」は、春の彼岸の頃に美味になる、また漁獲量が増えることから。地方名に「アカメフグ」があるが、標準和名「アカメフグ（*Takifugu chrysops*）」とは別種。地方名の「ナゴヤフグ」は毒にあたると死ぬので「尾張名古屋で終わり」とかけた、もしくは「毒にあたると美濃尾張（身の終わり）」という洒落から付いたといわれている。

Takifugu pardalis (Tetraodontiformes, Tetraodontidae). This fish is found along the coasts from Hokkaido to southern Kyushu, the Korean Peninsula, and the East China Sea. They typically measure 20 to 30 cm in length. There are small bumps on their skin. Their backs are brown with black spots. Generally speaking, their flesh is not poisonous, but poisonous individuals have been found in some parts of the Tohoku region. Their livers and egg sacs, however, are highly poisonous. Their Japanese name, "higanfugu," is said to come from them being especially delicious during the equinoctial week ("higan") in spring, or from catches being large during this time of the year.

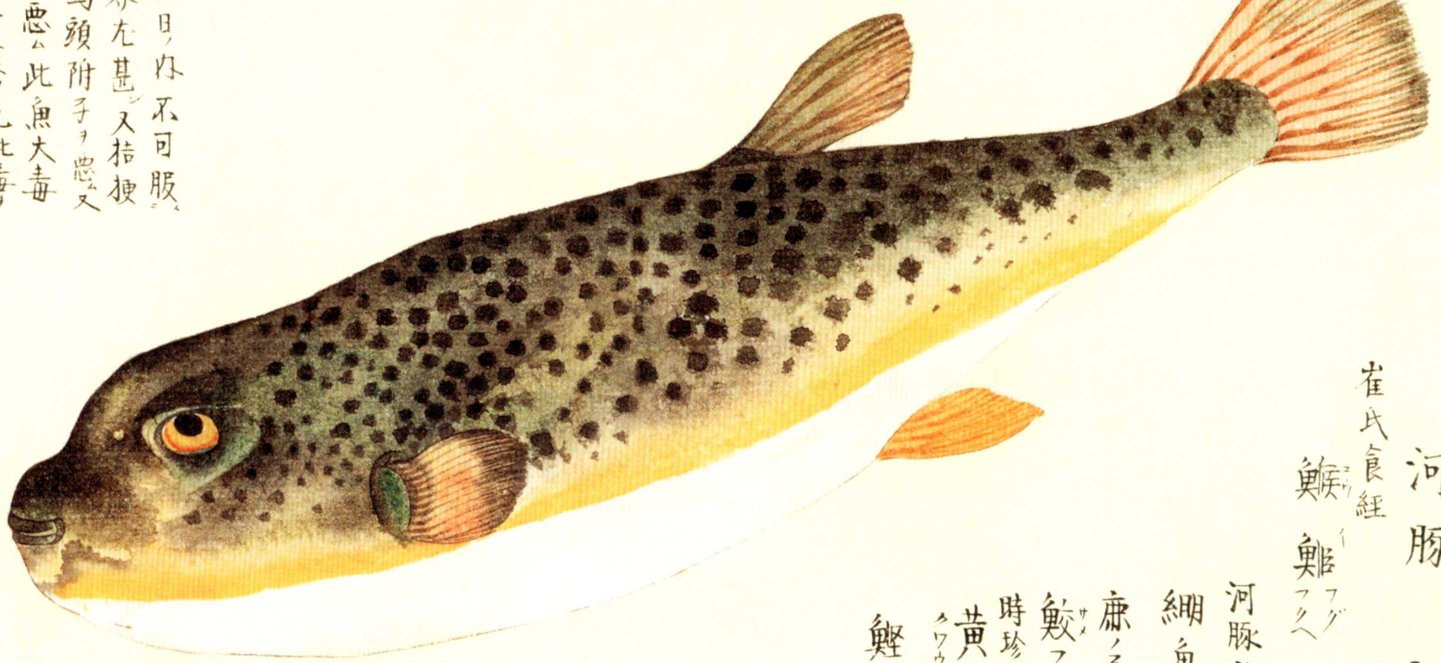

輟耕録ニ
凡食河豚一日ノ内不可服
湯薬ニ荊芥尤甚シ又拮梗
菊花甘州烏頭附子ヲ忌ム又
菠薐竹左悪ム此魚大毒
アレ此人多好ンテ食フ凡此毒ヲ
解スルニハ栗魚ヲ煎シ服ハ或ハ
生ニテ食ノ甚寄ナリ丹薬ニ勝
リ河豚慣食ノ膳ニハ必栗
魚ヲ付ルモ此故ナリ乾シテ河豚
毒絶テナシ端午ノ扇物ナリ

癸午十月廿二日麻布
龍士楼上三真寫

本草綱目　河豚　フグ　トミ　下総銚子
崔氏食経
鯸　フグ　テッホウ　江戸
鮐　フクヘ　マフグ
斑魚　把之則怒怒斯腰張浮出水上者也
河豚種類ヲタシ
緷魚　時珍食物本草出ス　ショサイフグ
廉ノ子フク　赤目フク　一名苗代フグ　大毒アリ
鮫フグ　虎フクノ一種　サメ
時珍ス
黄鑬　トラフク
鮭フク　フワウ
箱フク　薩州ニ産青色
島フク　堅魚ノ如シ
海牛フグ　スメ
裏カケフグ虎魚
針千本
針フグ

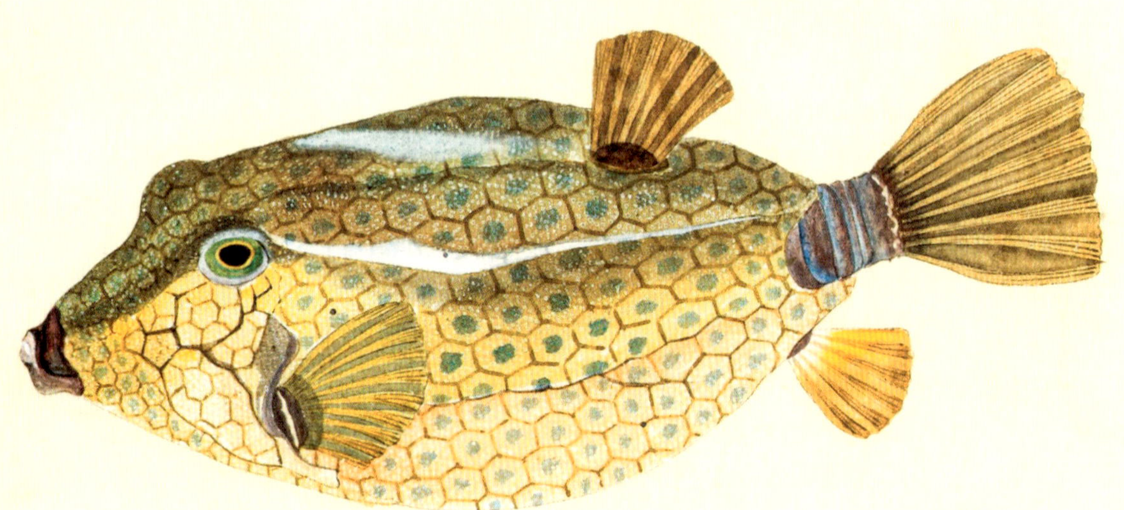

此者其惣身硬クシテ石ノ如ニ
其尾鬣有所ニ皆穴アリテ柔ニ
動ノ海牛ノ類也長崎ノ海ニ
多シ東武稀ナル者ニテ名ハ多
ク遠クヨリ喜ス生ナル者始親
見ス

乙未十月六日
名橋氏ヨリ送之
貞寫

箱河豚
(Hakofugu)

キツネ
(Kitsune)

シュウリ
(Shuri)

スッポ
(Suppo)

セキフグ
(Sekifugu)

モチゴメブク
(Mochigomebuku)

ハコフグ

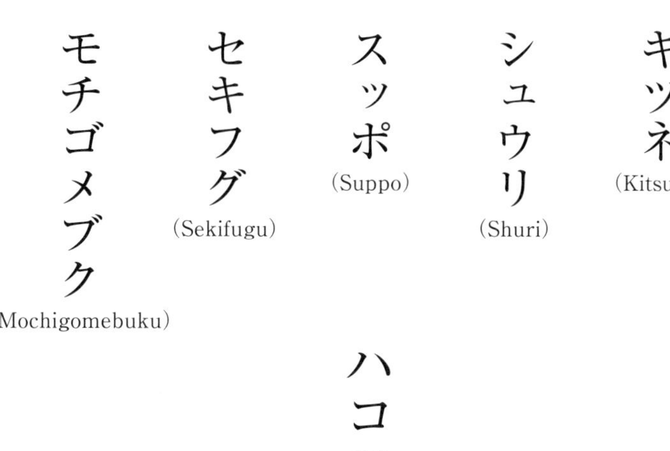

Bluespotted boxfish

フグ目ハコフグ科ハコフグ属。学名は*Ostracion immaculatum*。北海道から屋久島までの太平洋沿岸、青森県から九州南岸までの日本海・東シナ海沿岸、朝鮮半島南岸・東岸などに分布する。体長は20〜30cm。和名「ハコフグ」は、箱形のフグという意。英名の「Boxfish」、仏名の「Coffre」も箱やトランクの形に因む。属名の*Ostracion*はギリシャ語の「陶器、貝殻」に由来するが、これは体が硬いことから付けられた。外部から刺激されると魚に効く粘液毒を皮膚から分泌する。食用とされ、五島列島では名物料理とされるが、パリトキシン様毒での中毒が稀に発生している。観賞魚とすることもあるが、小さな水槽内では自身の粘液毒で死ぬことがあるので注意が必要。

Ostracion immaculatum (Tetraodontiformes, Ostraciidae). This fish is found along the Pacific coast from Hokkaido to Yakushima Island, along the coasts of the Sea of Japan and East China Sea from Aomori Prefecture to southern Kyushu, and the southern and eastern coasts of the Korean Peninsula. They typically measure 20 to 30 cm in length. Their Japanese name, "hakofugu," comes from them resembling a box-shaped ("hako") puffer ("fugu"). When threatened, their skin secretes poisonous mucus that is effective against other fish. They are sometimes kept as pets, but care must be taken, as in a small aquarium they can die from their own poisonous mucus.

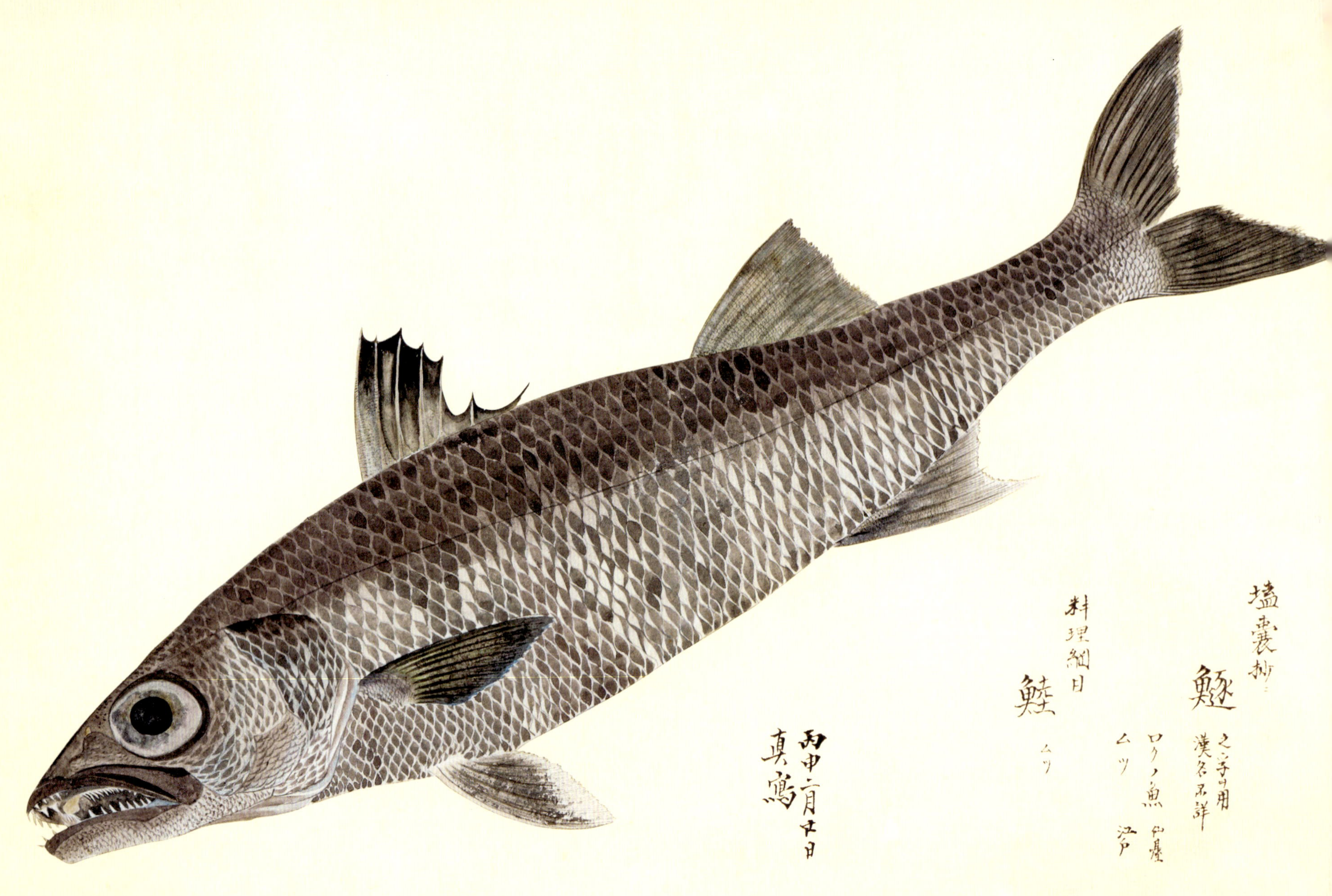

塩竈柳
鯥　之ヲ子ニ用　漢名ヲ不詳
ロクノ魚　和屋　ムツ　江戸
料理細目　鯥　ムツ
丙申二月廿日　真寫

鯥
（Mutsu）

鮏
（Mutsu）

六之魚
（Rokunouo）

オンシラズ
（Onshirazu）

ムツ

Gnomefish

スズキ目ムツ科ムツ属。学名は*Scombrops boops*。北海道から九州南岸までの日本周辺海域、朝鮮半島南岸などに分布する。体長は約60㎝。高級な食用魚とされ、特に冬は脂が乗り、美味である。和名「ムツ」は脂っこいことを意味する「むつっこい」「むつこい」という方言が語源といわれる。地方名も多数あり、相模湾周辺の呼び名に「オンシラズ」がある。幼魚は浅瀬に棲み、親魚のいる深い海にはいかないことから、この名前が付いたという。仙台では「ロクノウオ」と呼ばれるが、これは仙台の藩主であった伊達家が「陸奥守」という官職であったため、「ムツ」では藩主を呼び捨てにしてしまうという理由から「六ツ」にかけて「ロクノウオ」と呼ぶようになったという。

Scombrops boops (Perciformes, Scombropidae). This fish is found in the seas around Japan from Hokkaido to southern Kyushu, and along the southern coast of the Korean Peninsula. They typically measure 60 cm in length. They are considered delicacies, and are especially tasty in winter, when their fat content is highest. Their Japanese name, "mutsu," comes from "mutsukkoi" or "mutsukoi," which in one Japanese dialect means "fatty." In the Sagami Bay area they are sometimes called "onshirazu" ("ingrates") because young gnomefish live in the shallows and do not go to the deeper sea, where their parents are.

鰶
(Konoshiro)

都奈之
(Tsunashi)

小鰭
(Kohada)

鯯
(Konoshiro)

鮗
(Konoshiro)

子の代
(Konoshiro)

コノシロ

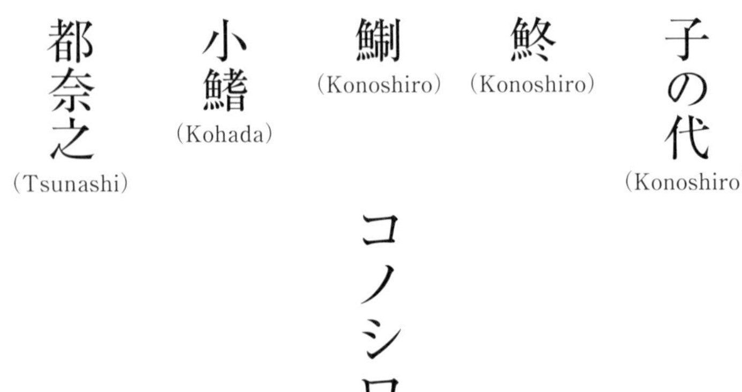

Dotted gizzard shad

ニシン目ニシン科コノシロ属。学名は*Konosirus punctatus*。新潟県および松島湾以南から南シナ海北部にかけて主に分布する。体長は20〜30cm。江戸後期の『物類称呼』によると、子どもが生まれても早逝する家では子どもが生まれたときに胞衣とコノシロを一緒に埋めるとその子は成長するが、その子には一生コノシロを食べさせてはいけないとあり、「子の代」と呼ばれるようになったという。さらに江戸後期の随筆『塵塚談』には「武家は決して食せざりしものなり」とあり、コノシロを食すのは「この城を食べる」ことになるため、武士は「コハダ」と呼んだとある。また、腹部が破れやすいため「切腹魚」と呼ばれ、武士の切腹で用いたことから忌み嫌われた魚だったという。

Konosirus punctatus (Clupeiformes, Clupeidae). This fish is primarily found in Niigata Prefecture and from Matsushima Bay southward to the northern reaches of the South China Sea. They typically measure 20 to 30 cm in length. Their Japanese name, "konoshiro," comes from a term meaning "child's replacement" because of a folk belief that if one's child dies shortly after birth, the next time one gives birth, one should bury the baby's placenta with a dotted gizzard shad so that the new child will grow healthily. However, the new child must never eat dotted gizzard shad.

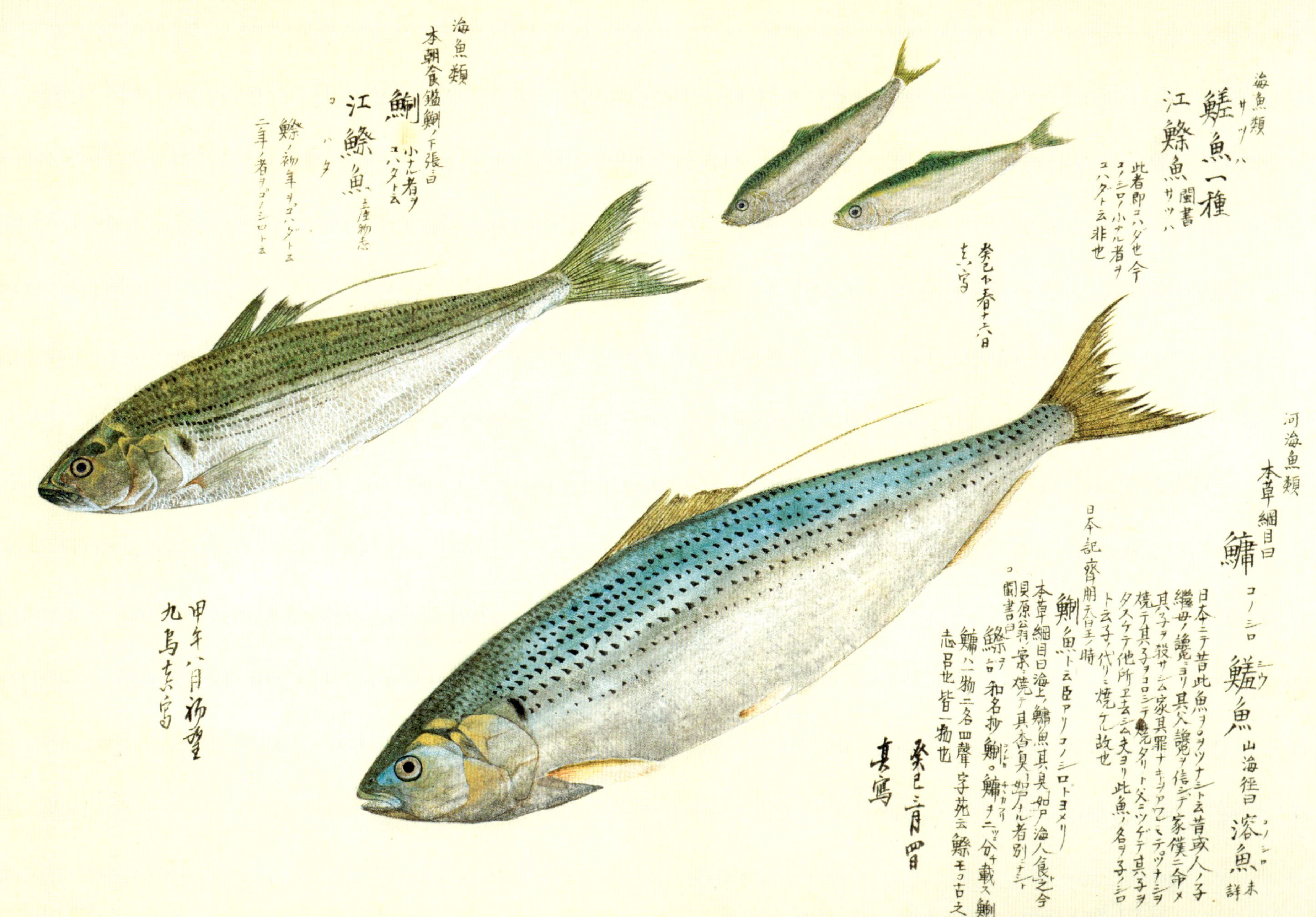

海魚類 サツパ
鯦魚一種
江鰶魚 閩書
江鰶魚 サツパ
海魚類
本朝食鑑鯦附下張曰
鯯
江鰶魚
河海魚類 本草綱目
鱅 コノシロ
鯦魚

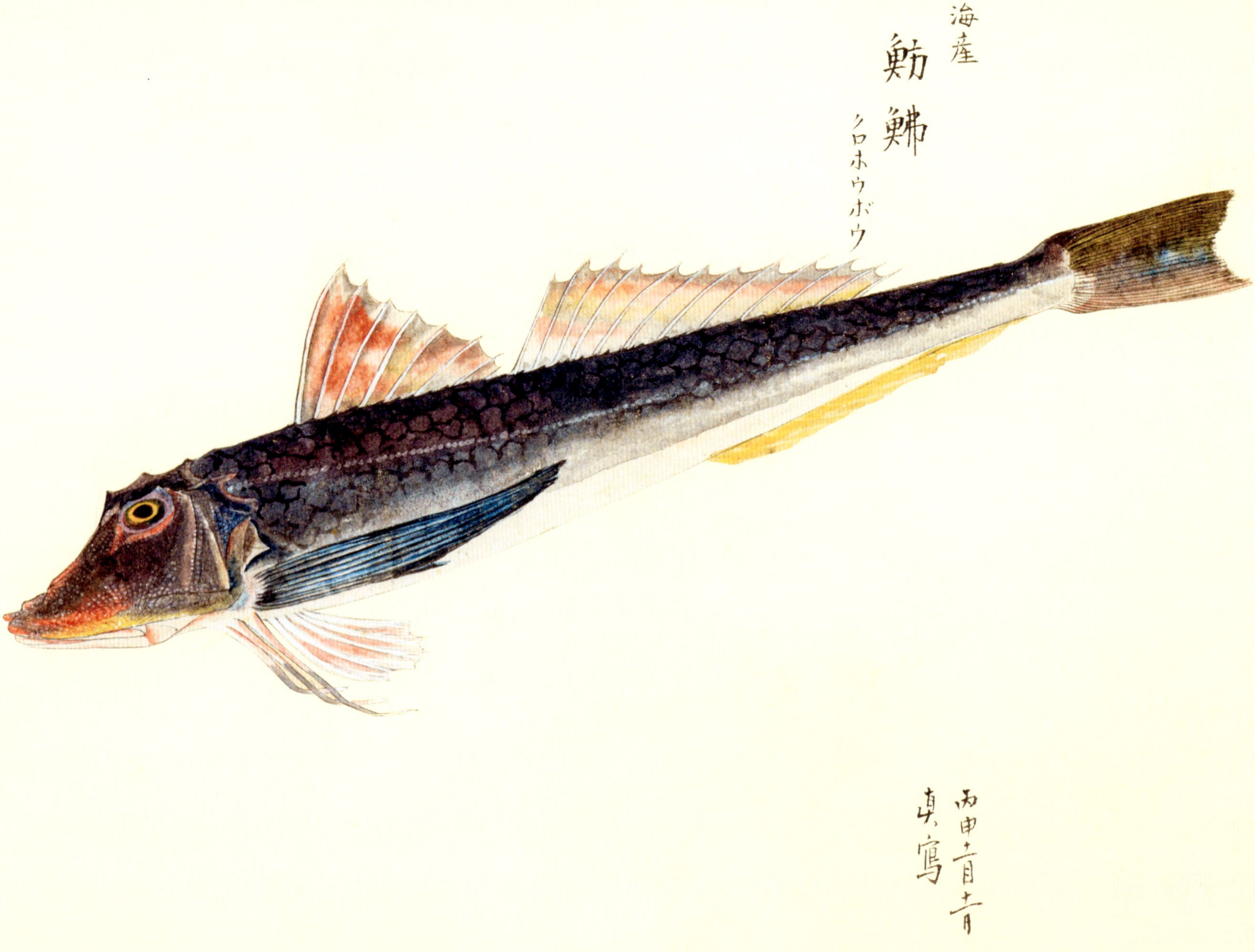

海産
魡鯡
クロホウボウ
丙申十一月十一
真寫

魴鮄
(Hobo)

琴弾 (Kotohiki)　金頭 (Kanagashira)　君魚 (Kimiyo)　竹麦魚 (Hobo)

ホウボウ

Spiny red gurnard

スズキ目ホウボウ科ホウボウ属。学名は*Chelidonichthys spinosus*。日本では北海道から九州南岸までの各沿岸などに分布する。体長は25〜30cm。硬い骨板に覆われた四角く大きい頭部と、胸びれの下方の軟条が遊離して発達しているのが特徴。和名「ホウボウ」は頭が角張っていることから「方帽（ホウボウ・四角い帽子）」「方頭（カナガシラ）」に由来するという説や、浮き袋による鳴き声がホウボウと聞こえるためという説などがある。また、新潟県などの地方名「キミヨ」は、藩主がホウボウを好んで食べたことから敬称で呼ぶようになったといわれている。江戸時代から食用とされていたようで、『和漢三才図会』には「炙って食べれば大へん美味」とある。

Chelidonichthys spinosus (Perciformes, Triglidae). This fish is found in Japan along the coasts from Hokkaido to southern Kyushu. They typically measure 25 to 30 cm in length. They are notable for the hard bone plate that covers their large, square head and for because the lower soft rays of their dorsal fins have developed to be separate from the other soft rays. Their Japanese name, "hobo" ("mortarboard"), is due to the angular shape of their head. They have been eaten since the Edo era (1603–1867), and the encyclopedia *Wakan Sansai Zue* says that they are delicious when grilled.

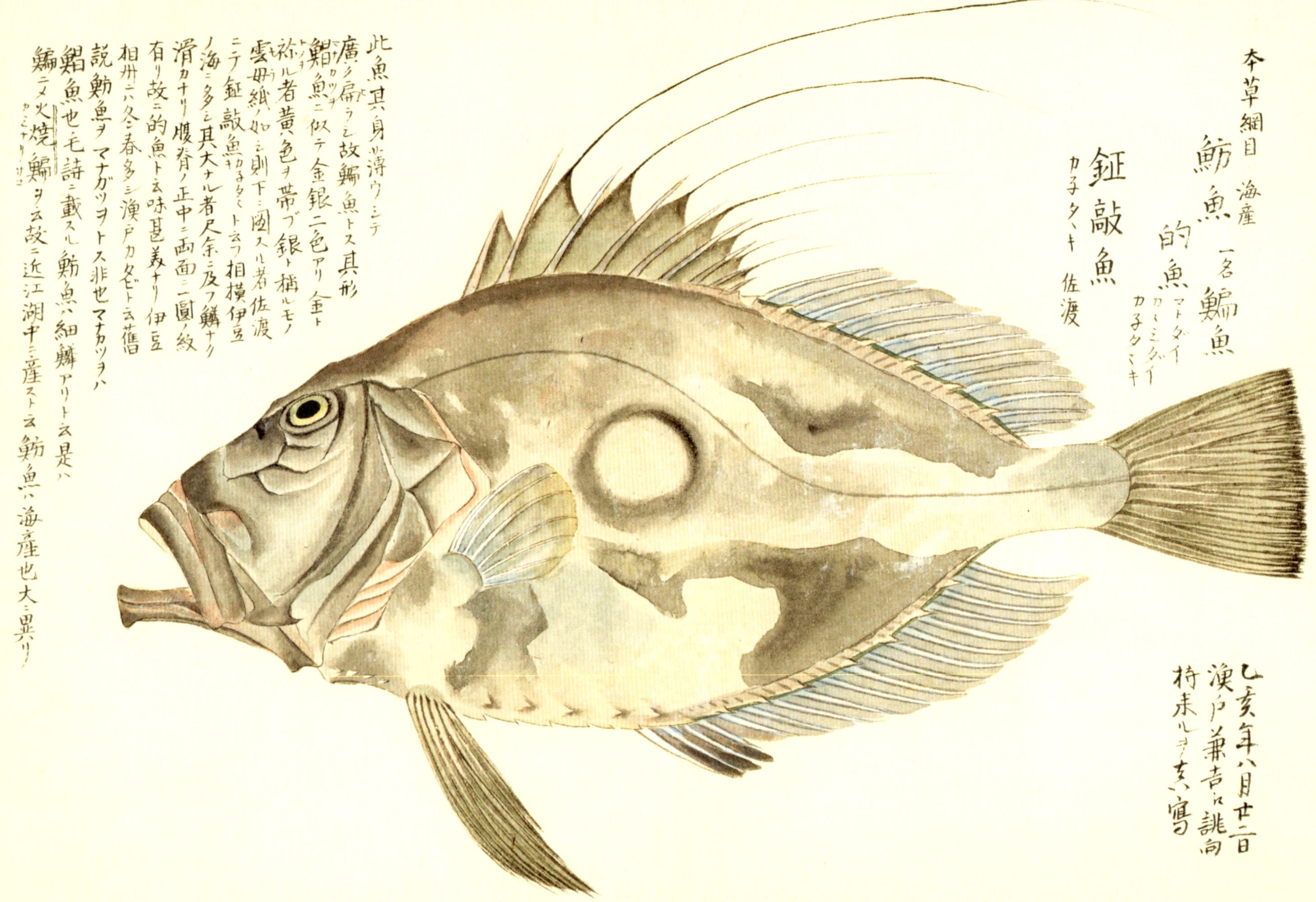

本草綱目　海産
鯮魚　一名　鯆魚
的魚　マトダイ　カヽミダイ　カネタヽキ
鉦敲魚　カ子タヽキ　佐渡
乙亥年八月廿二日
漁戸兼吉ニ誂ヒ
持来ルヲ以テ真寫

的鯛

（Matodai）

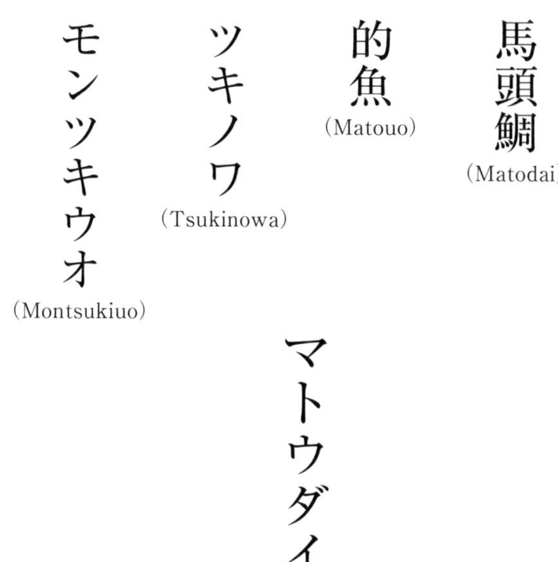

馬頭鯛
（Matodai）

的魚
（Matouo）

ツキノワ
（Tsukinowa）

モンツキウオ
（Montsukiuo）

マトウダイ

John Dory

マトウダイ目マトウダイ科マトウダイ属。学名は*Zeus faber*。日本では北海道から九州南岸までの各沿岸、東シナ海大陸棚域に分布する。体長は30〜40cmのものが多いが、50cmを超すものもいる。体側の中央部に大きな丸い黒褐色斑があるのが特徴で、和名「マトウダイ」は、この黒褐色斑を弓の的に見立てたことに由来する。他にも顔が馬の頭に似ていることから、「馬頭鯛」と呼ばれるようになったという説もある。「モンツキウオ」などの地方名もある。フランスでは、この黒褐色斑が聖ペテロがマトウダイの口からコインを取り出そうとしたときの指の跡という伝承から、「サン・ペテロの魚」という意味で「Saint pierre（サン・ピエール）」と呼ばれている。

Zeus faber (Zeiformes, Zeidae). This fish is found in Japan along the coasts from Hokkaido to southern Kyushu and around the East China Sea continental shelf. They typically measure 30 to 40 cm in length, but some exceed 50 cm in length. They are notable for a large round black spot at the center of each side of the body, and their Japanese name, "matodai," comes from the spot looking like an archery target ("mato"). In France, the legend is that the spots are from fingerprints of St. Peter trying to take a coin from the mouth of the John Dory, so in French they are called "Saint-Pierre."

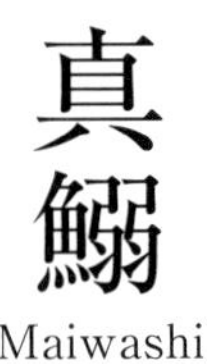

真鰯

(Maiwashi)

真鰮 (Maiwashi)

御紫 (Omura)

コバ (Koba)

ナナツボシ (Nanatsuboshi)

ヒラゴ (Hirago)

マイワシ

Japanese sardine

ニシン目ニシン科マイワシ属。学名は*Sardinops melanostictus*。日本では北海道から九州南岸までの各沿岸などに分布する。体長は20～30cm。「イワシ」の名前は「卑しい魚」で「いやし」や、水から揚げるとすぐに死んでしまうくらい弱いので「よわし」が転訛したといわれている。「マ」はイワシ類の代表種という意味。古くから食用とされてきたが、平安時代には卑しい魚といわれ、宮中ではその塩糟が紫黒くなることから「御紫」と呼ばれていた。それでも、紫式部や和泉式部はイワシが好物だったため、人目を忍んで食べていたという。また、節分の時期にはイワシのにおいとヒイラギの棘が鬼を祓う魔除けになるといわれ、イワシの頭をヒイラギの枝に刺して戸口に立てる風習がある。

Sardinops melanostictus (Clupeiformes, Clupeidae). This fish is found in Japan along the coasts from Hokkaido to southern Kyushu. They typically measure 20 to 30 cm in length. Their Japanese name, "maiwashi," is said to come from them being seen as lowly ("iyashi") fish or because they are weak ("yowashi"), dying quickly when taken out of the water. The "ma" indicates that they are a representative variety of "iwashi." They have long been used as food. It is said that the famous 10th century poets Murasaki Shikibu and Izumi Shikibu were great lovers of Japanese sardine and would eat them when no one was looking.

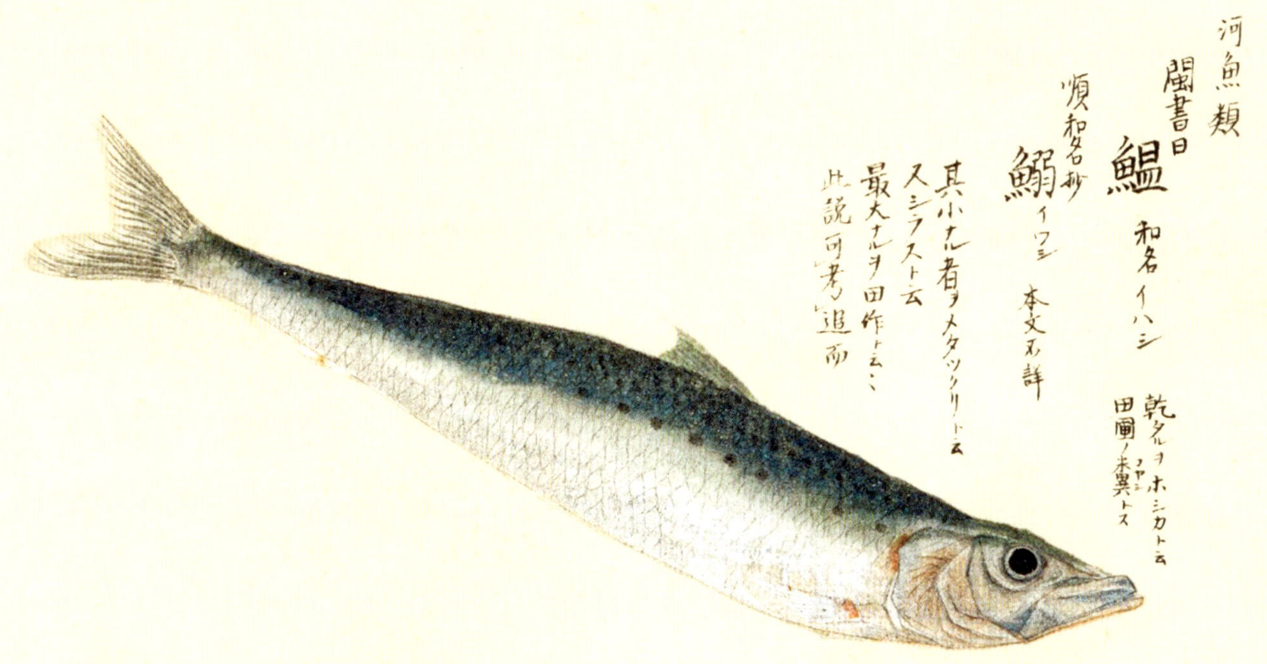

河魚類
闇書曰　鰮　和名イハシ
乾タルヲホシカトモ云
田圃ノ糞トス
順和名抄　鰯　イワシ　本文不詳
其小ナル者ヲメタツクリトモ云
最大ナルヲ田作ト云ヘハ
此説可考ノ迫而

楊梅大納言撰語抄ニ
鰯　イワシ　ヨホリ　又ハヲムラ

鰯所々ノ海ニ産スルト雖モ武州
内海ノ産ヲ所渭江都前ト
シ他国ノ産ニ勝リ化漢人ハ大
利ヲ得ル者クジラニ次ゲリ乾鰯
トシ稲ノタヤシトス紀州若州丹州
備中備後安藝周州讃州豊
後ヨリ多ク出ス是民用ニ利ノ者
他魚ニ勝リ塩漬久シキヲ歴テ
食フニ堪サル者ヲ赤イワシトモ云
今節分ノ夜柊ト共ニ門上
壁間ニ挿シテ邪鬼ヲ
避ル

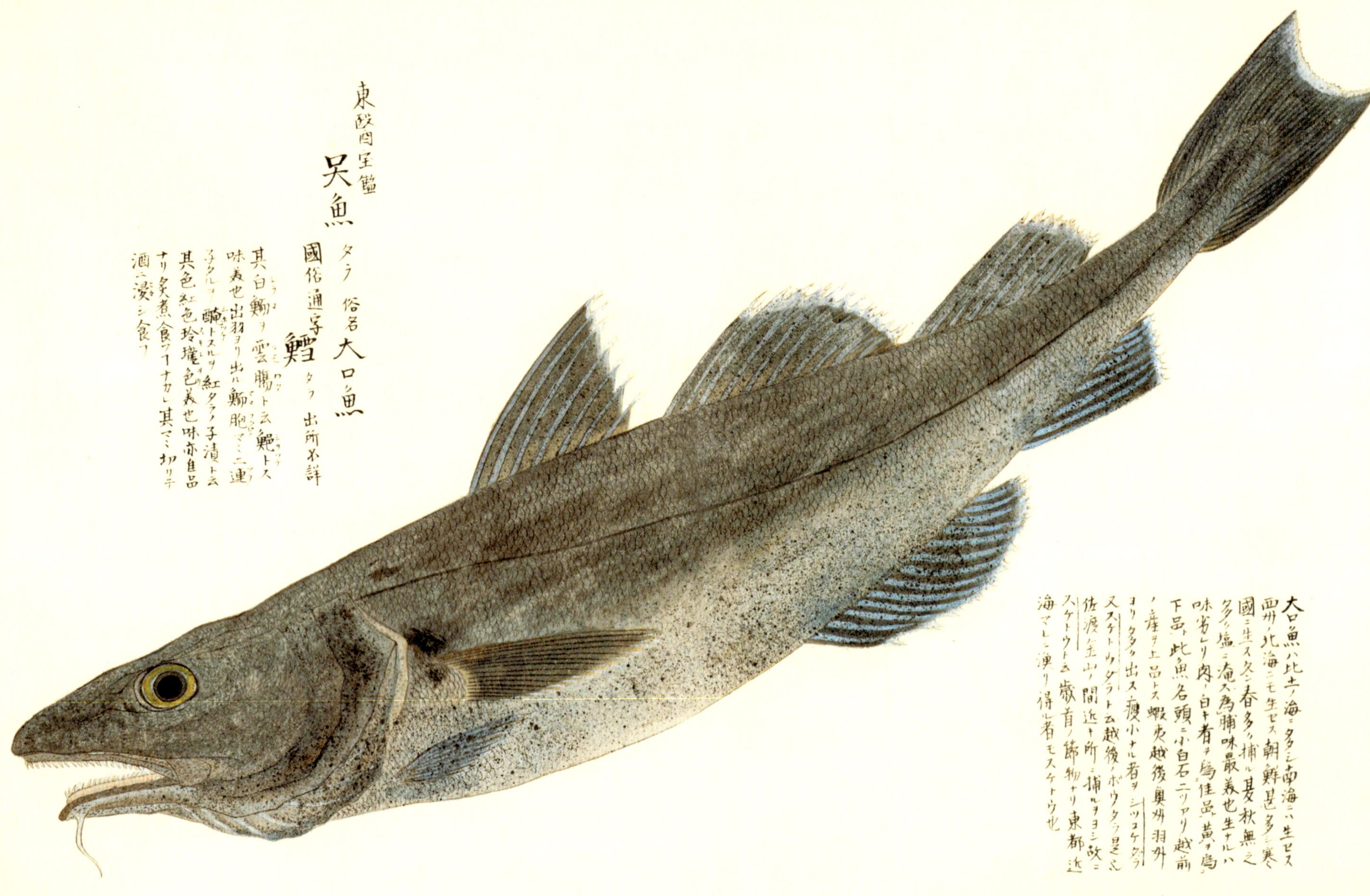

東腰間屋呈鹽
吳魚　タラ　俗名　大口ノ魚
國俗通字　鱈
其白蒻ヲ雲腸トス鰾トス
味美也出羽ヨリ出ス鰤腸ニ運
ブトイフ鮞トスル紅タラ子漬トス
其色紅色玲瓏色美也味赤佳品
ナリ又煮食ブイナカシ其ミ切リテ
酒ニ漬シ食フ
大口ノ魚ハ比ヒ十ノ海ニタヽシ南海ニハ生ゼス
西州ノ北海ニモ生ゼス多シ寒
國ニ生ス冬ヨリ春ニ多ク葛秋ニ無之
多ク塩ニ魚大為シ脯味最美也生ナルハ
味劣ニ肉ヲ白キ者ヲ為シ佳品黄ノ鳥
下品此魚名頭ニ小白石ニツアリ越前
ノ産ナリ上品トス蝦夷越後奥州羽州
ヨリクタク出ス渡小ナル者ヲシッケタラ
スケトヽダラト云越後ノボウタラ見ユ
佐渡ニ多シ出ノ間近キ所ニ捕ルヽチヨシ故ニ
スケトウト云歳ニヨリ東都近
海ニ多シ漁リ得ル者モスケトウ也

真鱈
（Madara）

大口魚
（Tara）

太羅
（Tara）

雪魚
（Tara）

鱈
（Tara）

マダラ

Pacific cod

タラ目タラ科マダラ属。学名は*Gadus macrocephalus*。北海道全沿岸、青森県から山口県までの日本海沿岸、青森県から茨城県までの太平洋沿岸、渤海、黄海などに分布する。体長は最大で120cmに達する大型魚。和名「マダラ」は、体表が斑であることに由来するという説など諸説ある。「鱈」の漢字は雪が降る時期の魚であることから作られたといわれ、江戸時代の『本朝食鑑』にも「初雪の後の冬に獲れるので鱈をあてると言われる」とある。身だけでなく卵や内臓も珍味とされる。江戸時代には縁起物として将軍家に献上された。タラの生命力の強さや切っても出血しないことから珍重されたという。「鱈腹食べる」という表現は、タラが大食いで腹が膨れていることから生まれた言葉。

Gadus macrocephalus (Gadiformes, Gadidae). This fish is found along the coast of Japan north of Yamaguchi and Ibaraki Prefectures, the Bohai Sea, and the Yellow Sea. The fish can grow up to 120 cm in length. One of many theories regarding their Japanese name, "madara," is that it comes from the spotted appearance ("madara") of their body. During the Edo era (1603–1867), they were sent to the family in line to accede to the shogunate as an auspicious gift. It is said that they were treasured because of their strong vitality and the fact that they do not bleed when cut.

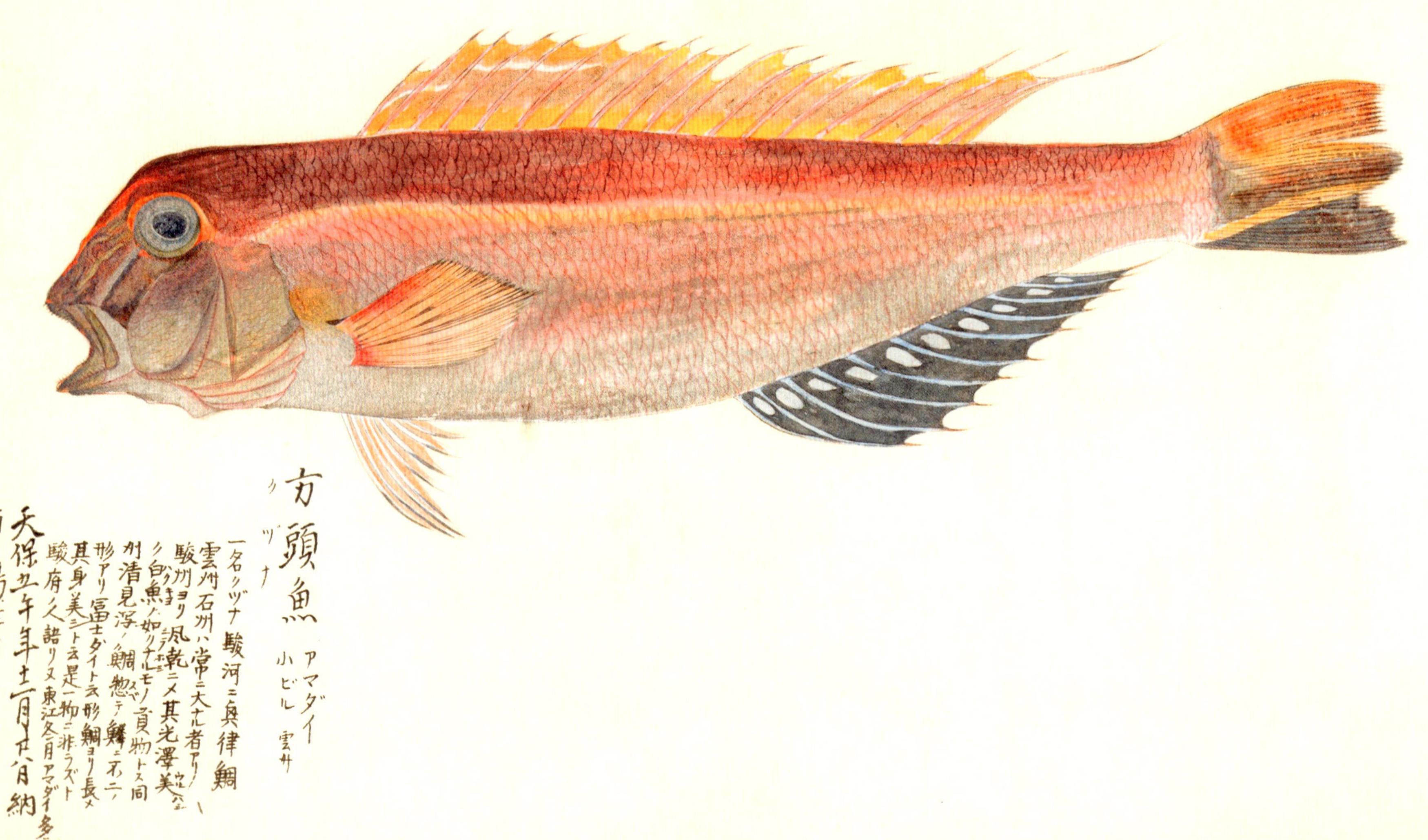

方頭魚　アマダイ
クヅナ
小ビル　雲州

一名クヅナ　駿河ニ兵律鯛
雲州石州ハ常ニ大ナル者アリ
駿州ヨリ汎乾シメ其光澤美
ク白魚ノ如クリモノ貢物トス同
形アリ冨士タイト云形ノ鯛ヨリ長メ
其身ハ美シトテ足一物ニ非ラズト
駿府ヘ語リヌ東江冬月アマダイ多シ
清見浦ノ鯛惣テ鱸ニ不二

天保五午年十二月廿六日納
貞鳥筆

黄甘鯛
（Kiamadai）

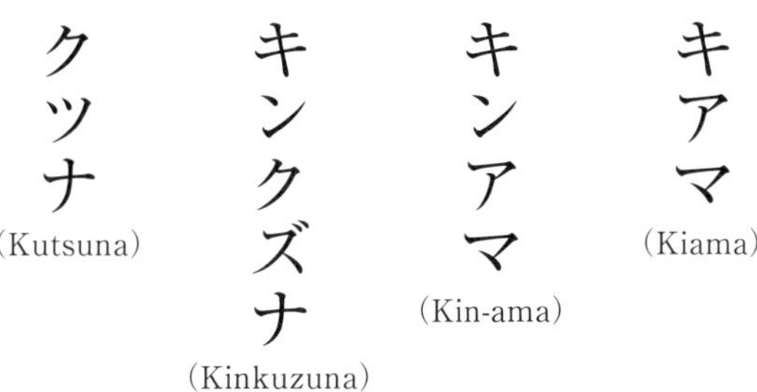

キアマ
（Kiama）

キンアマ
（Kin-ama）

キンクズナ
（Kinkuzuna）

クツナ
（Kutsuna）

キアマダイ

Yellow horsehead (Tilefish)

スズキ目アマダイ科アマダイ属。学名は*Branchiostegus auratus*。日本では千葉県銚子、紀伊水道から九州南岸までの太平洋沿岸、若狭湾以西の日本海沿岸、対馬、九州西岸、東シナ海大陸棚域などに分布する。体長は25〜30cmのものが多いが、大きいものでは50cmに達する。和名の由来は黄色を帯びたアマダイという意。外見はアカアマダイに似ているが、アカアマダイは眼の後下縁に三角形状の銀白色斑があり体の色も赤みが強く、キアマダイは眼の下から上顎にかけて銀白色の線が1本あり、体の色も黄色みが強いことで区別できる。静岡ではアマダイを生干ししたものを「オツキダイ」と呼ぶが、一説には徳川家康が駿河湾興津沖で獲れたものを「興津鯛」と言ったのが由来となったという。

Branchiostegus auratus (Perciformes, Branchiostegidae). This fish is found near Choshi in Chiba Prefecture, along the Pacific coast from Kii Channel to southern Kyushu, along the coast of the Sea of Japan west of Wakasa Bay, Tsushima, the western coast of Kyushu, and the East China Sea continental shelf area. They typically measure 25 to 30 cm in length. Their Japanese name, "kiamadai," comes from the fact that they are yellow ("ki") tilefish ("amadai"). In the Shizuoka area, dried tilefish are called "okitsudai." One theory is that this comes from Tokugawa Ieyasu catching them off the coast of Okitsu in the former province of Suruga.

鮟鱇
(Anko)

アンコモチ
(Ankomochi)

アンコ
(Anko)

アゴ
(Ago)

老婆魚
(Robagyo)

琵琶魚
(Biwauo)

華臍魚
(Kaseigyo)

アンコウ

Blackmouth angler

アンコウ目アンコウ科アンコウ属。学名は*Lophiomus setigerus*。北海道から九州南岸までの各沿岸、東シナ海、インド-西太平洋などに分布する。体長は約100cm。頭部は大きく、縦扁している。褐色で鱗はない。和名「アンコウ」の由来については諸説あるが、『新釈魚名考』によると「暗愚魚」の音便とある。食用とされ、身よりも肝臓（あん肝）が珍重されている。古くから食用とされてきた魚で、江戸時代には鮟鱇汁などにして食べていたという。『本朝食鑑』には「この魚、皮肉骨腸胆、皆食うべし」とある。他にも、江戸初期には冬のアンコウは献上物にされたこと、公家で食される高級魚であったこと、庶民は値下がりする春になってから食べていたことが記されている。

Lophiomus setigerus (Lophiiformes, Lophiidae). This fish is found in Japan along the coasts from Hokkaido to southern Kyushu, in the East China Sea, and in the Indian and western Pacific Oceans. They typically measure 100 cm in length. There are various theories of the origins of their Japanese name, "anko," one of which is that it is euphonic with "angu-uo," which literally translated would be "feebleminded fish." The Honchoshokkan states that during the early Edo era (which began in 1603), in winter anko were given as gifts to the shogun and were delicacies eaten by court nobles, but when their prices fell in the spring, commoners would also eat them.

背

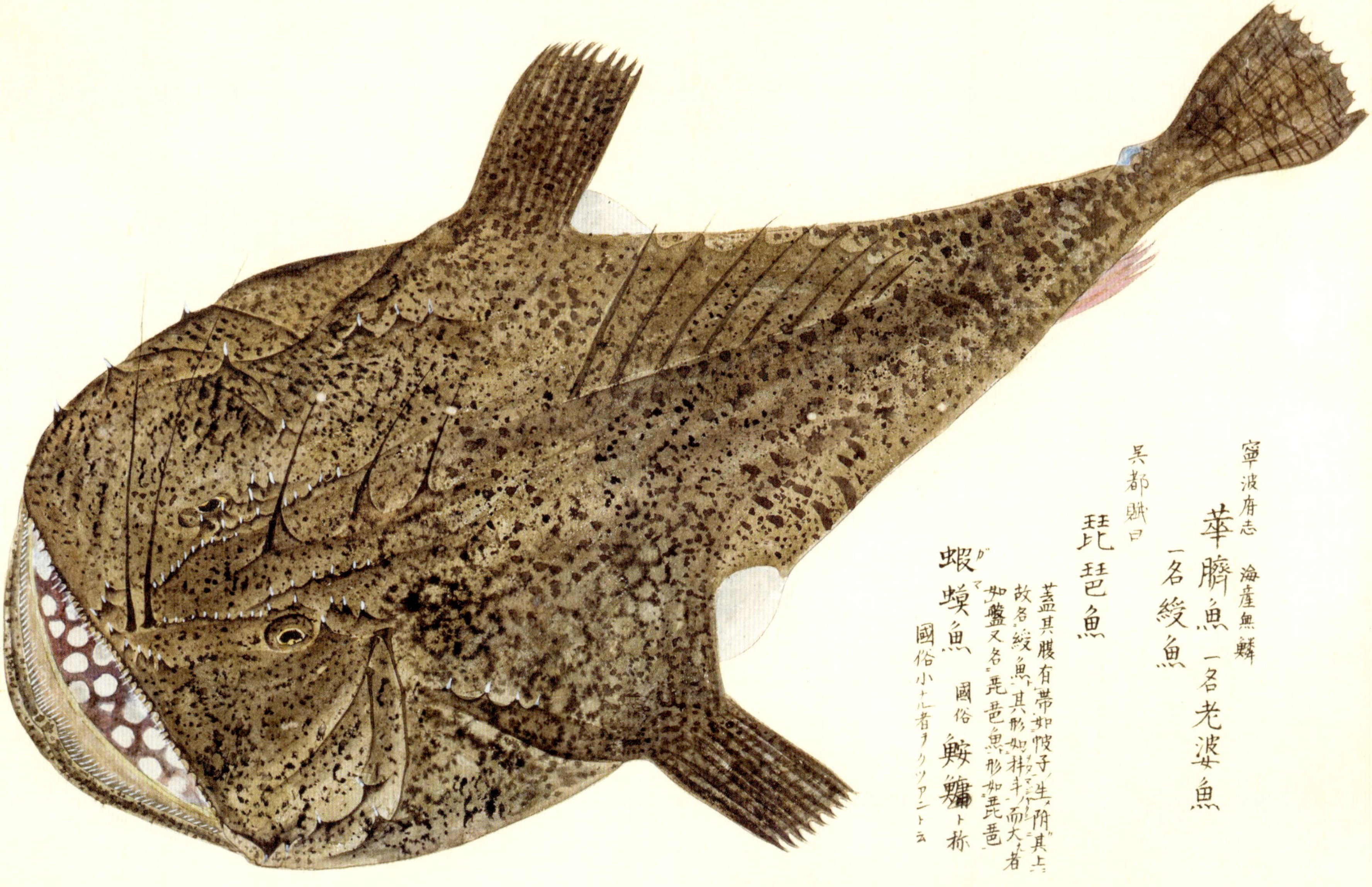

寧波府志　海產無鱗
華臍魚　一名老婆魚
一名綬魚

吳都賦曰
琵琶魚

蝦蟆魚、國俗
鮟鱇ト称

蓋其腹有帯如帨子生阶其上
故名綬魚　其形如枇杷而大者
如盤又名琵琶魚形如琵琶

國俗小ナル者ヲクツアニト云

Japanese sandfish

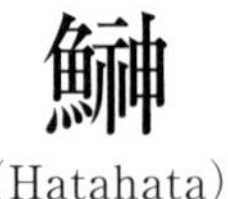

雷魚
（Kaminariuo）

燭魚
（Hatahata）

神鳴魚
（Hatahata）

霹靂魚
（Hatahata）

鱩
（Hatahata）

ハタハタ

スズキ目ハタハタ科ハタハタ属。学名は*Arctoscopus japonicus*。北海道から山口県までの日本海沿岸、朝鮮半島東岸などに分布する。体長は約20cm。「ハタハタ」の名前は、日本海で雷が多い冬に海岸に打ち寄せることから、雷神の古名「霹靂神（たかみ）」が遣わした魚として「霹靂魚」となったといわれている。波が多い時期に獲れることから「波多波多（ハタハタ）」、背に流紋があることから「斑斑（ハタハタ）」とする説もある。食用とされ、産卵期である厳冬期が旬。寒冷地では保存食にしたり、郷土料理の材料として使われてきたりした。秋田地方ではハタハタを塩漬けにした際の上澄み液を「しょっつる」と呼び、この魚醤とハタハタ、野菜などを煮込んだ鍋料理「しょっつる鍋」が有名。

Arctoscopus japonicus (Perciformes, Trichodontidae). This fish is found in the seas around Japan from Hokkaido to Yamaguchi Prefecture and along the eastern coast of the Korean Peninsula. They typically measure 20 cm in length. Their Japanese name, "hatahata," is said to relate to the fact that they come to the coast in the winter, when lightning is common in the Sea of Japan. They were called "hatahata" because they were sent out by Hatatakami, the ancient god of lightning. They are used for food and they are best in mid-winter, during the spawning season. In cold areas, they are used as a preserved food and eaten in regional dishes.

酉陽雑俎

雷魚

カミナリウヲ　奥州ノ奥外

釈名　神鳴魚　同上波多々（ハタハタ）云々同上
岩魚　同上此魚聞雷声則集
于海岸為群故名似水
踊無鱗頭面似魚背
薄青服淡赤色而在如木
目者大者到六七寸慶在
羽只秋田八盛濱多有之
出於物冬至臘月盛也又
此魚無之俗曰雷魚者佐
竹侯之家魚也先年領常
卅水戸故至今少有之矣
按往昔不聞有此魚漠及
異書不関有此奥也奥羽
津軽領鰺筒沢與八盛隣
濱也故此魚有之耳気味
甘冷有小毒主冷益気和
中多食発瘧毒如小児虚人
病人不可以食又暖有子
如小豆而色淡赤也束之
如柘榴子之大貫之以細縄
以貨四方也売如大珠数主
用漫水二三日許而作鮓食
之方言曰之武刺子並施赦
子曰東魚譜

雷魚ハ南海ニ住ホ河魚也首尤ノ鼻尖テ鋸ノ如ニ左右ニ羽異ヲ
鰭アリ惣身ニ針ヲ植タルカ如ク水中ヨリクル事スミヤカ也怒睛ハ海中
鳴動スルト云大ナル首ハ大ニ先ニスル小ナル者ハ三五尺有其膽ヲ酒
ニ浸ニテ人ニ飲マ毒有テ先畜田類ニ飲シムレハ能言ト也
此説ハ分ニ非ス他魚也可考　雷ノ名ヲ得ル者

魚ニ有雷魚　鳥ニ有雷鳥　獣ニ有雷獣
木ニ有雷木　一云桙樹　石ニ有雷斧　皆雷気ヲ除ク
者也其具一雷歟ハ雷気ニ発スレハ乗雲ニテ雷ノ気ニ随ヒ走
雷ヲ好ムル者也蓋雷ヲ陳ルー草木花譜ニ詳ナリ

ハタ／＼往古ハ常陸水戸ニ産ス今ハ
出羽秋田ニ多ク産ス此魚雷ノ声
アレハ好ニテ多ク集ル故ニカミナリ魚
ト云首ノ中ニ釼アリ他ノ魚ニ釼骨
ナシ此魚佐竹矣参ノ府ノ時ニハ
江戸ニ向ッテ游行ス佐竹帰府
ノ年ハ佐竹ノ城ニ向テ行游ストス
佐竹ノ家ニ此魚付ル故也

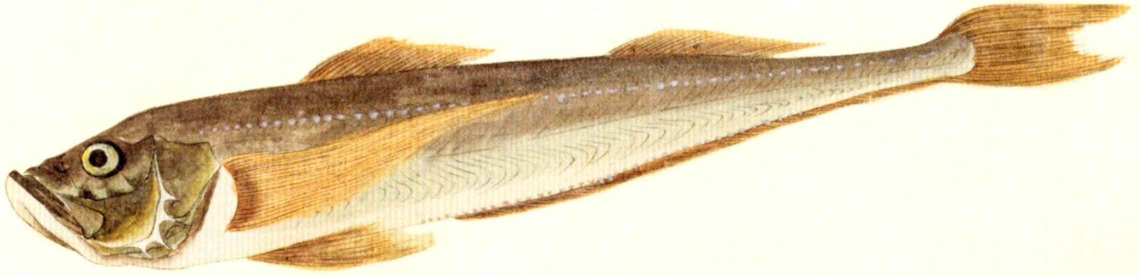

首中釼骨

首中釼骨

丁酉二月九日大舘
仁山子送之真寫

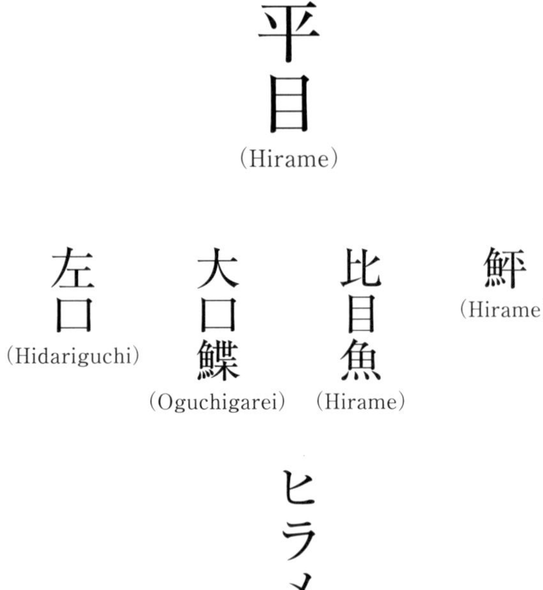

平目
（Hirame）

鮃
（Hirame）

比目魚
（Hirame）

大口鰈
（Oguchigarei）

左口
（Hidariguchi）

ヒラメ

Bastard halibut

ヒラメ目ヒラメ科ヒラメ属。学名は*Paralichthys olivaceus*。日本では北海道から九州南岸までの各沿岸などに分布する。体長は80〜100cm。カレイ類と体形が似ているが「左ヒラメの右カレイ」といわれるように、両眼が体の左側にあるのが特徴。和名「ヒラメ」の由来は「扁平な魚」の意とする説、眼が並んでいることから「比目魚」という説などがある。江戸時代の方言辞典『物類称呼』には「畿内、西国ともにカレイと称し、江戸にては大なるものをヒラメ、小なるものをカレイと呼ぶけれども、類同じくして種異也」とあり、当時は正確に区別する方法がなかったことがうかがえる。食用とされるが、最近では漁獲量が少ないため高級魚となっている。

Paralichthys olivaceus (Pleuronectiformes, Paralichthyidae). This fish is found in Japan along the coasts from Hokkaido to southern Kyushu. They typically measure 80 to 100 cm in length. Bastard halibut have both eyes on their left side. Their Japanese name, "hirame," is said to come from their flat shape ("hira") or from the fact that their eyes are on the same side of their head, so their name was written with the Chinese characters for "compare eyes fish". While they are used for food, recently catches have been small and they have become a delicacy.

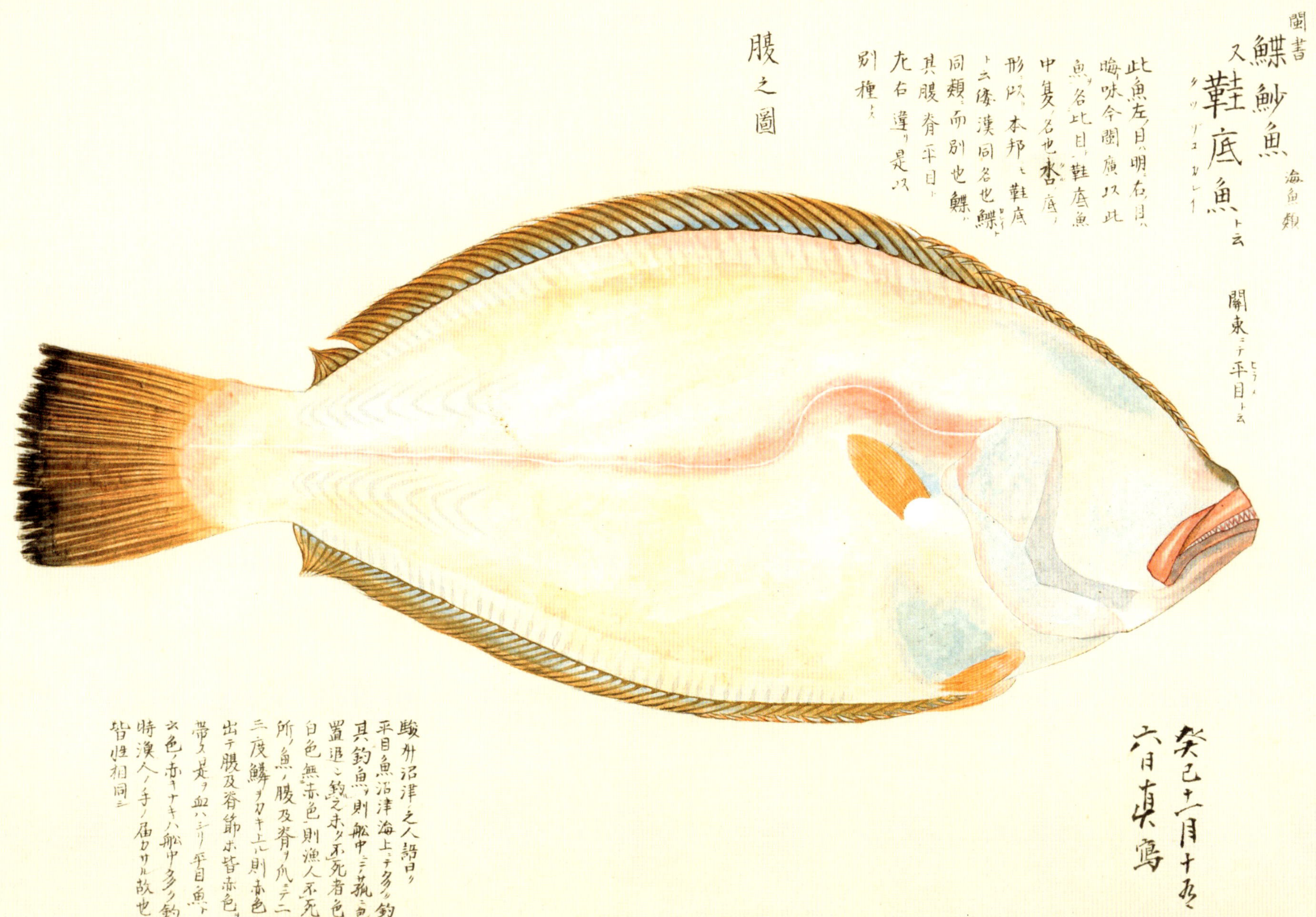
腹之圖
闥書
鰈魦魚　海魚類
又　鞋底魚ト云
クツゾコヒラメ
關東ニテ平目ト云

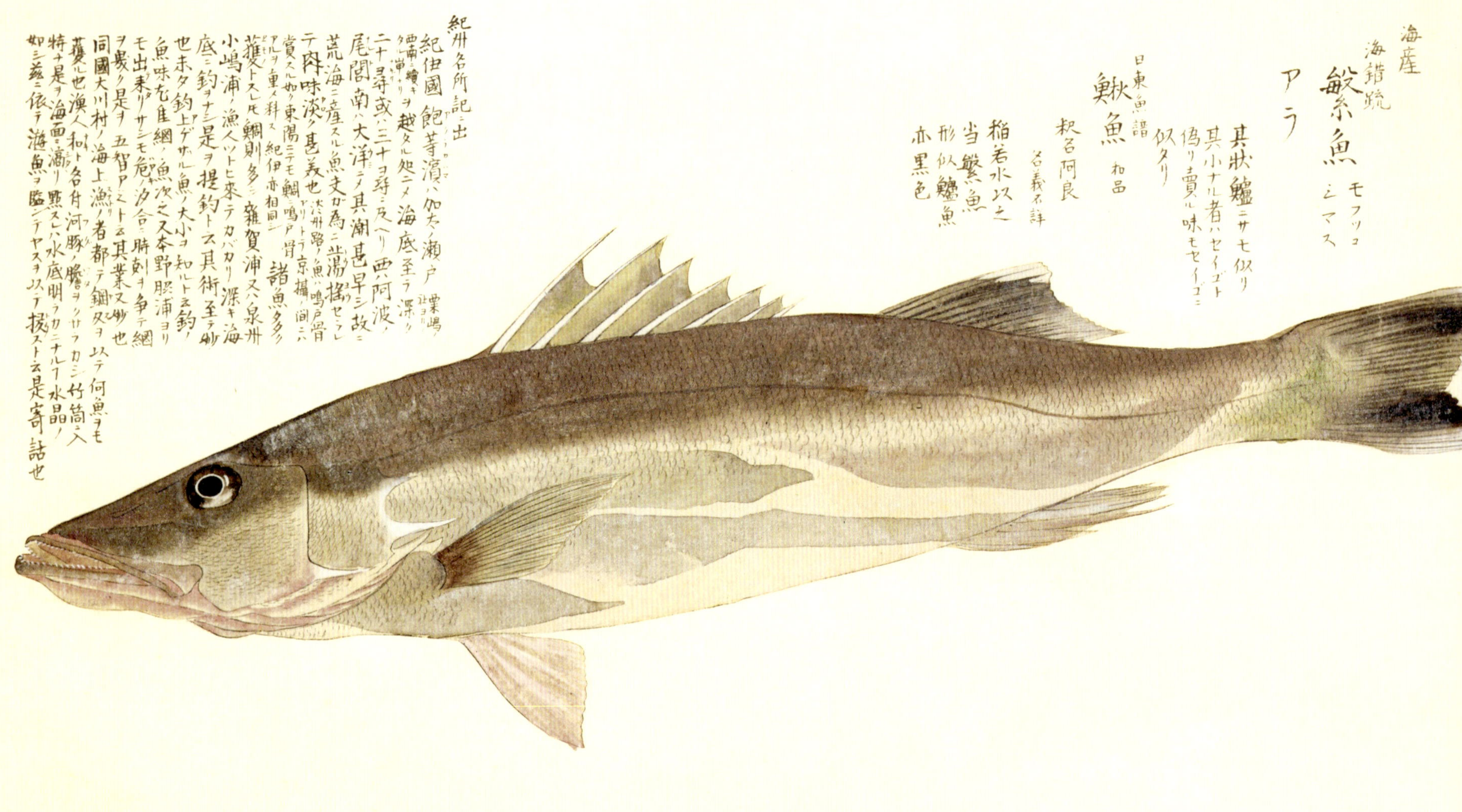

海産
海錯號
綬糸魚　モフツコ
　　　　ニマス
アラ

其状鱸ニサモ似タリ
其小ナル者ハセイゴト
偽リ賣ル味モセイゴニ
似タリ

日東魚譜
鮲魚　和品
釈名阿良
名義不詳

稲若水以之
当鱶魚
形似鱧魚
亦黒色

鯎
（Ara）

ホタ
(Hota)　　沖鱸
(Okisuzuki)　　白鱒
(Shiromasu)　　浜田鱈
(Hamadatara)　　阿羅
(Ara)　　阿良
(Ara)

アラ

Sawedged perch

スズキ目アラ科（またはハタ科）アラ属。学名は*Niphon spinosus*。日本では北海道から九州南岸までの各沿岸、東シナ海沿岸などに分布する。体長は80〜100cm。体形はスズキに似て側扁している。その体形から以前はスズキ科、後にハタ科に分類されていたが、近年はハタ科が細分化され、アラ科に属するとすることが多い。和名「アラ」の由来は不詳だが、一般的に荒々しい習性や外貌からと推測されている。江戸時代には薬効があると考えられ、『魚鑑』には産後の眩暈や出血を治療し、切り傷、破傷風を治す、『和漢三才図会』には血をよく止め、血を清涼にする効果があると記されている。現在では最高級魚で料理店へ直送されることが多く、市場に出回ることは少ない。

Niphon spinosus (Perciformes, Niphonidae). This fish is found in Japan along the coasts from Hokkaido to southern Kyushu and along the coast of the East China Sea. They typically measure 80 to 100 cm in length. The origin of their Japanese name, "ara," is unknown, but it is generally believed to be from their wild ("araarashii") behavior and appearance. During the Edo era (1603–1867), they were believed to have medical properties. The *Uo-kagami* says that they can be used to treat postpartum vertigo and blooding, cuts, and tetanus. The *Wakan Sansai Zue* says they can be used to stop blooding and to refresh blood.

真魚鰹

（Managatsuo）

鯧（Managatsuo）

魚味鰹（Managatsuo）

真味鰹（Managatsuo）

マナガツオ

Harvest fish

スズキ目マナガツオ科マナガツオ属。学名は*Pampus punctatissimus*。日本では新潟県から九州西岸までの日本海・東シナ海沿岸、相模湾から土佐湾までの太平洋沿岸などに分布する。体長は30〜60cm。和名の由来は、瀬戸内海ではカツオが獲れないため、この魚を初ガツオに見立てて「マネ（真似）ガツオ」と呼んだのが転訛したという説や、美味であることから親愛の意を表す「真名」に由来するという説など、諸説ある。食用とされ、主に和歌山と瀬戸内海が産地。関東よりも産地から近い関西で特に好まれ、高級魚として珍重されている。刺身や西京漬けにすると絶品といわれているが、江戸時代の百科事典『和漢三才図会』にも「さしみにすると最もよい」と記されている。

Pampus punctatissimus (Perciformes, Stromateidae). This fish is found along the coasts of the Sea of Japan and the East China Sea from Niigata Prefecture to western Kyushu, along with the Pacific coast from Sagami Bay to Tosa Bay. They typically measure 30 to 60 cm in length. Their Japanese name, "managatsuo," is said to come from "manegatsuo" ("imitation skipjack tuna" : *Katsuwonus pelamis*) because skipjack tuna are not found in the Seto Inland Sea, so those in the area treated harvest fish like the first skipjack tuna (*Katsuwonus pelamis*) of the season. The *Wakan Sansai Zue*, an encyclopedia from the Edo era (1603–1867), says that they are delicious when eaten as sashimi.

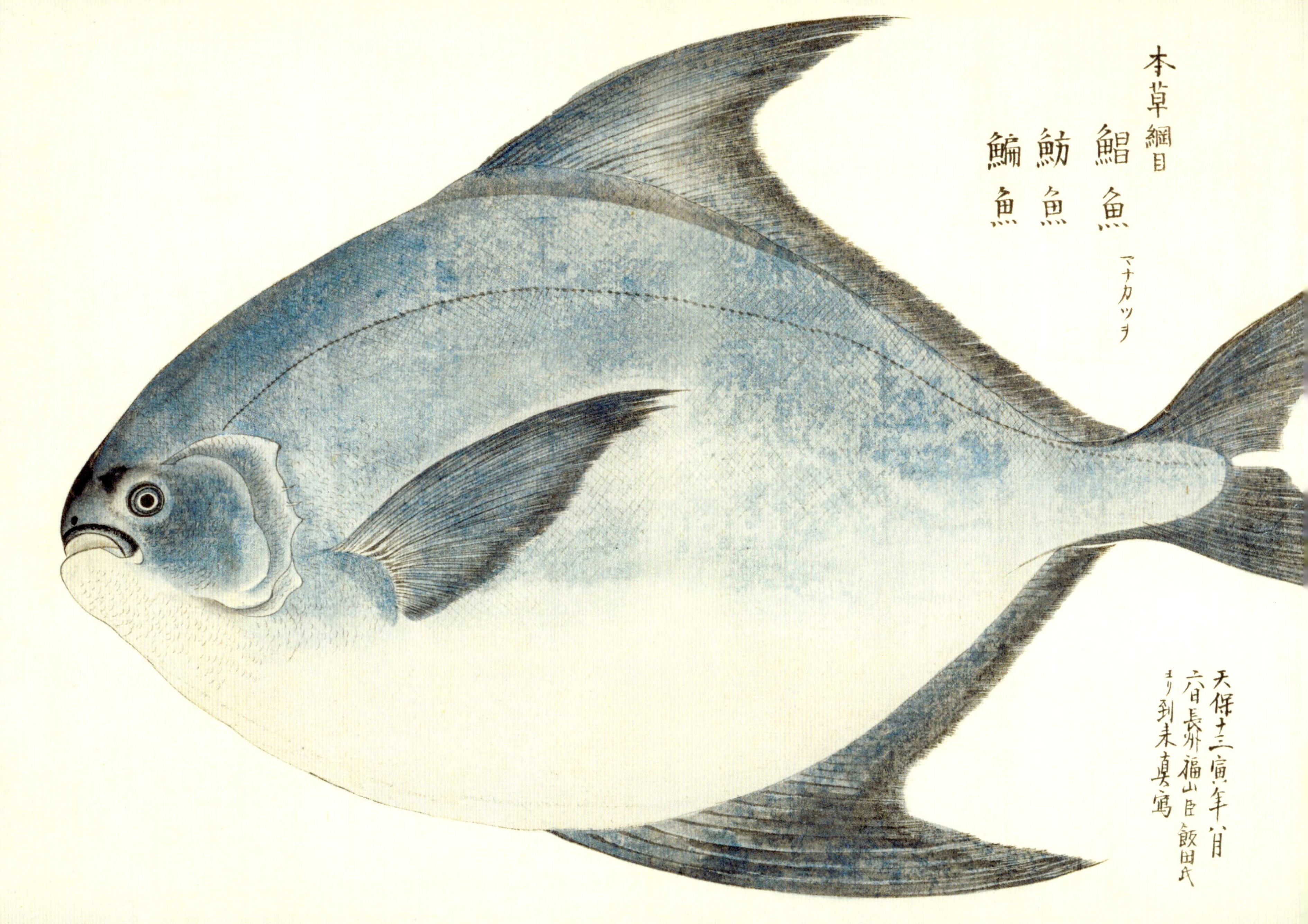

本草綱目
鯧魚　マナカツヲ
魴魚
鯿魚
天保十三寅年八月
六日長州福山臣飯田氏
より到来真寫

猫鮫

（Nekozame）

トラブカ
（Torabuka）

サザエワニ
（Sazaewani）

ネコブカ
（Nekobuka）

栄螺割
（Sazaewari）

ネコザメ

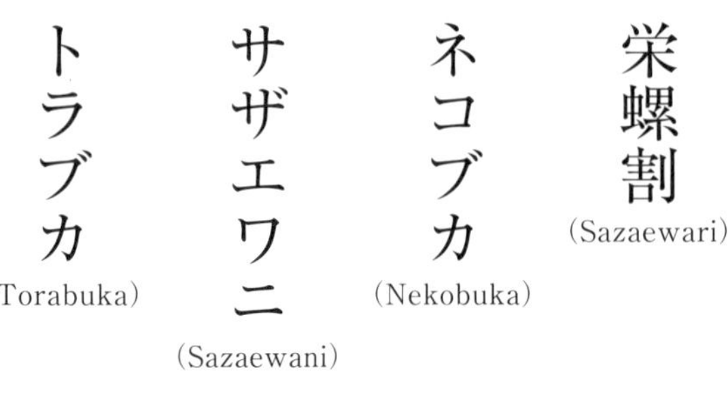

Japanese bullhead shark

ネコザメ目ネコザメ科ネコザメ属。学名は*Heterodontus japonicus*。岩手県から九州南岸までの太平洋沿岸、新潟県から九州南岸までの日本海・東シナ海、朝鮮半島、台湾などに分布する。体長は最大で約120cm。体色は茶褐色で横縞がある。和名「ネコザメ」の由来は、丸く大きい頭部が猫の顔に似ていることから名付けられた。サザエなどの貝類を噛み砕いて食べるので「サザエワリ」、サメをワニ・フカと呼ぶ地域では「サザエワニ」「ネコブカ」とも呼ばれる。食用とされるが、そのまま食べられることはなく、練り製品の材料とされる。江戸時代の百科事典『和漢三才図会』には「頭の形は猫に似ていて扁たく、身体には虎斑文がある。歯がある。味はよくない」とある。

Heterodontus japonicus (Heterodontiformes, Heterodontidae). This fish is found along the Pacific coast from Iwate Prefecture to southern Kyushu, along the coasts of the Sea of Japan and East China Sea from Niigata Prefecture to southern Kyushu, the Korean Peninsula, and Taiwan. They typically measure up to 120 cm in length. Their Japanese name, "nekozame," comes from the fact that they are a shark ("same") with a large round head that resembles the face of a cat ("neko"). The Edo era (1603–1867) encyclopedia *Wakan Sansai Zue* says "Their heads are flat, like a cat's, and their bodies are striped, like a tiger's."

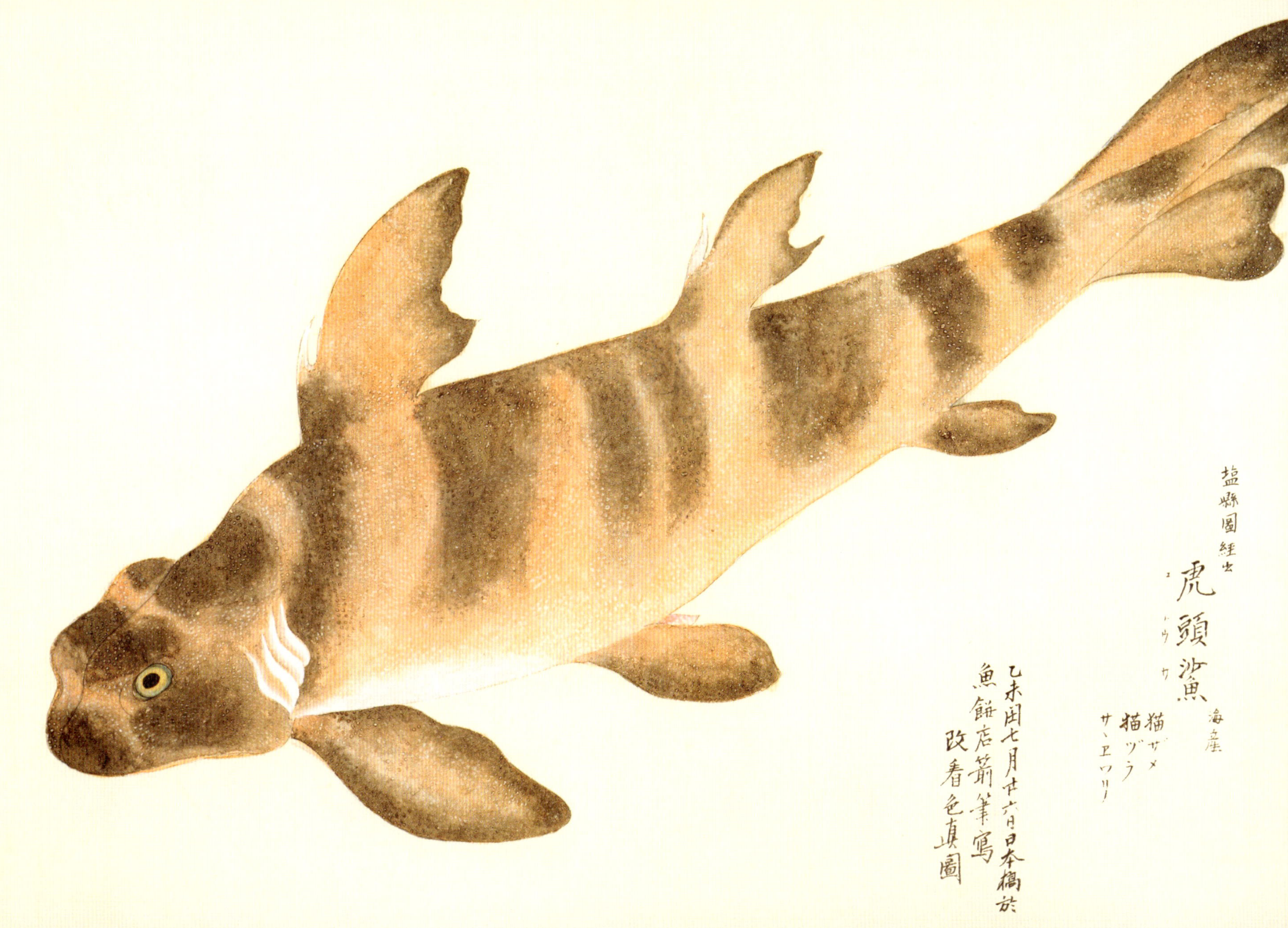
塩縣圖経出
虎頭鯊　海立産
トウ
猫サメ
猫ヅラ
サヽエワリ
乙未閏七月廿六日日本橋於
魚餌店箭筆寫
改看色真圖

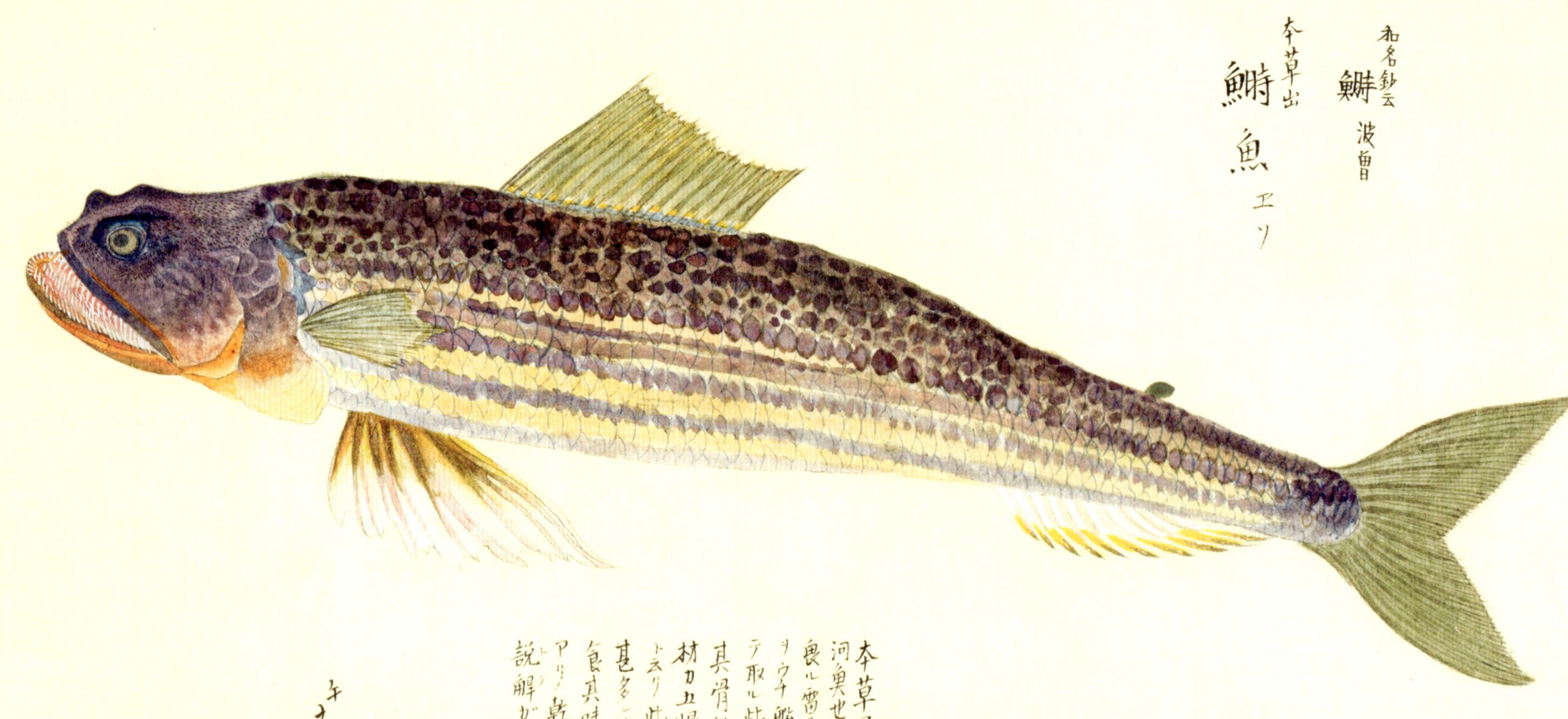
和名鈔云　鱗　波曽

本草出

鱒魚
エソ

本草曰大河ノ下潮ニ通スル處ニアリ
河奥也夏間多ニ大鼓ナリノ物ヲ
喰ル雷ヲモヨソル是ヲ取ル漢人大鼓
ヲウチ舩ヲタヽキ板ヲナスニ一方ニ遣ヨセ
テ取ル此魚肉小骨多ニ乾ニカハケレバ
其骨外ニアラハ此魚味ヨキ故ニ彭淵
材力五恨ニ鱠魚ニ骨多キヲ恨ム
トヱリ此説最然リゾア味ノ之肉ノ小骨
甚多ニ肉子バリ多ニ乾ク是ヲアブク
食其味甚ニ美ナリ生魚ナルハ臭気
アリノ乾タルハ省ヒナシニ上品也条本草ニ
説解ガ如シ

十二月二日真写

沖狗母魚
（Okieso）

沖鱚
（Okieso）

イソギス
（Isogisu）

トラギス
（Toragisu）

ハダカヨソ
（Hadakayoso）

オキエソ

Bluntnose lizardfish

ヒメ目エソ科オキエソ属。学名は *Trachinocephalus trachinus*。新潟県から九州南岸までの日本海沿岸・東シナ海沿岸、岩手県から九州南岸までの太平洋岸、沖縄島、台湾など、インド-西太平洋に分布する。体長は30〜40cm。体は細長い。背側は薄黄色、腹側は白色で、体側に3〜4本の青い縦帯がある。頭頂近くに小さい眼があるのと、口のすぐ上に眼が付いているように見えるほど、大きな口が特徴。主に沿岸から200m以浅の砂泥底に生息する。和名「オキエソ」の由来は不詳だが、沖合で獲れるエソという意だと考えられる。食用とされ、主に底曳網で漁獲されて練り製品の材料とされるが、他のエソ類と比べると味が劣るため漁獲量は少ない。

Trachinocephalus trachinus (Aulopiformes, Synodontidae). This fish is found along the coasts of the Sea of Japan and East China Sea from Niigata Prefecture to southern Kyushu, along the Pacific coast from Iwate Prefecture to southern Kyushu, around Okinawa-jima Island, Taiwan, and the Indian to western Pacific Oceans. They typically measure 30 to 40 cm in length. They have small eyes near the top of their heads, and their mouths are so large that it looks like their eyes are located right over their mouth. The origin of their Japanese name, "okieso," is unknown, but it is believed to be because they are lizardfishes ("eso") caught offshore ("oki").

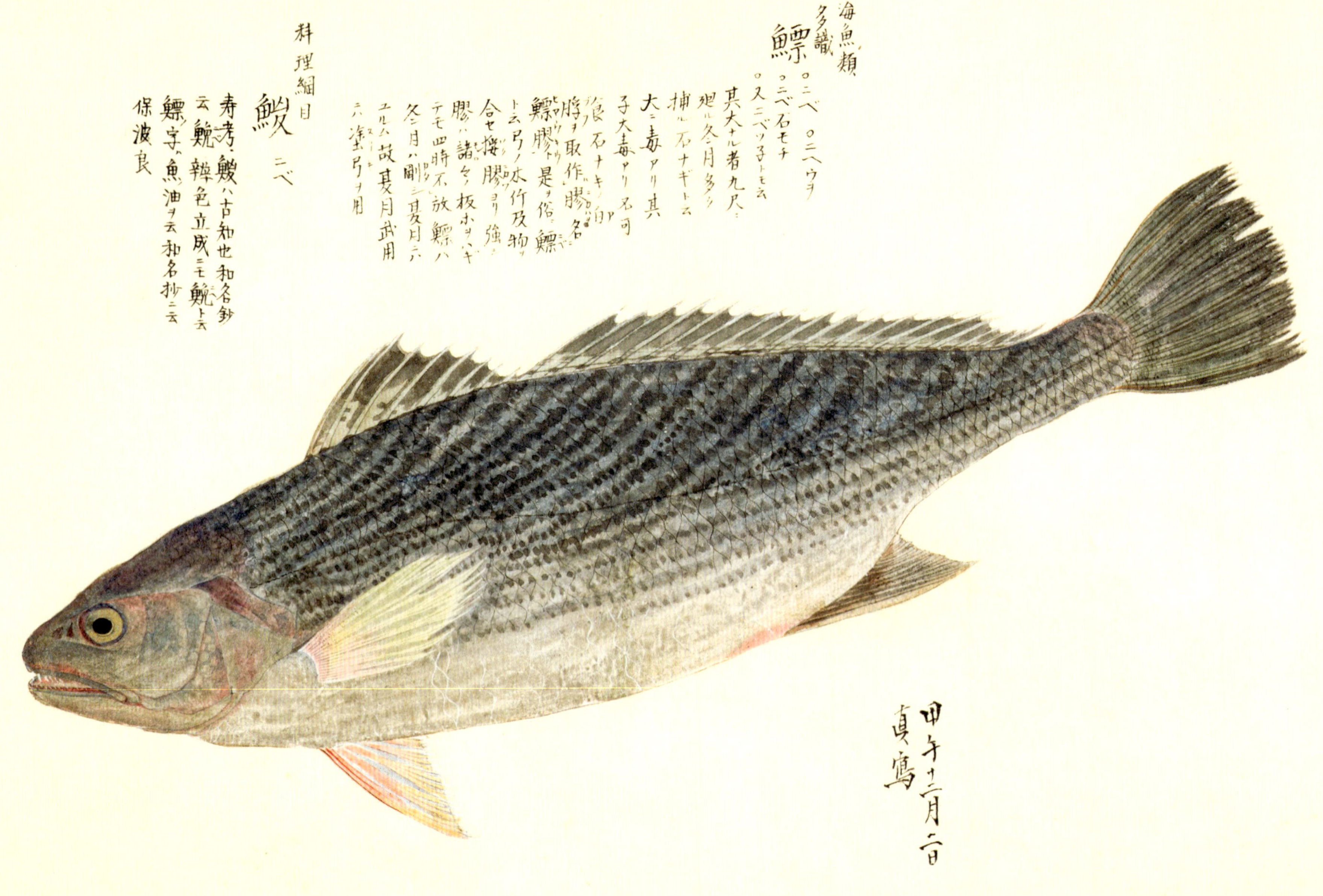

海魚類
多識
鱞 ○ニベ ○ニベウヲ
○ニベ石モチ
○又ニベツトモ云
其大ナル者九尺ニ
捕ハ冬月多ク
捕ニ石ナキニ石ヲ
大ニ毒アリ其
子大毒ヨリ石ヲ
将テ取作ル勝名
鱞膠是ヲ俗ニ鱞
トス弓ノ水竹及物ニ
合セ接膠引強
膠ハ諸々ノ板ホシハギ
テモ四時不放鱞ハ
冬月ハ剛ニ夏月六
ユルハ故其夏月武用
二塗弓ヲ用

料理綱目
鰸 ニベ
寿考・鰸ハ古知世和名鈔
云鰸辨色立成ニモ鰸ト云
鱞字魚油ヲ云和名抄ニ云
保波良

甲午十二月二日
真寫

鮸
（Nibe）

鮠
（Koichi）

爾陪魚
（Nibeuo）

ニベ

スズキ目ニベ科ニベ属。学名は*Nibea mitsukurii*。日本では仙台湾から九州までの太平洋沿岸、新潟県から島根県までの日本海沿岸などに分布する。体長は約40cmだが、大きいものは70cmに達する。和名「ニベ」は膠の俗称で、かつてニベのうきぶくろから魚膠を作り、接着剤として職人らに重宝されていたことなどに因んでいる。ニベから作られた魚膠は粘着力が強いことから人間関係の親密さを示す言葉として使われ、転じて不愛想なことを「にべもない」と言うようになったという。夏の産卵期には雌雄で群れを作り、グーグーとうきぶくろで音を立てる。『和漢三才図会』には「その声、雷のごとく、海人は竹筒をもって、水底を探り、声をききて網をおろす」と記されている。

Nibea mitsukurii (Perciformes, Sciaenidae). This fish is found along the Pacific coast from Sendai Bay to Kyushu, along with the coast of the Sea of Japan from Niigata Prefecture to Shimane Prefecture. They typically measure 40 cm in length. Their Japanese name, "nibe," comes from the old colloquial term for the fish glue ("Nihe", "Nibe") that could be made from their swim bladder. The *Wakan Sansai Zue* says that the sound of nibe croakers was like thunder, and fishermen would use bamboo tubes to explore the sea floor, listening for the sound of the nibe croakers to determine where to cast their nets.

Nibe croaker

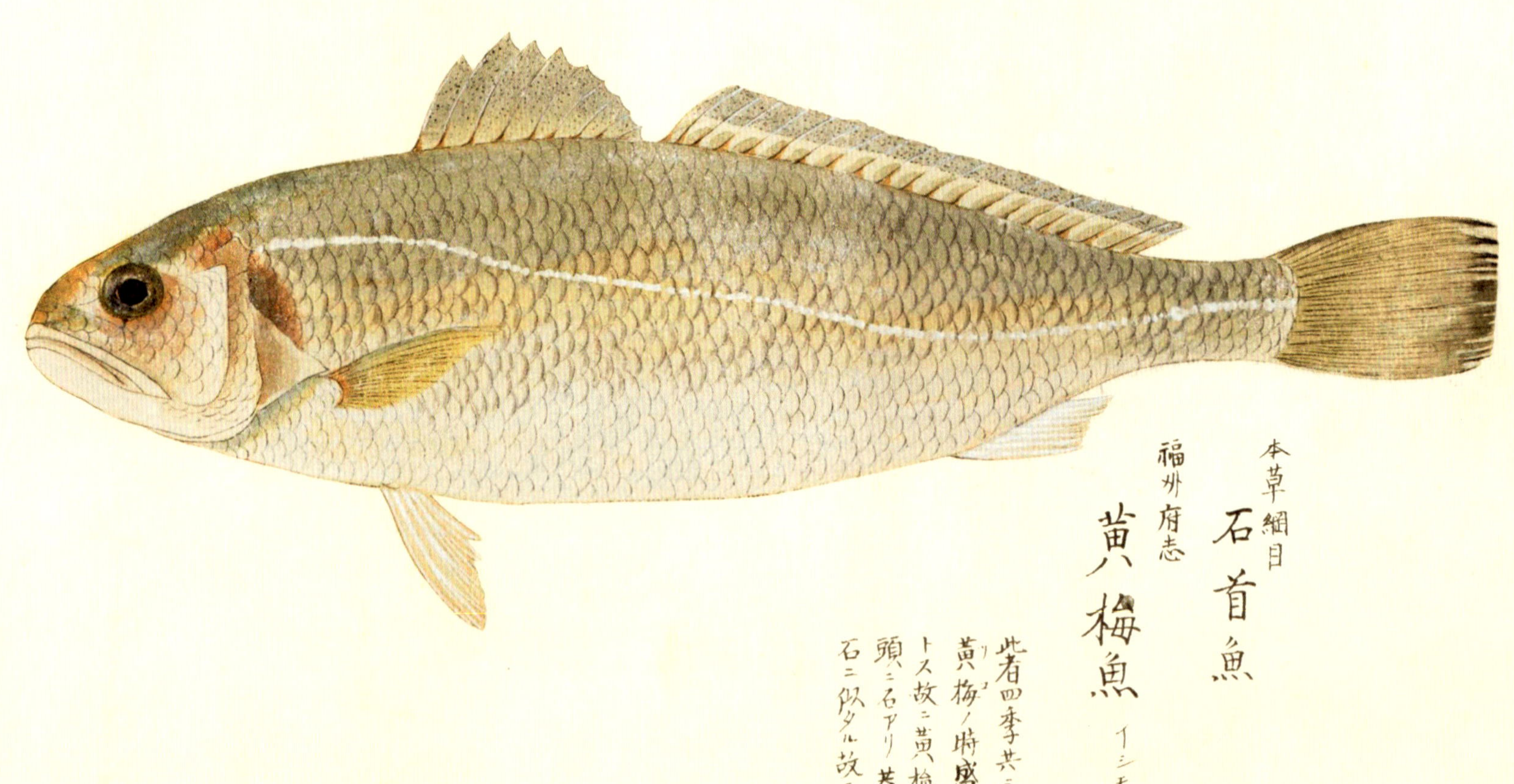

本草綱目　石首魚

福州府志　黃ハ梅魚　イシモチ

此者四季共ニ有之五月
黃梅ノ時盛ニ出ル尤飾
トス故ニ黃梅魚トモ云各
頭ニ石アリ盞骨ノ形
石ニ似タル故ニ名トス
石ニ似タル故ニ名トス

白愚痴
(Shiroguchi)

石首魚
(Ishimochi)

石持
(Ishimochi)

白久智
(Shiroguchi)

シログチ

Silver croaker

スズキ目ニベ科シログチ属。学名は*Pennahia argentata*。日本では青森県から九州南岸までの周辺海域に分布する。体長は20〜40cm。名前にある「グチ」はニベ科の魚を釣り上げたときに、うきぶくろの筋肉を振動させてグーグーと音を出す様子が愚痴をこぼしているように聞こえることに由来し、本種の体色が銀白色なので「シログチ」の名が付いたといわれている。別名「イシモチ」は、頭蓋骨の中にある耳石が非常に大きいことに由来する。古来この耳石は霊能があると信じられていた。また、江戸時代の本草書である『本朝食鑑』には生薬として用いられていたことが記されている。現在でも食用とされ、新鮮なものは刺身で食べられるが、一般的には塩焼きや干物にすることが多い。

Pennahia argentata (Perciformes, Sciaenidae). This fish is found in the waters around Japan from Aomori Prefecture to the southern coast of Kyushu. They typically measure 20 to 40 cm in length. Their Japanese name, "shiroguchi," comes from the fact that the sound they make when caught, by vibrating the muscles around their swim bladder, makes it sound like they are complaining ("guchi"), and their bodies are a silvery white ("shiro"). The *Honchoshokkan*, a book of dietary medicines from the Edo era (1603–1867), says that silver croakers were used as medicine.

"

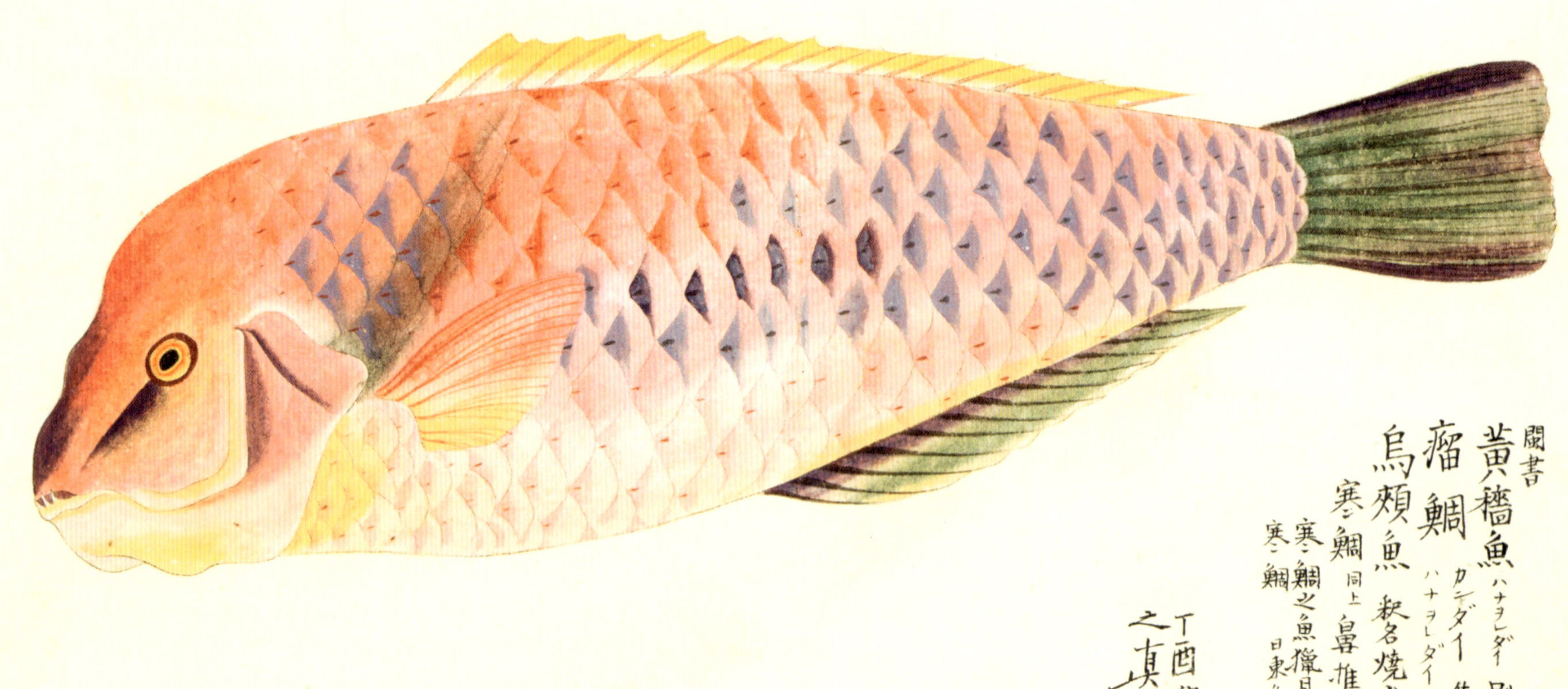

閨書
黄櫚魚 ハナヲレダイ 別一種同各
瘤鯛 カテダイ 佐渡
ハナヲレダイ 黒キ色ノ者ヲサスミ ヤキトヒ云黒鯛各同
烏頬魚 釈名焼炭鯛 和名
寒鯛 同上 鼻堆鯛 同上 両頬魚
寒鯛之魚 獵月盛出故又名 日東魚譜
寒鯛
丁酉如月三日未
之真寫

伊良
（Ira）

モクズ
（Mokuzu）

ホテイ
（Hotei）

テス イラ
（Tesu）

寒鯛
（Kandai）

磯甘鯛
（Isoamadai）

Scarbreast tuskfin

スズキ目ベラ科イラ属。学名は*Choerodon azurio*。新潟県から九州南岸までの日本海・東シナ海沿岸、千葉県館山から九州南岸までの太平洋沿岸、朝鮮半島南岸、台湾などに分布する。体長は30〜40cm。ベラ科のなかでも体高があり、体色は全体的に紅褐色。胸びれから背びれにかけて暗色の帯が斜めにあるのが特徴だが、個体差があるため色彩が異なるものもいる。雄は成長とともに前頭部が張り出すようになる。和名「イラ」の由来は、捕らえようとするとかみつく性質から「苛魚」の意からとする説、「イザ（斑紋）」が転訛したという説などがある。磯臭いため食用とされることは少ないが、身は柔らかく、旬の時期には味噌汁や煮物、ちり鍋などにして食べられる。

Choerodon azurio (Perciformes, Labridae). This fish is found along the coasts of the Sea of Japan and the East China Sea from Niigata Prefecture to southern Kyushu, along the Pacific coast from Chiba Prefecture's Tateyama to southern Kyushu, the Korean Peninsula, and Taiwan. They typically measure 30 to 40 cm in length. They have a diagonal dark band from their pectoral fin to their dorsal fin, but the color varies by individual. The foreheads of the males grow as they get older. Their Japanese name, "ira," is said to come from "ira-uo" ("irritated fish") because they bite when someone tries to catch them.

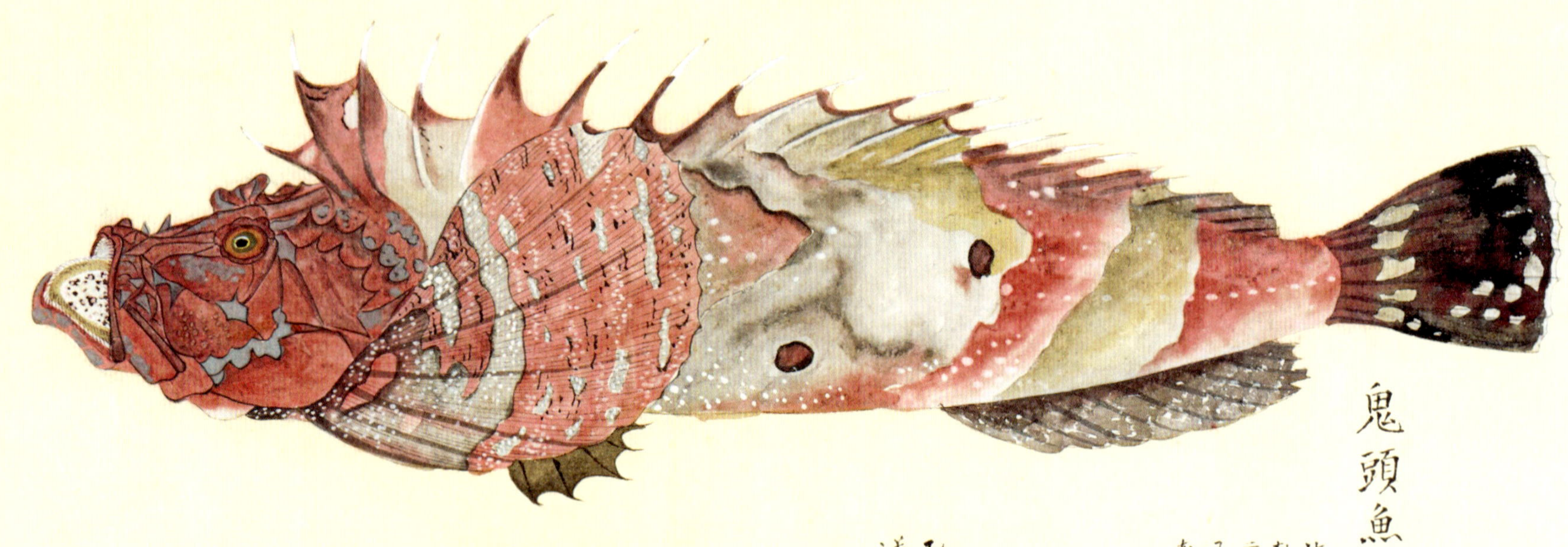

鬼頭魚　一種

鬼カサゴ　山神ヲコセトモ云

此者漁人風雨ニテ時無テ家ニ三十
乾シテ藏置其時取出シ山神ヲ祈リ
テ大櫂ノ有ハコノ願フ山神ヲ祭ル
コトハ風雨ヲ晴ラシメニカ烏也魚商
ノ外ニ説ナス非也

乙未十二月廿七日從倉橋氏
送之真寫

鬼鰧

（Oniokoze）

オニオコゼ

鬼虎魚（Oniokoze）

アカオコゼ（Akaokoze）

オクジ（Okuji）

オコジョ（Okojo）

Devil stinger

スズキ目オニオコゼ科オニオコゼ属。学名は*Inimicus japonicus*。日本では青森県から九州南岸までの各沿岸などに分布する。体長は20〜30cm。背びれの棘に毒腺があり刺されると激しい痛みが出る危険な魚だが、味は良く、食用とされる。「オニオコゼ」の名前の由来は、「オニ」は奇怪な顔かたちであること、「オコ（痴）」は容姿が醜いこと、「ゼ（魚）」は魚名語尾であるといわれている。他にも矛のような背びれから「ホコセ（矛背）」が転訛したという説など、諸説ある。オニオコゼは古くから山の神への供え物にされたり、狩りのときに持参されたりしたが、これは「山の神は嫉妬深い醜女のため、自分よりも醜いオニオコゼを見ると喜ぶ」という伝承に因る。

Inimicus japonicus (Perciformes, Synanceiidae). This fish is found in Japan along the coasts from Aomori Prefecture to southern Kyushu. They typically measure 20 to 30 cm in length. Their Japanese name, "oniokoze," is said to be because of their unusual face ("oni" means "ogre") and their ugly appearance ("oko" is an old Japanese word for "ugly"), with the suffix "ze," used at the end of fish names. They have long been offered to the goddess of mountains, and were taken along on hunts. There is a legend that this is because the mountain goddess was a jealous, ugly woman, so she would be happy when she saw the even uglier devil stinger.

鯔
（Bora）

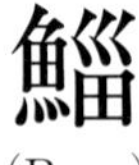

鯔
（Bora）

口女
（Kuchime）

名吉
（Myogichi）

目白鯔
（Mejirobora）

シュクチ
（Shukuchi）

マボラ
（Mabora）

ボラ

Black mullet

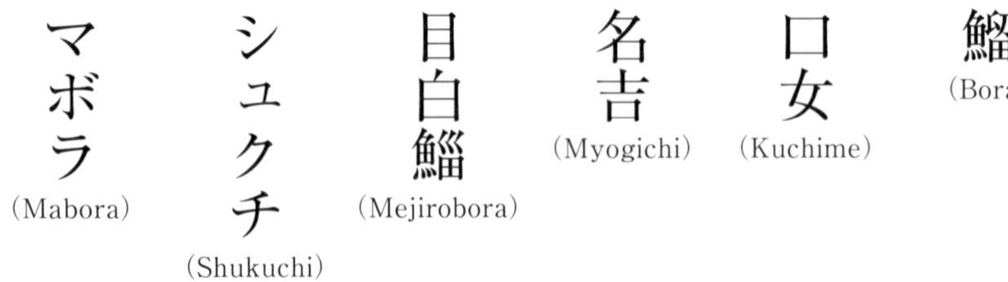

ボラ目ボラ科ボラ属。学名は*Mugil cephalus cephalus*。全世界の熱帯・暖海域に分布し、日本でも北海道から九州南岸までの各沿岸、琉球列島、小笠原諸島など広い範囲で見られる。体長は50〜60cmのものが多いが、大きいものでは80cmを超える。和名「ボラ」の由来は「ホバラ（太腹）」の転訛という説など、諸説ある。食用とされ、卵巣は珍味として有名な「からすみ」の原料となる。日本におけるからすみの起源は今から約400年前、ギリシャ、トルコで考案されたものが中国を経て伝来したといわれている。長崎の代官が豊臣秀吉に献上する際にその名を問われ、中国の墨石に似ていたので咄嗟に「唐墨」と答えてしまったのが全国に広がったという。

Mugil cephalus cephalus (Mugiliformes, Mugilidae). This fish is found in tropical and warm seas around the world. In Japan, they are found over a wide area, including the coasts from Hokkaido to southern Kyushu, around the Ryukyu Islands, and around the Ogasawara Islands. They typically measure 50 to 60 cm in length. Their Japanese name, "bora," is said to come from "hobara," meaning "pot belly." They are used as food and their roe are used in the famous delicacy "karasumi." Karasumi is said to go back roughly 400 years ago, and the method of preparing it was developed in Greece and Turkey, reaching Japan via China.

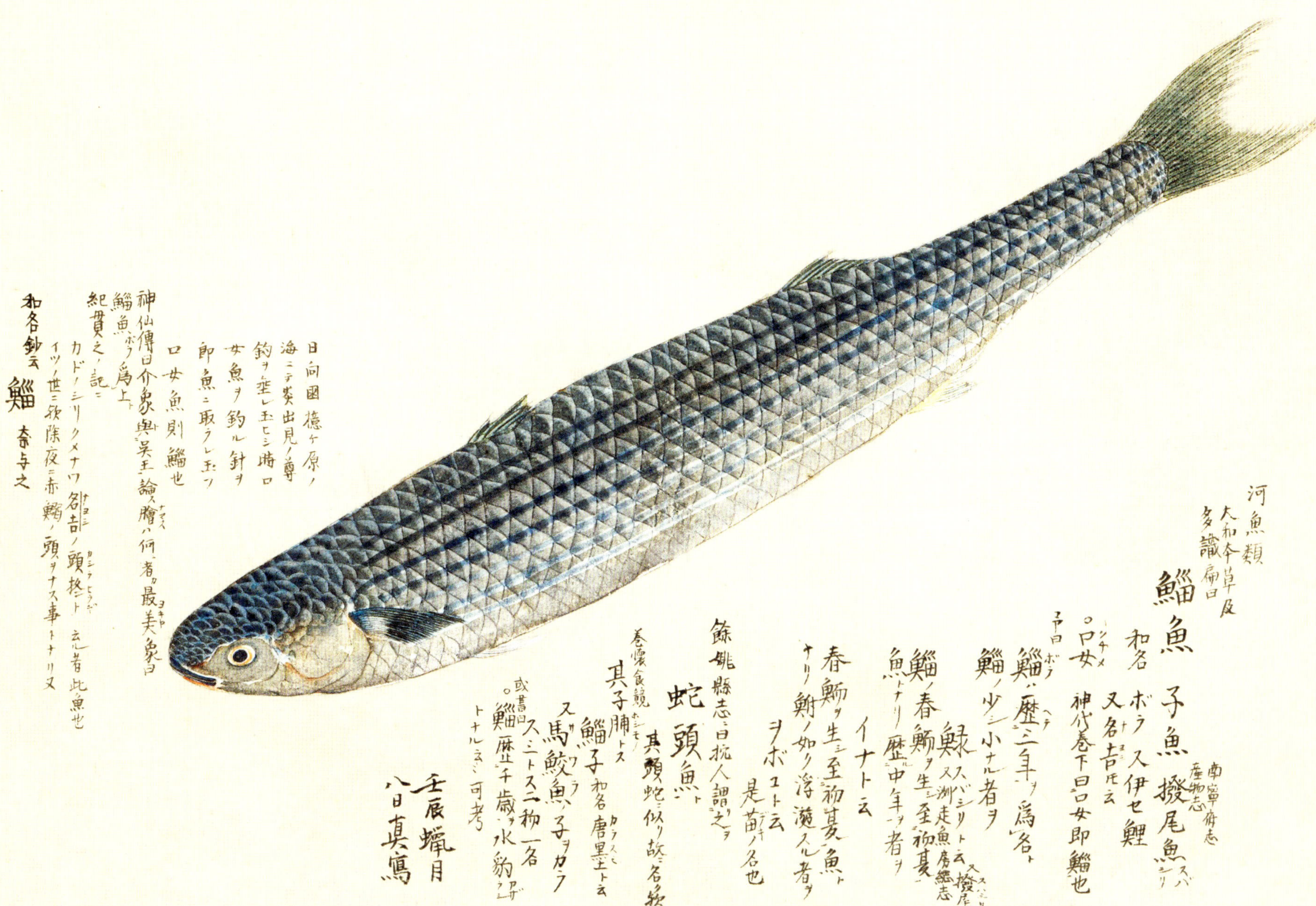
河魚類
大和本草及
多識扁曰
鯔魚 子魚 撥尾魚 スバシリ
和名 ボラ ス伊セ鯉
又名 吉元云
ロ女 神代巻下曰ロ女即鯔也
鯔ハ歴三年ヲ為名
鯔ノ少シ小ナル者ヲ
鯐 又入洲走魚房総志
鯔ノ春鯐ヲ生ニ至初夏
魚トナリ歴中年ノ者ヲ
南寧府志
産物志
日向國憶ヶ原ノ
海ニテ葵出見ノ尊
釣ヲ垂レ玉ヒシ時口
女魚ヲ釣ル針ヲ
即魚ニ取ラレ玉フ
口女魚則鯔也
神仙傳曰介象與呉王論膾ハ何者ヲ最美象曰
鯔魚ヲ為上
紀貫之ノ記ニ
カド ノシリクメナワ名吉ノ頭挫ト云ル者此魚也
イツ世ニ須陳夜ニ赤鯔ノ頭ヲナス事トナリヌ
和名鈔云
鯔 春与之

参考文献

魚介類別名辞典（日外アソシエーツ）

さかな・釣り検索（つり人社）

魚の事典
（能勢幸雄 監修 / 能勢幸雄、羽生 功、岩井 保、清水 誠 編集 / 東京堂出版）

魚の手帖（尚学図書 編集 / 小学館）

魚の名前（中村庸夫 著 / 東京書籍）

魚の日本史　シリーズ自然と人間の日本史1（新人物往来社）

小学館の図鑑Z　日本魚類館（中坊徹次 編、監修 / 小学館）

図説　魚と貝の事典
（望月賢二 監修 / 魚類文化研究会、雅麗 編者 / 柏書房）

精選版 日本国語大辞典（小学館）

世界大博物図鑑2［魚類］（荒俣 宏 著 / 平凡社）

大辞泉（小学館）

動植物名よみかた辞典　普及版（日外アソシエーツ）

難読／誤読　魚介類漢字よみかた辞典（日外アソシエーツ）

日本産魚名大辞典（日本魚類学会 編 / 三省堂）

日本大百科全書（小学館）

日本の博物図譜—十九世紀から現代まで
（国立科学博物館 編者 / 東海大学出版会）

日本方言大辞典（小学館）

企画・アートディレクション
田島一彦（たじま かずひこ）
1946年東京生まれ。1969年多摩美術大学デザイン科卒業後、資生堂宣伝部入社。2005年同社部長クリエイティブディレクターを経て独立、現在フリー。受賞歴：朝日広告賞、毎日広告賞、読売広告賞、フジサンケイ広告大賞、日経広告賞、電通賞、ACC賞、日本雑誌広告賞、ニューヨークフェスティバル等。

Planning, Art Director
Kazuhiko Tajima
Born 1946, Tokyo. Graduated in design from Tama Art University in 1969. After working in the advertising department of Shiseido, eventually as creative director, Tajima began working as an independent art director in 2005. Among his many awards are the Asahi Advertising Award, Mainichi Advertisement Design Award, Yomiuri Advertising Award, Fuji Sankei Advertising Award, Nikkei Advertising Award, Dentsu Award, ACC Award, Japan Magazine Advertising Award, and New York Festival Award.

監修
中江雅典（なかえ まさのり）
国立科学博物館動物研究部脊椎動物研究グループ・研究主幹、理学博士。専門は魚類の形態学。なぜこのように多様な形の魚類が存在するのか、その要因を明らかにしようと研究をしている。『新魚類解剖図鑑』（緑書房）、『顔の百科事典』、『魚類学の百科事典』（ともに丸善出版）、『ぐんぐん頭のよい子に育つよみきかせ いきもののお話25』（西東社）、『Fish Diversity of Japan: Evolution, Zoogeography, and Conservation』（Springer）などを分担執筆。

Supervisor
Masanori Nakae
National Museum of Nature and Science, Department of Zoology, Division of Vertebrates, Chief Researcher, Senior Curator. Specialist of fish morphology. He studies fish morphology, particularly lateral line system of bony fishes. He is also the co-author of various books including *"Shin-Gyorui-Kaibozukan (New Atlas of Fish Anatomy)"* (Midori Shobo), *"Kao-no-Hyakkajiten"* and *"Gyoruigaku-no-Hyakkajiten (The Encyclopedia of Ichthyology)"* (both from Maruzen Shuppan), *"Gungun-Atama-no-Yoiko-ni-Sodatsu Yomi-Kikase Ikimono-no-Ohanashi 25"* (Seitosha), and *"Fish Diversity of Japan: Evolution, Zoogeography, and Conservation"* (Springer).

美し、をかし、和名由来の
江戸魚図鑑

2024年5月21日　初版第1刷発行

企画 / アートディレクション　田島一彦
監修　中江雅典
デザイン　淡海季史子
文　門司智子
　　山口未和子
翻訳　マイケル・ブルーシャ
　　名取祥子
　　ブレインウッズ株式会社
校正　株式会社 鷗来堂
編集　杵淵恵子

発行人　三芳寛要
発行元　株式会社 パイ インターナショナル
〒170-0005　東京都豊島区南大塚2-32-4
TEL 03-3944-3981
FAX 03-5395-4830
sales@pie.co.jp

印刷・製本　図書印刷株式会社

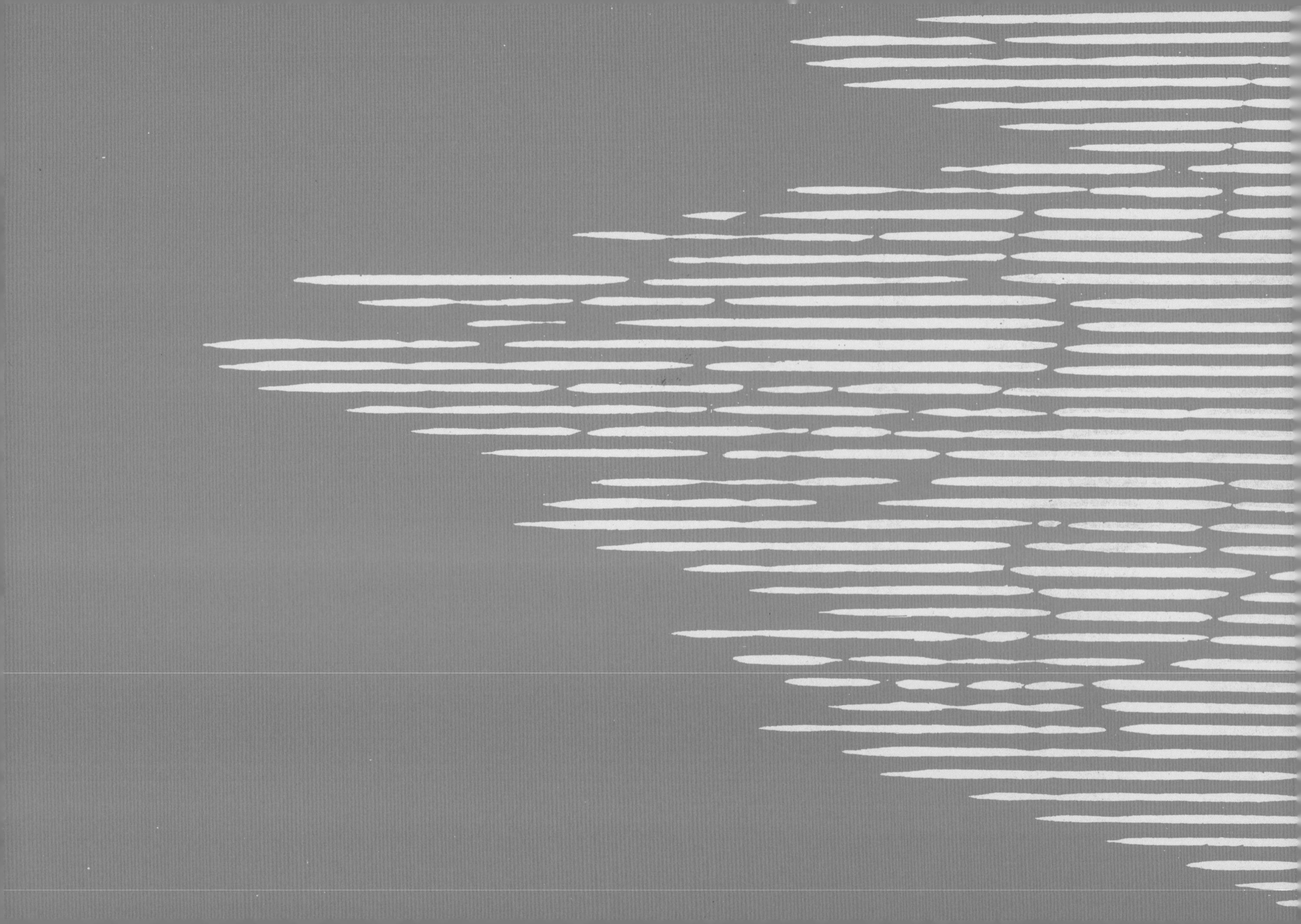

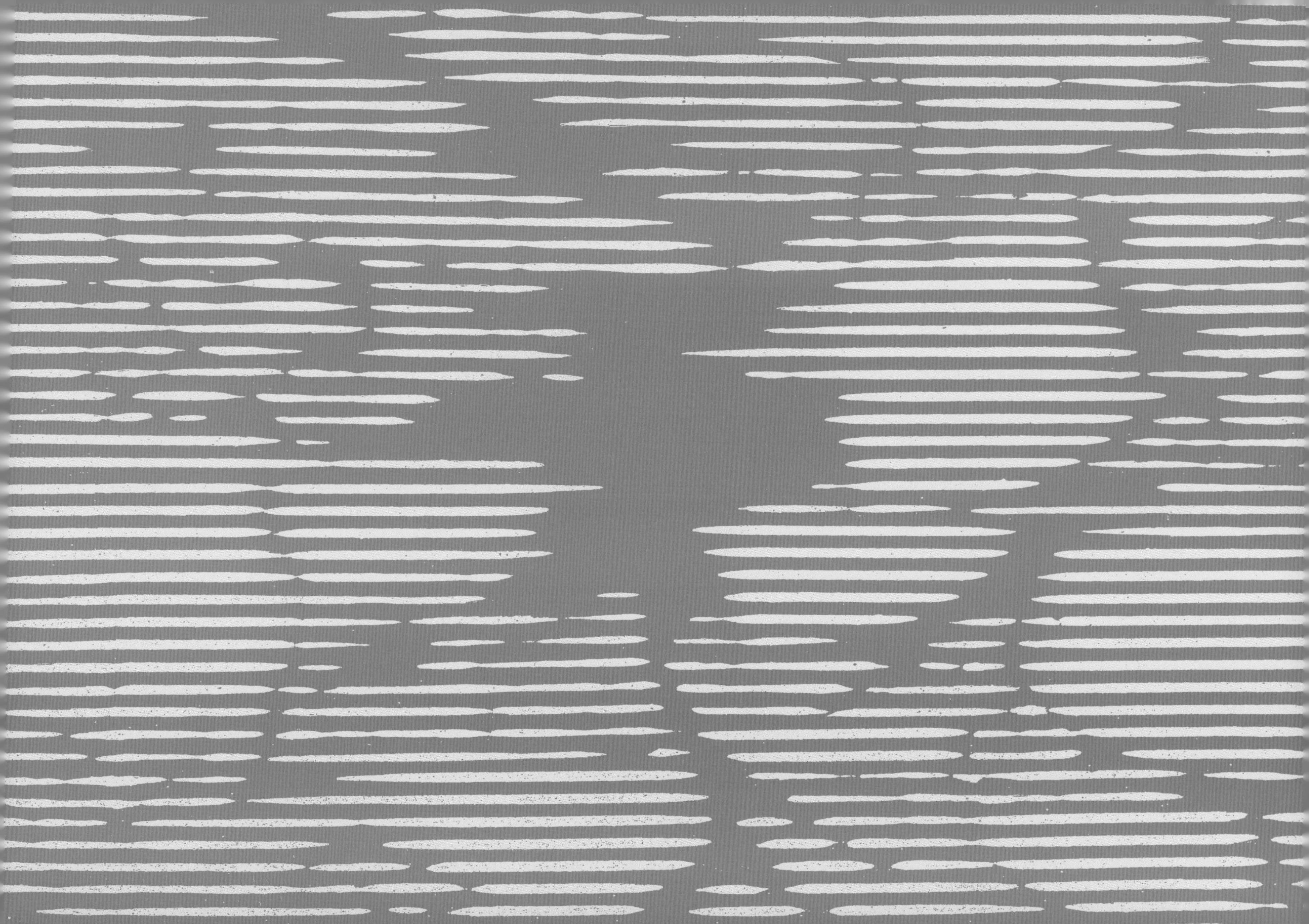